The First Book of

MS-DOS® 6

The First Book of
MS-DOS® 6

Joe Kraynak

alpha
books

A Division of Prentice Hall Computer Publishing
11711 North College Ave., Carmel, Indiana 46032 USA

To my sister, Kathy, for staying close even when she's thousands of miles away.

© **1993 by Alpha Books**

International Standard Book Number: 1-56761-124-9
Library of Congress Catalog Card Number: 92-75151

95 94 93   8 7 6 5 4 3 2 1

Interpretation of the printing code: the rightmost number of the first series of numbers is the year of the book's printing; the rightmost number of the second series of numbers is the number of the book's printing. For example, a printing code of 93-1 shows that the first printing of the book occurred in 1993.

Screen reproductions in this book were created by means of the program Collage Plus from Inner Media, Inc., Hollis, NH.

Printed in the United States of America

Publisher
Marie Butler-Knight

Associate Publisher
Lisa A. Bucki

Managing Editor
Elizabeth Keaffaber

Acquisitions Manager
Stephen R. Poland

Development Editor
Faithe Wempen

Production Editor
Annalise N. Di Paolo

Copy Editor
San Dee Phillips

Cover Designer
Susan Kniola

Designer
Amy Peppler-Adams

Indexer
Jeanne Clark

Production Team
Diana Bigham, Julie Brown,
Scott Cook, Tim Cox,
Mark Enochs, Tom Loveman,
Joe Ramon, Carrie Roth,
Barbara Webster,
Kelli Widdifield

*Special thanks to Kelly Oliver for ensuring the technical
accuracy of this book.*

Contents

1 Understanding Your Computer and DOS 3

The Parts of a Computer 3
   The System Unit 4
   Input Devices 5
   Output Devices 8
What DOS Does 9
How a Computer Works 10
   What Happens When You Start
     Your Computer? 10
   Booting Your Computer 12
   Running an Application Program 12
   Typing Text or Other Information 13
   Saving Your Work to a Disk 14
   Getting Your Work from Disk 14
Is That All? 15

**2 Understanding Disks, Files,
and Directories 17**

The Purpose of Disks 18
   Disk Drives: It's As Easy As A B C 18
   Working with Floppy Disks 19
   Working with Hard Disks 22
Understanding Files 22
   Naming Files 23
   Why Save Files onto a Disk? 23
Organizing Your Files 23
   Organizing Files on Floppy Disks 24
   Organizing Files on a Hard Disk 24
Moving On to DOS 26

3 Installing MS-DOS 6 29

Do You Have the Right Disks? 29
Write-Protect the Floppy Disks 30
   Write-Protecting 3 1/2-Inch Disks 30
   Write-Protecting 5 1/4-Inch Disks 31

Set Aside Blank Disks 32
Back Up Your Hard Disk 32
Installing DOS on a New Computer's Hard Disk 32
Replacing an Earlier Version of DOS 33
Uninstalling DOS 6 37
Installing DOS on Floppy Disks 38
Booting Your Computer 39
Booting from a Hard Disk 40
Booting from Floppy Disks 40
Performing a Warm Boot 41
Moving On from the DOS Prompt 41

4 Working in the DOS Shell   43

Starting the DOS Shell 44
Parts of the DOS Shell 44
Working in the Shell 46
Moving Around in the Shell 46
Selecting Commands from Menus 47
Changing Disk Drives 49
Working in the Directory Tree 50
Working in the File List 53
Working with Dialog Boxes 54
Going to the DOS Prompt 55
Displaying the Program List 56
Changing the Appearance of the Shell 58
Getting Help in the DOS Shell 61
Getting Around in a Help Window 62
Getting Context-Sensitive Help 62
Exiting the DOS Shell 63
Is That All? 63

5 Working at the DOS Prompt   65

Entering Commands at the DOS Prompt 66
The Parts of a DOS Command 66
Does Capitalization Matter? 67
Being Grammatical in DOS 67
A Brief Course in DOS Syntax 67
Conventions Used in This Book 68
Editing a Command 69

Cancelling or Stopping a Command 69
Entering Some Commonly Used DOS Commands ...70
    Choosing a Disk Drive 70
    Changing Directories 70
    Viewing a Directory Tree 71
    Viewing a List of Files 73
Getting Help at the DOS Prompt 75
    Accessing the MS-DOS Help: Command
        Reference 76
    Getting Help About a Specific Command 79
Saving Time with DOSKey 79
Is That All? 81

6 Working with Disks   83

Changing Disk Drives 83
Preparing a Disk for Storing Data 84
    Types of Floppy Disks and Drives 84
    Using the DOS Format Program 85
    Unformatting a Disk 89
Renaming a Disk 91
Copying Disks 92
Comparing Disks 95
Is That All? 97

7 Organizing Your Disk with Directories   99

Changing to a Directory 100
Adding Directories 100
    Planning Ahead 101
    Creating a Directory 102
Renaming a Directory 104
Removing a Directory 106
    DELTREE, New to DOS 6 108
Practice, Practice, Practice 109

8 Managing Your Files   111

Changing the Way Files Are Listed in the Shell 112
    Setting the File Display Options 112
    Opening More Windows 115

Selecting Files 117
  Selecting Individual Files 117
  Selecting and Deselecting All Files
    in a Directory 117
  Selecting a Group of Neighboring Files 118
  Selecting a Group of Non-Neighboring Files 119
  Selecting Files in Different Directories 121
Copying Files 122
  Copying to the Same Directory and Disk 122
  Copying Files to a Different Subdirectory
    or Disk 124
  Fast File Copying with a Mouse 125
  Name Conflicts 127
Moving Files 127
Renaming Files 130
Deleting Files 132
Undeleting Files 133
  Running Undelete 134
  Enhancing File Recovery 138
Viewing a File's Contents 140
Printing a File 141
Changing File Attributes 142
Locating Files 144
Is That All? 146

9 Running Programs
from the DOS Shell   149

How to Run Programs from Shell 150
Using the Run Command 150
Using the Open Command 152
Running Programs from the Program List 153
  Running a Program 154
  Adding Programs to a Program List 156
  Editing a Program Group or Item 160
  Using Advanced Program Options 160
  Creating Custom Dialog Boxes
    for Your Programs 162
  Deleting a Program from a Program List 164
  Moving a Program in a Program List 164
Associating Document Files with Programs 165

Running Several Programs at the Same Time 168
   Switching Between Programs 169
   Quitting a Program 169
Is That All? 170

10 Backing Up Files on Your Hard Disk   173

Establishing a Backup Strategy 174
   Backup Types and Why They Matter 174
Setting Up Microsoft Backup for Your System 177
Running Microsoft Backup 182
   Selecting the Drive You Want to Back Up 183
   Selecting a Drive for Storing the Backups 183
   Selecting a Backup Type 184
   Selecting Additional Backup Options 184
Backing Up All Files on a Hard Disk 186
Backing Up Modified Files 189
Backing Up Selected Directories and Files 191
   Selecting a Drive to Back Up 192
   Including and Excluding Groups of Files 192
   Choosing Directories from the Tree 194
   Selecting and Deselecting Files 195
   Excluding Special Groups of Files 196
   Accepting Your File Selections 197
   Saving Your File Selections 197
Running Backup for Windows 199
Backups: Past, Present, and Future 200

11 Comparing and Restoring Backup Files   203

Comparing Backup Files to the Originals 203
   Choosing a Backup Set Catalog 204
   Choosing a Compare Source and Destination 206
   Selecting the Files to Compare 207
   Starting the Compare Operation 209
Restoring Files to Your Hard Disk 210
   Setting the Restore Options 211
   Restoring All the Files on Your Hard Disk 212
   Restoring Selected Files to Your Hard Disk 215
It's All in the Catalog 219
Summing It Up 219

12 Optimizing Your Hard Disk   221

Reclaiming Pieces of Files with CHKDSK 222
Eliminating File Fragmentation with Defrag 223
  Starting Defrag 224
  Configuring Defrag 227
Getting More Disk Space with DoubleSpace 228
  Setting Up DoubleSpace: Express
    or Custom Setup? 229
  Setting Up DoubleSpace the Easy Way 230
  Taking More Control over
    the DoubleSpace Setup 233
Managing a Compressed Disk 235
  Working with a Compressed Disk 236
  Maintaining a Compressed Disk 239
Compressing Additional Disks
  with DoubleSpace 240
  Creating a New Compressed Disk
    on Your Hard Drive 240
  Compressing a Floppy Disk 241
What's Next? 243

13 Making the Most of Your Computer's Memory   245

Understanding the Different Memory Types 246
Disk Caching with SmartDrive 248
  Using SmartDrive: What Is Involved? 248
  Taking Control of SmartDrive 249
Freeing up Conventional Memory
  with MemMaker 251
  What You Need to Use MemMaker 252
  Setting Up MemMaker: Express
    or Custom Setup? 252
  Setting Up MemMaker the Easy Way 253
  Taking More Control Over
    the MemMaker Setup 256
  Undoing MemMaker's Changes 259
Summing It Up 261

14 Protecting Your System Against Viruses   **263**

How Susceptible Is Your System? 264
  Preventions and Cures 264
Microsoft Anti-Virus and Anti-Virus
  for Windows 265
  What Does Anti-Virus Do? 266
  Scanning the Files on a Disk for Viruses 267
  Setting Anti-Virus Scanning Options 269
Creating an Emergency Virus Disk 271
Running Anti-Virus at Startup 272
Running VSafe for Continuous Anti-Virus
  Protection 272
  Changing the VSafe Settings 273
  Unloading VSafe from Memory 274
Summing It Up 275

15 Configuring Your System with AUTOEXEC.BAT and CONFIG.SYS   **277**

Making a Copy of AUTOEXEC.BAT
  and CONFIG.SYS 278
Viewing the Contents of AUTOEXEC.BAT
  or CONFIG.SYS 279
Using the DOS Editor 281
Editing Your AUTOEXEC.BAT File 283
  Changing the Look of the DOS Prompt 283
  Helping Your Computer Locate Files
    with a Path Statement 284
  Preventing Commands from Appearing
    On-Screen 285
  Setting Up Programs to Run Automatically 285
  Running DOSKey 286
  Running VSafe 287
  Using the REM Command to Temporarily
    Disable a Command Line 287
Editing Your CONFIG.SYS File 288
  Device Commands and What They Do 289
  Setting the Number of Buffers and Files 290

Allowing DOS to Use Upper Memory 291
Turning Your NumLock Key Off at Startup 291
Other CONFIG.SYS Commands 292
Rebooting Your Computer to Put Your
   Changes into Effect 292
Troubleshooting Startup Problems 293
Summing It Up 294

16 Special Programs for Laptop Computers

297

Using Interlnk to Transfer Files
   between Two Computers 298
   What You Need to Use Interlnk 298
   Connecting the Two Computers 299
   Setting Up the Client and Server 300
   Using the Remote Copy Procedure 303
   Establishing the Connection
      Between Computers 304
   Using the Redirected Drives 305
   Breaking the Connection Between
      Computers 305
Conserving Power on Your Laptop Computer 306
Summing It Up 307

DOS Command Reference

309

APPEND 310
ATTRIB 310
BREAK 310
BUFFERS 311
CD (CHDIR) 311
CHKDSK 312
CLS 312
COPY 312
DATE 313
DEFRAG 313
DEL (ERASE) 313
DELOLDDOS 314
DELTREE 314

DEVICE and DEVICEHIGH 314
DIR 315
DISKCOMP 315
DISKCOPY 316
DOSHELP 316
DOSKEY 316
DOSSHELL 317
DBLSPACE 317
ECHO 317
EDIT 318
EXIT 318
FORMAT 319
HELP 319
INTERLNK and INTERSVR 319
LABEL 320
LH (LOADHIGH) 320
MEM 320
MEMMAKER 321
MD (MKDIR) 321
PATH 321
PROMPT 322
REM 322
REN (RENAME) 322
RD (RMDIR) 323
SETVER 323
SMARTDRV 323
TIME 324
TREE 324
TYPE 325
UNDELETE 325
UNFORMAT 325
VER 326
VERIFY 326
VOL 326

Index   **327**

What's New with MS-DOS 6

To Learn About This New DOS Feature

See Chapter

Anti-Virus
14

Anti-Virus scans your computer's memory and hard disk to detect and remove any viruses from your system.

Anti-Virus for Windows
14

If you use Windows, try the Windows version of Anti-Virus.

Defragmenter
12

Defragmenter pulls all the pieces of each individual file together and places the pieces on neighboring areas of the disk. This makes it easier for your disk drive to read files.

DELTREE
7

DELTREE allows you to delete directories and subdirectories from the DOS prompt even if the directories contain files.

DoubleSpace
12

DoubleSpace compresses the files on your hard disk so they take up less disk space. After you run DoubleSpace, your disk will have 50 to 100 percent more disk space.

Interlnk
16

Interlnk allows you to connect two computers (usually a laptop and desktop computer) to transfer files directly from one computer to the other.

MemMaker
13

MemMaker optimizes your computer's memory by loading some programs in a previously reserved portion of memory.

Microsoft Backup   **10, 11**

Microsoft Backup allows you to back up your hard disk almost effortlessly.

Microsoft Backup for Windows   **10**

If you use Microsoft Windows, Backup for Windows allows you to back up your files as you are working in other Windows programs.

MS-DOS Help   **5**

DOS has a new Help system that provides more and better information about the various DOS commands, including helpful examples for each command.

Power   **16**

Power helps conserve battery power on a laptop computer. Your computer will experience a savings of 5 to 25 percent.

Step-by-Step CONFIG.SYS Startup   **15**

When you start your computer, you can have DOS execute each command in your CONFIG.SYS file one at a time, asking you to confirm each command. This can help you troubleshoot any problems in CONFIG.SYS.

Undelete   **8**

This improved Undelete program provides increased protection for your files, with features that save additional information about each file.

Undelete for Windows   **8**

If you use Microsoft Windows, use Undelete for Windows. It displays a complete list of all recoverable files; undeleting a file is as simple as selecting it from the list.

VSafe   **14**

VSafe stays in your computer's memory and warns you if it notices any suspicious activity that might be caused by a computer virus.

Introduction

Congratulations! You now have the latest, greatest version of MS-DOS 6, a program that contains an incredible array of features for managing your computer and files. That's the good news. The bad news is that you now have to learn how to use those features to become more productive. Where do you start?

To help, we at Alpha Books have put together the *First Book of MS-DOS 6*. In this book, you will learn everything from installing MS-DOS on your computer's hard disk to using MS-DOS for running programs and for managing disks, directories, and files. You will also learn how to use the nifty, new DOS 6 features, including Microsoft Backup, Anti-Virus, DoubleSpace (a program that makes files take up less room on your hard disk), and a host of Windows programs. And you will learn all this (the simple and the complex tasks) in an easy-to-follow format presented in plain English.

How to Use This Book

The chapters in this book are organized in the same manner that you are likely to use the various DOS features and programs. You can proceed through the chapters from beginning to end or skip around, if you prefer.

Although you don't have to read this book from cover to cover and in order, at the very least you should start by reading

Chapters 1 to 5. These chapters provide an overview of your computer and DOS and explain in detail how to access its features and capabilities.

Conventions Used in This Book

As you use this book, you will notice that it includes several special elements to highlight important information.

- Actions that you take, whether it's pressing a key or selecting a menu, will appear in color.

- Characters that you see on-screen appear in `computer font like this`.

- Text that you should type in is printed in a **`bold, color, computer font like this`**.

- Keys that you press are shown as keycaps, like `↵Enter` and `Tab↹`.

- Many commands are activated by pressing two or more keys at the same time. These key presses or selections are separated by a plus sign (+) in the text. For example, "press `Alt`+`F1`" means that you should hold down the `Alt` key while you press the `F1` key. (You don't type the plus sign.)

- Other commands are activated by selecting a menu and then an option. A command like "select File New" means that you should open the File menu and select the New option from it. In this book, the selection letter is printed in boldface for easy recognition.

QUICK STEPS   Look for this icon for Quick Steps that tell you how to perform important tasks in DOS 6. Quick Steps and the page numbers on which they appear are listed on the inside front cover of this book.

TIP: Helpful tips and shortcuts are included in TIP boxes.

Practical ideas for using MS-DOS 6 are outlined in these boxes.

NOTE: Important information that should be noted when using MS-DOS 6 is included here.

These are potential pitfalls and problems which you should avoid when using MS-DOS 6.

This book focuses mostly on the DOS Shell, but for diehard DOS prompt users, special boxed notes give the command line equivalents.

Acknowledgments

I'd like to give special thanks to Faithe Wempen, my development editor, for her insights, enthusiasm, and direction, and for constantly motivating me to write in plain English. I also owe Faithe thanks (and money?) for her late-inning relief work.

Thanks to the editorial staff at Alpha Books for fine-tuning the book. Thanks to Kelly Oliver for checking the book for technical accuracy. Thanks to Annalise Di Paolo, Lisa Bucki, and

Liz Keaffaber for coordinating the production of the book, and to San Dee Phillips and Linda Hawkins, the copy editors, for making sure everything made sense grammatically.

Thanks also to our wonderful, unheralded production department at Prentice Hall Computer Publishing for transforming a stack of pages into an attractive, bound book.

Trademarks

All terms mentioned in this book that are known to be trademarks or service marks are listed below. In addition, terms suspected of being trademarks or service marks have been appropriately capitalized. Alpha Books cannot attest to the accuracy of this information. Use of a term in this book should not be regarded as affecting the validity of any trademark or service mark.

Bernoulli is a registered trademark of Iomega Corporation.

IBM is a registered trademark of International Business Machines Corporation.

Microsoft, MS, and MS-DOS are registered trademarks, and Windows is a trademark of Microsoft Corporation.

WordPerfect is a registered trademark of WordPerfect Corporation.

In This Chapter

Understanding the Parts of the Computer

What Is DOS?

How DOS Interacts with Your Computer

What Happens When You Start Your Computer

Parts of a Computer

- *System unit*—Contains the brains of the computer. It processes all information.
- *Keyboard*—Allows you to type information and commands into the computer.
- *Mouse*—Allows you to point to and select commands or objects on-screen.
- *Monitor*—Displays a program and your work on-screen, so you can see what you are doing.
- *Printer*—Prints information from the computer onto paper.

The Role of MS-DOS

- MS-DOS stands for *Microsoft disk operating system* and is pronounced "em-ess-DAWSS."
- DOS is a set of instructions that tells a computer how to operate.
- DOS allows you to run applications—programs that help perform practical tasks, such as typing a letter.
- DOS contains several programs that help you manage and maintain your computer system, programs, and information.

What a Computer Does at Startup

- When you start the computer, it first reads a set of built-in instructions.
- Next, the computer looks for DOS and loads the instructions from DOS into its memory.
- The computer displays a prompt (short message) on-screen, showing that it is ready to start work.

Chapter 1

Understanding Your Computer and DOS

If this is your first time using a computer, this chapter will help you become a little more comfortable with computers. You will learn about the basic parts of the computer and how the parts work together. You will also learn why your computer needs DOS.

The Parts of a Computer

A computer consists of several components that work together to perform various tasks (see Figure 1.1). Before you start working with DOS, you should have a general understanding of the components that make up a computer and how they work together. The following sections provide a brief overview.

Figure 1.1

A computer system is made up of several components.

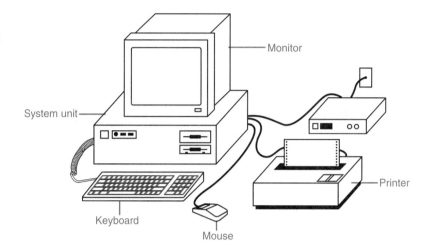

Monitor

System unit

Printer

Keyboard

Mouse

The System Unit

The *system unit* is the central component of your computer (see Figure 1.2). Although it doesn't look like much from the outside, the system unit contains the following elements, which allow your computer to carry out the most complex of computer operations:

Memory chips   Memory chips store instructions and data temporarily while your computer is using them. Whenever you run a program, the program's instructions are kept in memory so the computer can read and follow the instructions. Whatever you type into the computer is stored in memory so your computer can process that information.

Central processing unit   The central processing unit (CPU) is the brain of the computer. The CPU carries out the program instructions and processes the information you enter.

Input and output ports   At the back of the system unit are several receptacles into which you can plug your keyboard, mouse, display monitor, printer, modem, and other devices. Input ports are for input devices, such as a keyboard or mouse. Output ports are for output devices, such as a monitor or printer.

Disk drives Disk drives allow you to feed program instructions to your computer. When you purchase a program, you get several magnetic disks on which the program instructions are stored. When you run the program, the system unit reads the instructions from disk and stores them in memory. The disk drives also allow you to save any data you typed into the computer to disk and read previously stored data from disk into the computer's memory.

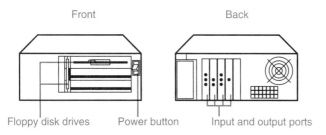

Figure 1.2
The system unit.

Input Devices

Input devices allow you, the user, to communicate with the computer. The two most common input devices are the keyboard and the mouse, as explained in the following sections.

Keyboard

The *keyboard* plugs into the keyboard port (usually at the back of the system unit). You use the keyboard to enter data (numbers or text) or to enter commands that tell the computer or a program what to do. A typical keyboard is shown in Figure 1.3. Although the locations of keys on your keyboard may vary, all IBM and compatible keyboards contain the following keys:

Alphanumeric keys The alphanumeric keys are like the keys on any typewriter; you use them to type numbers and letters. This area of the keyboard also includes ⚡Shift (for uppercase letters), ↵Enter (or Return), Spacebar, Tab↹, and ←Backspace.

Function keys   The function keys are the 10 or 12 F keys at the top or left side of the keyboard. These keys are numbered F1, F2, F3, and so on. They are used for entering commands.

Arrow keys   Also known as cursor-movement keys, the arrow keys are used for moving around on-screen.

Numeric keypad   The numeric keypad consists of a group of number keys that are set up like the keys on an adding machine. This keypad includes Num Lock. With Num Lock off, you use the numeric keypad to move around on-screen. With Num Lock on, you use the keypad to type numbers.

Ctrl and Alt   Ctrl (Control) and Alt (Alternative) are used to make the other keys on the keyboard act differently from the way they normally act. For example, if you press F1 by itself, the computer may display a help screen, but if you hold down Ctrl while pressing F1, the computer will carry out an entirely different command.

Esc   Esc (Escape) is used by most programs to back out of or quit whatever you are currently doing.

Figure 1.3
A typical IBM-compatible keyboard.

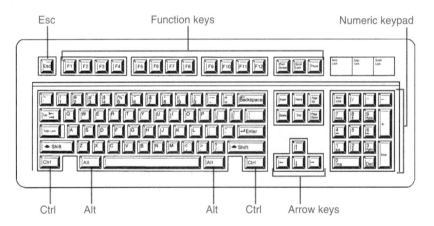

Mouse

A *mouse* is a pointing device that enables you to move around quickly and select commands rather than typing them. A typical mouse is shown in Figure 1.4. If you have a program that enables you to use a mouse, a mouse pointer will appear on-screen when you start the program. You can use the mouse to perform the following actions:

Point   To point to something on-screen, you roll the mouse on your desktop or table until the tip of the mouse pointer is touching the desired area or command.

Click   To select a command or move to an area on-screen, you must point to the command or area and hold the mouse still while pressing and releasing the left mouse button.

Double-click   Double-clicking consists of pressing and releasing the left mouse button twice quickly without moving the mouse. You usually double-click to execute a command.

Drag   Dragging consists of holding down the mouse button while moving the mouse. You usually drag to select text, move an object on-screen, or draw a line or shape.

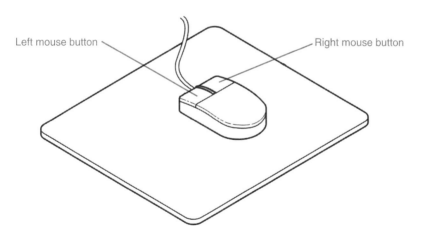

Left mouse button   Right mouse button

Figure 1.4

A mouse enables you to point to objects on-screen.

Special Input Devices

Although the keyboard and mouse are the bread and butter of input devices, there are many other specialized input devices. These include musical instruments, microphones, drawing tablets, and even movie cameras. Any device that enables you to input any sort of data into your computer is an input device.

Output Devices

Output devices allow a computer to communicate with the user and present information in a usable form. The two most common output devices are the monitor and printer, as described in the following sections.

Monitor

A *monitor* is like a pair of eyes—it enables you to see what you and your computer are doing as you are doing it (see Figure 1.5). Whenever you run a program, the program displays a screen, menu, or prompt that enables you to enter a command or type text. Whatever you type appears on-screen, allowing you to see exactly which keys you are pressing.

Figure 1.5

The monitor lets you see what you are doing.

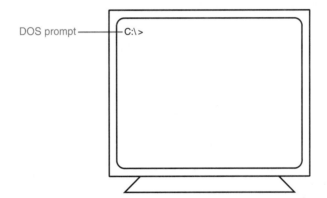

DOS prompt ———— C:\>

Printer

The *printer* transforms the electronic information from your computer into a paper printout (see Figure 1.6). Printers range from inexpensive dot-matrix types, which print each character as a series of dots, to expensive laser printers, which operate like copy machines.

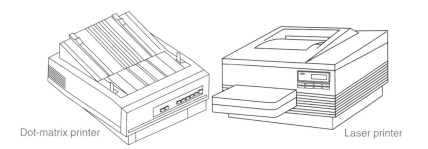

Figure 1.6

The printer prints information from the computer onto the paper.

Special Output Devices

Although the monitor and printer are the standard output devices, any device that presents information in an understandable form is an output device. These devices include speakers (which provide audible output) and cameras that can record data on video tape.

What DOS Does

No matter how complex your computer is, no matter how many parts it has, it can't do more than warm its chips without instructions that tell it what to do. MS-DOS provides those instructions.

Think of DOS as the boss, the supervisor, of your computer. It tells your computer how to interpret input (from the keyboard and mouse), how to process the data, how to produce output (on the display screen or printer, for instance), and how to store programs and information. DOS also enables you to run other programs on the computer to perform specific tasks, such as writing a letter or balancing your checkbook.

In addition, DOS comes with several programs of its own that allow you to take care of your computer, including programs for backing up your work, protecting your system against computer viruses, and managing your computer's memory.

NOTE: MS-DOS stands for *Microsoft disk operating system* and is pronounced "em-ess-DAWSS," or "DAWSS" for short. An *operating system* is a set of instructions that tells a computer how to function.

NOTE: The number after MS-DOS (the 6 in MS-DOS 6) is called the *version* number. Every time Microsoft Corporation releases an updated version of MS-DOS, the version number increases. This book covers the most recent version of MS-DOS, MS-DOS 6.

How a Computer Works

Now that we've dissected the computer and looked at DOS all by itself, let's take a more practical view of what goes on inside the computer as you work.

What Happens When You Start Your Computer?

Every computer comes with a built-in set of very basic instructions. These instructions tell the computer how to control traffic between the various elements that make up the computer, including disk drives, the printer, the communications ports, and the display. When you turn on your computer, it first reads these instructions to determine what to do next. The computer then looks for an operating system, in this case DOS.

If the DOS files are on the computer's hard disk or on a disk that is in the computer's floppy drive, then the computer reads

DOS and stores its instructions in memory. A *prompt* appears on-screen, as shown in Figure 1.7. You can now use your computer to run other programs.

If the DOS files are not on the computer's hard disk or on a disk in the computer's floppy drive, the computer will display a message on-screen telling you to Insert a system disk in drive A. In other words, the computer needs the DOS files before it can do anything else.

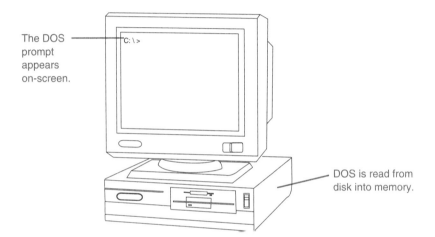

The DOS prompt appears on-screen.

DOS is read from disk into memory.

Figure 1.7

The computer loads DOS from disk into memory and is ready to start work.

NOTE: A computer's startup instructions are called the BIOS (pronounced "BUY-ose"), which stands for basic input-output system. These instructions are stored in the computer's ROM (pronounced "RAHM"), which stands for read-only memory; the computer can read the instructions but cannot change them in any way.

Booting Your Computer

When you start your computer with the DOS files in place, the computer is said to have *booted* itself. That is, the computer "has pulled itself up by its own bootstraps" and is ready to operate.

What happens to DOS once the computer is booted? DOS remains in your computer's memory until you turn off the computer. DOS runs in the background, performing any of the steps required for your other programs to operate.

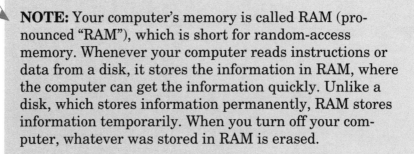

NOTE: Your computer's memory is called RAM (pronounced "RAM"), which is short for random-access memory. Whenever your computer reads instructions or data from a disk, it stores the information in RAM, where the computer can get the information quickly. Unlike a disk, which stores information permanently, RAM stores information temporarily. When you turn off your computer, whatever was stored in RAM is erased.

Running an Application Program

Once DOS is running, you can run specialized programs, such as word processing, spreadsheet, or database programs. These programs are called *applications* because they allow you to use the computer to perform a specific task, such as writing a letter, balancing your budget, or playing a game.

When you run an application, your computer reads the program's instructions from disk and stores them in RAM (see Figure 1.8). You can then use the program to do your work or play a game. When you quit the program, it is removed from RAM.

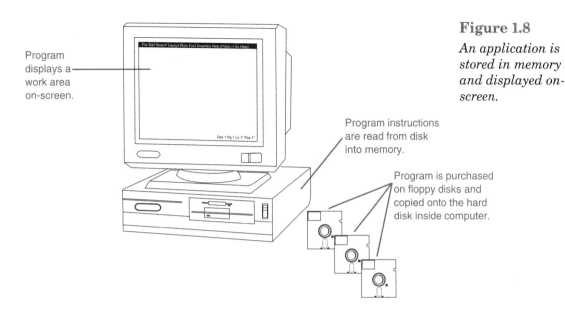

Program displays a work area on-screen.

Program instructions are read from disk into memory.

Program is purchased on floppy disks and copied onto the hard disk inside computer.

Figure 1.8

An application is stored in memory and displayed on-screen.

Typing Text or Other Information

Once DOS and your application are running, you can use your application to type a letter, enter numbers, create a picture, or perform some other task (see Figure 1.9). As you work, however, keep in mind that whatever you create is stored electronically in RAM. If you turn off your computer (or if the power goes out) before you save your work, your work will be lost forever.

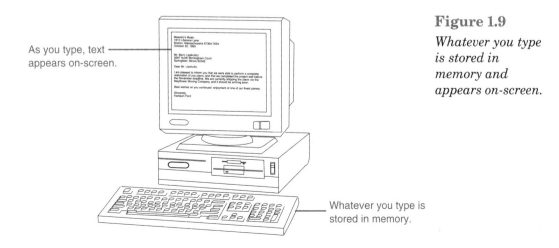

As you type, text appears on-screen.

Whatever you type is stored in memory.

Figure 1.9

Whatever you type is stored in memory and appears on-screen.

Saving Your Work to a Disk

As explained in the preceding section, whatever you type is stored only in RAM—a temporary, electronic storage area. To prevent your work from getting lost, you must save it to a disk—a permanent, magnetic storage device. Whenever you save your work, it is saved in a special *file*, which you must name. During the save operation, the computer writes the electronic data from RAM to the magnetic disk (see Figure 1.10).

TIP: Think of a magnetic disk as a cassette tape. With a cassette tape, you can save sounds and play them back later. With a disk, you can save data and "play it back later" on the computer.

Figure 1.10

When you save information, it is written from memory to a file on a magnetic disk.

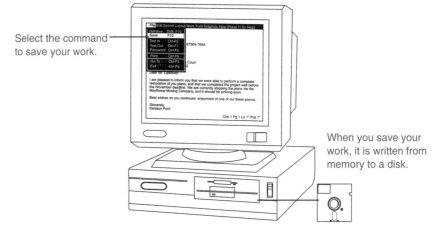

Select the command to save your work.

When you save your work, it is written from memory to a disk.

Getting Your Work from Disk

Once your work is saved on disk, you can read your work from disk and continue working on it later. However, in order to open the file you saved, you must first run the application in which you created the file. When you open the file, your work will appear on-screen, ready for your changes (see Figure 1.11). For example, to open a document you have previously saved in WordPerfect, you would first run the WordPerfect application, and then open the file.

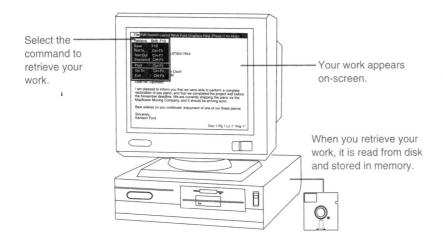

Select the command to retrieve your work.

Your work appears on-screen.

When you retrieve your work, it is read from disk and stored in memory.

Figure 1.11

Whenever you want to work with your file, you have to read it from disk into memory.

Is That All?

In this chapter, you have learned some basic information about computers, including how a computer works. In the next chapter, you will learn how DOS and your computer store information on disk.

In This Chapter

How Your Computer Stores Information on Disk

Understanding the Different Disk Drives

Working with Floppy Disks

Working with Hard Disks

Naming Files

Organizing Files on a Hard Disk

DOS Disk-Drive Letters

- DOS assigns a letter to each disk drive: A, B, C, and so on.
- The top or left floppy disk drive is drive A.
- The bottom or right floppy disk drive is drive B.
- Hard disk drives are labeled C, D, E, and so on.

Files and File Names

- Whenever you save information to disk, you save the information in a separate file.
- Each file must have a unique name.
- DOS file names consist of a base name (up to eight characters), a period, and an extension (up to three characters).
- DOS does not allow you to use any of the following characters in a file name:

  ” . / \ [ ] : * < > | + ; , ? space

Directories and Paths

- Directories allow you to store related files in a separate group.
- Each directory must have a unique name consisting of up to eight characters.
- Directories can have subdirectories.
- The entire directory listing for a drive is referred to as a *directory tree*.
- To specify the location of a directory in the tree, you type a *path* consisting of all the directory names that lead to the desired directory.

Understanding Disks, Files, and Directories

Although DOS can perform many complex tasks, you will most commonly use DOS to perform the following tasks:

- To prepare a new disk to store information.

- To create separate directories on your hard disk for storing related files.

- To view a list of files that are stored on a disk or in a directory.

- To copy files from one disk or directory to another.

In short, you will use DOS to manage your disks and the information stored on those disks. In this chapter, you will learn some general information about disks, directories, and files.

The Purpose of Disks

To understand the purpose of computer disks, you must understand the relationship between information stored on disk and information stored in your computer's memory. Think of it as the relationship between a book and your own memory. Your memory can work with information quickly, but it has a tendency to forget things. On the other hand, a book stores information permanently but does not have the tools for processing that information.

In the computer world, disks are used to store information permanently. The computer reads instructions or other information from the disk and stores it in memory, where the computer can quickly work with that information. When you turn the power off to your computer, everything that was stored in memory is erased, so you need to store the information on disk before turning off the computer.

Disk Drives: It's As Easy As A B C

Most computers have three disk drives, which DOS refers to as A, B, and C (see Figure 2.1). The two drives on the front of the computer are the *floppy disk drives*. The top drive (or left drive, on some computers) is drive A. The bottom drive (or right drive, on some computers) is drive B. If your computer has only one disk drive, it is drive A, and you have no drive B.

Figure 2.1

DOS uses letters from the alphabet to refer to disk drives.

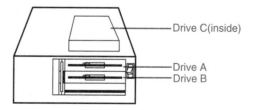

The drive shown inside the computer is the *hard drive*. Some computers have an *external* hard drive, which sits outside of the computer and is connected to the system unit by a cable. This drive can be divided (or *partitioned*) into one or more drives, which DOS refers to as drive C, drive D, drive E, and so on. The actual unit is called the *physical* drive; whereas each partition is called a *logical* drive.

Whenever you save or get information from one of the disks, you must tell DOS where the information is stored by specifying the drive letter: A, B, C, D, and so on.

Working with Floppy Disks

Floppy disks are the disks you insert into your computer's floppy disk drive. There are two kinds of floppy disks: 5 1/4-inch disks and 3 1/2-inch disks, as shown in Figure 2.2.

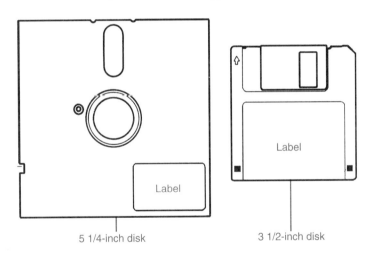

Figure 2.2

The two types of floppy disks.

5 1/4-inch disk

3 1/2-inch disk

Two characteristics describe floppy disks: *size* and *capacity*. The size of a disk refers to its physical measurements (its dimensions) and dictates what kind of disk drive it fits into. The capacity of a disk refers to the maximum amount of information the disk can hold. This capacity is measured in *kilobytes (K)* and *megabytes (M)*. Each *byte* consists of eight *bits* and is used to store a single character. A kilobyte is 1,024 bytes—1,024 characters. A megabyte is roughly one million bytes. Maximum is important here.

A disk's capacity depends on whether it stores information on one side (single-sided) or both sides (double-sided) and how much information it lets you cram into a given amount of space (the disk's density). Table 2.1 shows the types of floppy disks that are available and how much information they hold.

Table 2.1
Types of Floppy Disks

Disk Size	Disk Type	Disk Capacity
5 1/4-inch	Double-sided Double-density (DS/DD)	360K
5 1/4-inch	Double-sided High-density (DS/HD)	1.2M
3 1/2-inch	Double-sided Double-density (DS/DD)	720K
3 1/2-inch	Double-sided High-density (DS/HD)	1.44M

In general, a disk drive can read disks that are equal to or less than its own density. A high-density disk drive can read low-density disks, but the reverse will not work—a low-density disk drive cannot read high-density disks.

Proper Care and Handling of Floppy Disks

Floppy disks are fragile. If you damage a disk, you may destroy the data that's stored on the disk, or the disk may not reliably store information. You should follow a few simple precautions to prevent damage:

- Keep the disk in a clean place. Dust, dirt, coffee, fingerprints, and any foreign matter can damage a disk.

- When labeling a disk, write on the label before sticking it to the disk. Any pressure from a pen tip may damage the disk. If you've already stuck the label on the disk, write on it gently with a felt-tip marker.

- Keep disks away from heat sources, such as the top of your monitor or a photocopy machine. Heat or excessive cold can damage disks, so store them at a temperature between 50 and 140 degrees Fahrenheit.

- Keep disks away from magnetic fields. (Your telephone has a magnet in it.) Disks store information magnetically, so a magnet can erase information from a disk.

Inserting and Removing Floppy Disks

A disk will fit into a floppy drive in any number of ways—upside down, sideways, backwards—but it will work only if inserted properly. To insert the disk, hold it by its label, label facing up, and insert the disk into the drive, as shown in Figure 2.3. If the floppy drive has a lever or a door, you must flip the lever or close the door so it covers the slot.

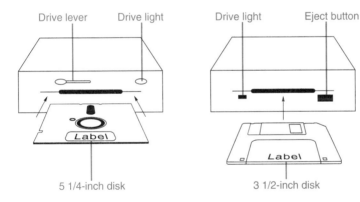

Drive lever   Drive light   Drive light   Eject button

5 1/4-inch disk   3 1/2-inch disk

Figure 2.3

A disk drive cannot read a disk unless the disk is inserted properly.

The procedure for removing the disk from the drive varies, depending on the type of drive. But no matter what type of drive you have, you should make sure the drive light is off before removing a disk from the drive. If the drive light is on, the drive is reading information off the disk or writing information to the disk. Removing the disk during either of these operations may damage the disk and drive and may cause you to lose data.

Once you're sure the drive light is off, you can eject the disk. Most 3 1/2-inch drives have an eject button. Press the button to eject the disk, and then gently pull the disk from the drive. Most 5 1/4-inch drives have a lever or door. Flip the lever up or open the door, and then gently pull the disk from the drive.

Formatting a Floppy Disk

Before you can store information on a new floppy disk, you must *format* the disk. The formatting operation creates a map on the disk that allows the computer to keep track of any information that will be stored on the disk. You will learn how to format disks in Chapter 6.

Working with Hard Disks

The hard disk acts like a giant floppy disk that's permanently installed in the computer or connected to the computer with a cable. Although the hard disk is not an essential component, it does make working with a computer much easier.

Even the smallest hard disk can store large amounts of data. For example, a 20M hard disk (the smallest) can store the same amount of data as sixty 5 1/4-inch, double-density floppy disks.

If you don't have a hard disk, you have to *swap* disks—eject one floppy disk from the disk drive and insert another. Every time your computer needs information that's not on a disk in one of your disk drives, it displays a message like `Please insert disk into drive A` or `Please insert program disk into drive B`. With a hard disk, the information is readily available, making disk swapping unnecessary.

Understanding Files

Whenever you save information to a disk, the computer saves the information as a separate *file*, just as you might place all the pages of a report in a single manila folder. The computer asks you to name the file, and then it stores the named file on disk.

Your computer uses two types of files: *data* files and *program* files. Data files are the files you create and save—your business letters, your reports, or the pictures you draw. Program files are the files you get when you purchase a program. These files contain the instructions that tell your computer how to perform a task.

Naming Files

Every file on a single disk must have a separate name to distinguish it from other files on the same disk. DOS file names consist of a *base name* (up to eight characters) and an *extension* (up to three characters)—for example, CH5-ART.PCX. The extension identifies the type of file. (In this case, a picture that can be opened in a Paintbrush program.)

DOS is particular about the file names it allows. The base name must be eight characters or less, the extension must be three characters or less and must be preceded by a period (this is the only place a period can appear in the file name), and the following characters are not allowed:

```
" . / \ [ ] : * < > ¦ + ; , ? space
```

Why Save Files onto a Disk?

When you begin typing information into your computer, the information is initially stored in RAM, the electronic storage facility. If you blow a fuse or accidentally turn off your computer, it's bye-bye document! To prevent such a loss of important information, you must store your work in a more stable location—on a disk.

Organizing Your Files

When you save files to disk, you can store hundreds or thousands of files. It's great that disks can hold so much information, but it also results in a problem—keeping all these files organized. The following sections explain some techniques for keeping your files organized on both floppy disks and hard disks.

Organizing Files on Floppy Disks

Organizing files on a floppy disk is not all that difficult, because you normally don't store very many files per disk. Even if you store as many as 100 files on a single disk, you can manage to search through a list of files fairly quickly.

Even so, you should follow three standard procedures to make the information more accessible:

- Give each file a unique name that helps you remember what's in the file. For example, JOHNSON.LTR tells you the name of the person the document concerns (Johnson) and the type of document (LTR for Letter).

- Label the outside of each disk with the names of the files stored on that disk and the date. That way, you'll know what's on the disk and which disk holds the most recent revisions.

- Copy any files you don't use very often to separate disks, and erase the original files from the disks you use often.

Organizing Files on a Hard Disk

Because hard disks can store thousands of files, you need to create *directories* and *subdirectories* to help organize your files. To understand directories, think of your disk as a filing cabinet. Each directory is like a drawer in the filing cabinet. The subdirectories are like dividers in the drawers. Each divider marks a group of files. Directories and subdirectories form a tree structure, shown in Figure 2.4, that looks like a family tree.

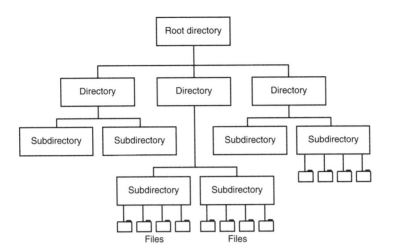

Figure 2.4
A directory tree illustrates how a hard disk is organized.

To understand how your computer locates files, it's helpful to look at the directory tree in terms of a *path*. Whenever you tell your computer where a file is located, you're essentially telling it to follow a specific path through the directory tree. For example, you may need to tell your computer to get the CUB file that's in subdirectory LION, in the directory ZOO, on drive C. The path would look like this:

```
c:\zoo\lion\cub
```

Figure 2.5 shows a schematic of how the disk drive uses the path above to locate the CUB file.

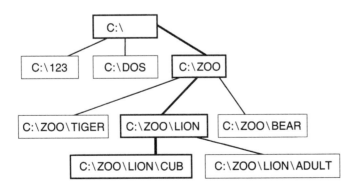

Figure 2.5
A schematic of a directory path.

Once you get accustomed to using directories, they're pretty straightforward; just weave through your directory tree to your destination.

Moving On to DOS

In Chapters 1 and 2, you learned the basics of how a computer operates, the purpose of DOS, and how your computer stores information on disks. In the next chapter, you will learn how to install DOS if it is not already installed on your computer.

In This Chapter

Preliminary Installation Steps

Installing MS-DOS 6 on a New Computer

Installing MS-DOS 6 over a Previous Version of DOS

Installing MS-DOS 6 on Floppy Disks

Starting Your Computer with DOS

Preparing for Installation

- Make sure you have the right size and density of MS-DOS 6 disks for your computer.
- Write-protect the MS-DOS 6 disks you purchased.
- Set one or two blank disks aside for uninstall disks.
- Make backup copies of the installation disks.

Installing MS-DOS 6 over an Earlier Version

1. Turn on your computer.
2. Insert Setup Disk 1 into floppy drive A or B.
3. Type a: or b: and press ↵Enter.
4. Type setup and press ↵Enter.
5. Follow the on-screen prompts and perform the steps as instructed.

Installing MS-DOS 6 on a New Computer

1. Insert Setup Disk 1 into floppy drive A.
2. Turn on your computer.
3. Follow the on-screen prompts and perform the steps as instructed.

Booting Your Computer from a Hard Disk

1. Turn on your monitor.
2. Turn on your computer.

Booting Your Computer from a Floppy Disk

1. Turn on your monitor.
2. Insert the Startup/Support disk into floppy drive A.
3. Turn on your computer.
4. Remove the Startup disk from drive A.

Installing MS-DOS 6

Installing MS-DOS 6 is not as intimidating as it sounds. Installation consists of transferring the files from the disks that you purchased to your computer's hard disk or to a different set of floppy disks. MS-DOS comes with a setup program that performs the installation process for you.

Before you start the installation, you must take some steps to prepare for the installation. The following sections lead you through the essential steps.

Do You Have the Right Disks?

DOS comes on high-density floppy disks—either 5 1/4-inch high-density floppy disks or 3 1/2-inch high-density disks. If your computer is equipped with only low-density floppy disk drives, you cannot use the original disks. If this is the case, you must send in a special coupon (at the back of the DOS documentation) to Microsoft Corporation to get the right disks.

Write-Protect the Floppy Disks

Before you install any program, you should write-protect the floppy disks on which the program files are stored. By write-protecting the disks, you protect the disk in two ways:

- You prevent any files from being accidently changed or deleted from the disk during installation.

- You prevent any viruses that may already be on your computer from infecting the disk.

Your computer can still read a write-protected disk, but it cannot write to the protected disk or change it in any way.

The procedure for write-protecting disks varies depending on the type of disks that you have. The following sections explain the two different procedures.

CAUTION All floppy disks consist of a case that contains the magnetic disk on which the data is stored. When handling the disk, touch only the case; do not touch any of the exposed areas of the magnetic disk.

Write-Protecting 3 1/2-Inch Disks

The 3 1/2-inch disk has a write-protect tab that slides back and forth on the disk, as shown in Figure 3.1. To write-protect the disk, slide the tab so that you can see through the window that the tab covers.

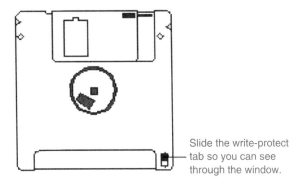

Figure 3.1
Use the write-protect tab on a 3 1/2-inch disk.

Slide the write-protect tab so you can see through the window.

Write-Protecting 5 1/4-Inch Disks

The 5 1/4-inch disk has a notch in the side of the disk, as shown in Figure 3.2. To write-protect the disk, apply a write-protect sticker over the notch, as shown.

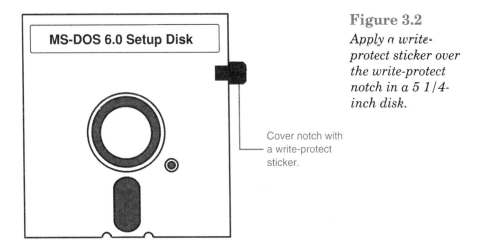

MS-DOS 6.0 Setup Disk

Figure 3.2
Apply a write-protect sticker over the write-protect notch in a 5 1/4-inch disk.

Cover notch with a write-protect sticker.

Most boxes of new 5 1/4-inch disks come with write-protect stickers. If you do not have a write-protect sticker, cut a section of a disk label or mailing label 1 inch by 1/2 inch, and use it for a write-protect sticker.

Set Aside Blank Disks

If you are installing MS-DOS 6 over a previous version of DOS on your hard disk, you need one or two blank disks on which to store uninstall files. (The uninstall files allow you to return to the previous DOS version if you have problems running MS-DOS 6.)

If you have only 360K (5 1/4-inch, double-density) disks, label two blank disks UNINSTALL 1 and UNINSTALL 2. If you have 720K, 1.2M, or 1.44M disks, you will need only one blank disk. If you do not have a blank disk, use a disk that contains data that you will never need.

Back Up Your Hard Disk

If you are installing MS-DOS 6 over a previous version of DOS, you probably have many important program and data files on your hard disk as well. Although the installation process is fairly safe, it is a good idea to perform a full backup of your hard disk drive before installing MS-DOS 6.

To back up your hard disk drive, use a backup program such as Central Point Backup, Norton Backup, or Fastback Plus. Or use the backup program that was included with the version of DOS that is currently on your computer. See your old DOS manual for details.

Installing DOS on a New Computer's Hard Disk

Most new computers come with DOS already installed on the hard drive. (The manufacturer installs DOS in order to test the disk before shipping it.) If you've just purchased the computer, don't install DOS 6 yet. Get everything connected and plugged in, and then turn on your computer. If you get a DOS prompt, such as C:> or C>, or if some other program appears on-screen, then DOS is already installed. If the computer starts and displays Insert system disk in drive A or a similar message, then you need to install DOS.

Installing DOS on a new computer is fairly simple, as described in the following steps:

1. Make sure your computer is turned off.

2. Insert the DOS setup disk in floppy drive A. If you have two floppy disk drives, the top or left drive is A, and the bottom or right drive is B. If you have only one floppy disk drive, it is A.

3. Turn on the power to your computer. (The position of the power switch varies.)

4. Make sure the power to your monitor is turned on, so you can see the information that the setup program displays.

5. When the DOS prompt A> appears, type setup and press ⏎Enter. This starts the DOS Setup program.

6. Follow the on-screen instructions to complete the setup.

Replacing an Earlier Version of DOS

If an earlier version of DOS is already on your computer, you can replace it with MS-DOS 6. The setup program will copy the files from the floppy disk to your hard disk and save any information you may need to uninstall the newer version. To install MS-DOS 6 over an earlier version, perform the following steps:

1. Turn on your computer.

2. Insert Setup Disk 1 into floppy drive A or B. If you have two floppy disk drives, the top or left drive is A, and the bottom or right drive is B. If you have only one floppy disk drive, it is A.

3. If the Setup disk is in drive A, type **a:** and press ↵Enter. If the Setup disk is in drive B, type **b:** and press ↵Enter. This activates the drive that contains the Setup disk.

4. Type **setup** and press ↵Enter. A message appears, asking you to type information about yourself.

5. Type the requested information, and press ↵Enter after each entry. After you have entered the last piece of information, the first MS-DOS 6 Setup screen appears, as in Figure 3.3.

Figure 3.3

The Welcome screen for the MS-DOS 6 Setup program.

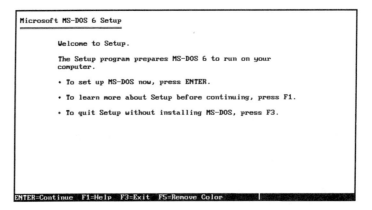

6. Press ↵Enter to continue with the installation, or press F1 to view additional information, or press F3 to cancel the installation. If you press ↵Enter, another screen appears, telling you to prepare uninstall disks, which you have already done.

7. Press ↵Enter to continue. The next screen asks you to specify the manufacturer of the current version of DOS that is on your computer, the directory where you want the new DOS files stored, and the type of monitor you have (see Figure 3.4).

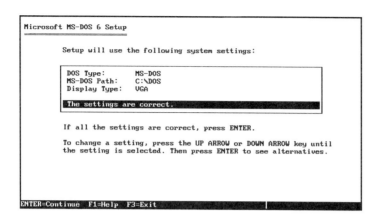

Figure 3.4
Make sure the current settings are correct.

8. In most cases, you can simply press ⏎Enter to continue. However, if you know that one of the settings is wrong, perform the following steps:

- Use ↑ to move up to the setting you want to change, and press ⏎Enter.

- Use the arrow keys to highlight the correct setting, and press ⏎Enter.

- When all the settings are correct, use the arrow keys to move to The settings are correct and press ⏎Enter.

The next setup screen allows you to choose additional DOS programs to install: Backup, Undelete, and Anti-Virus (see Figure 3.5).

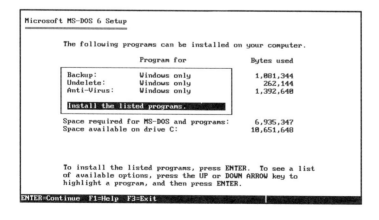

Figure 3.5
You can install DOS and/or Windows versions of Backup, Undelete, and Anti-Virus.

9. To install only the Microsoft Windows versions of Backup, Undelete, and Anti-Virus, press ⏎Enter. Otherwise, perform the following steps to install the DOS version or both the DOS and Windows versions:

   - Use ↑ to move up to the setting you want to change, and press ⏎Enter.

   - Use the arrow keys to highlight the correct setting, and press ⏎Enter.

   - When all the settings are correct, use the arrow keys to move to Install the listed programs and press ⏎Enter.

10. If Microsoft Windows is installed on your computer, a screen will appear asking you to verify the location of the Windows files. If the suggested directory is wrong, type the correct name of the directory and press ⏎Enter.

11. The next screen informs you that your system is about to be upgraded to MS-DOS 6. Press Y to continue or F3 to stop the installation. If you pressed Y, the Setup program starts copying the files from the floppy disk to your hard disk.

12. When Setup displays a message telling you to insert Uninstall Disk 1 in drive A, insert one of the Uninstall disks you prepared into drive A and press ⏎Enter. Setup copies the necessary files to the Uninstall disk and then proceeds to copy the DOS files to your hard disk.

13. When Setup is done copying files from the first disk, it displays a message telling you to insert the next disk. Remove the old disk, insert the next disk, and press ⏎Enter.

14. Repeat step 13 until the Setup program displays a message telling you to remove all floppy disks.

15. Remove the floppy disk(s) from the floppy drive(s), and press ⏎Enter. A message appears, indicating the installation is complete.

16. Press ⏎Enter. The Setup program restarts your computer with MS-DOS 6.

If your computer doesn't start correctly after installing DOS 6, see Uninstalling DOS 6 later in this chapter.

Uninstalling DOS 6

If you installed DOS 6 over a previous version of DOS, the Setup program copied your old DOS files to a directory named OLD_DOS.1 on your hard drive. (You will learn more about directories in Chapter 6.) If you did not finish the installation process, or if you have problems running other programs after installation, you can use the Uninstall disk to copy the old DOS files back to their original directory and return your computer to its original condition.

To return to the previous version of DOS, perform the following steps:

1. With your computer on, insert Uninstall Disk 1 into drive A.

2. Hold down Ctrl and Alt while pressing Del. This restarts your computer using the Uninstall disk. A warning screen appears, indicating that if you continue, the MS-DOS 6 files will be removed from your hard disk (see Figure 3.6).

3. Press R to restore the original version of DOS, or remove the Uninstall disk from drive A and press E.

4. If you pressed R, Uninstall deletes the MS-DOS 6 files from your hard disk and copies the original DOS files back to the DOS directory. A message appears when the operation is complete.

5. Remove the Uninstall disk from drive A and press any key. This restarts your computer with the original version of DOS.

Figure 3.6

*The Uninstall
MS-DOS 6
Warning screen.*

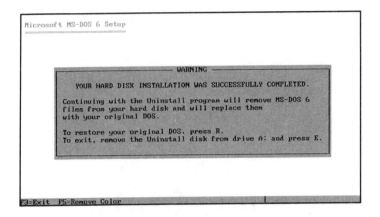

```
Microsoft MS-DOS 6 Setup
━━━━━━━━━━━━━━━━━━━━━━━━

                  ─── WARNING ───
      YOUR HARD DISK INSTALLATION WAS SUCCESSFULLY COMPLETED.

      Continuing with the Uninstall program will remove MS-DOS 6
      files from your hard disk and will replace them
      with your original DOS.

      To restore your original DOS, press R.
      To exit, remove the Uninstall disk from drive A: and press E.


F3=Exit   F5=Remove Color
```

Installing DOS on Floppy Disks

If you have a computer without a hard disk drive, you can install DOS on floppy disks. However, if you run DOS from floppy disks, you won't be able to use many of the advanced features of MS-DOS 6 described in this book.

To install MS-DOS 6 on a set of floppy disks, perform the following steps:

1. Label three blank high-density disks for use in drive A (the disks do not have to be formatted). Use the following labels:

   STARTUP/SUPPORT

   HELP/BASIC/EDIT/UTILITY

   SUPPLEMENTAL

2. Put the DOS Setup Disk 1 in drive A or B.

3. If the Setup disk is in drive A, type a: and press ⏎Enter. If the Setup disk is in drive B, type b: and press ⏎Enter. This activates the drive that contains the Setup disk.

4. Type setup /f and press ⏎Enter. A message appears, telling you to label three disks for the installation, which you have already done.

5. Press [↵Enter]. The next screen prompts you to specify the drive on which you want to install DOS (usually drive A) and the type of monitor you have.

6. In most cases, you can simply press [↵Enter] to continue. However, if you know that one of the settings is wrong, perform the following steps:

   • Use [↑] to move up to the setting you want to change, and press [↵Enter].

   • Use the arrow keys to highlight the correct setting, and press [↵Enter].

   • When all the settings are correct, use the arrow keys to move to The settings are correct and press [↵Enter].

7. Follow the on-screen messages, and insert the requested disks. The Setup program copies files from the MS-DOS 6 setup disks to the disks you labeled. When the operation is complete, the Setup program displays a message telling you what to do next.

8. Remove the floppy disk(s) from the floppy disk drive(s).

9. Write-protect the disks you created, as explained earlier in this chapter.

10. Insert the Startup/Support disk you created into drive A, and press [↵Enter]. The Setup program restarts your computer from the disk in drive A.

Booting Your Computer

As you learned in Chapter 1, your computer cannot perform a task until you start your computer with DOS. This is called *booting* the computer. When you boot your computer, the computer reads the DOS instructions from disk and stores them in its memory. The following sections explain how to boot your computer from a hard disk and from a floppy disk. You will also learn how to reboot (*warm boot*) a computer which you have already booted.

Booting from a Hard Disk

Booting from a hard disk is simple, because the DOS files are already on your hard disk. When you turn on your computer, the computer reads the DOS files automatically. To boot from a hard disk, perform the following steps:

1. Turn on your monitor. (If your monitor is off, you will not be able to view the progress of the boot.)

2. Turn on your computer. The computer will start to make sounds, and the hard disk drive light will come on, indicating that the computer is reading the DOS files. Several messages may appear on-screen followed by a DOS prompt, as shown in Figure 3.7.

Figure 3.7

When you boot your computer, a DOS prompt will appear.

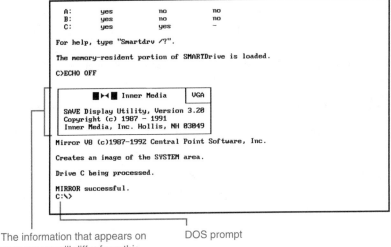

```
A:      yes        no         no
B:      yes        no         no
C:      yes        yes        —

For help, type "Smartdrv /?".

The memory-resident portion of SMARTDrive is loaded.

C>ECHO OFF

    ■►◄■ Inner Media     VGA

SAVE Display Utility, Version 3.20
Copyright (c) 1987 - 1991
Inner Media, Inc. Hollis, NH 03049

Mirror V8 (c)1987-1992 Central Point Software, Inc.

Creates an image of the SYSTEM area.

Drive C being processed.

MIRROR successful.
C:\>
```

The information that appears on your screen will differ from this.

DOS prompt

Booting from Floppy Disks

If your computer does not have a hard disk drive, you can boot from the floppy disks you created earlier in this chapter. To boot from floppy disks, perform the following steps:

1. Turn on your monitor.

2. Insert the Startup/Support disk you created earlier into floppy drive A (the top or left drive).

3. Turn on your computer. The computer will start to make sounds, and the floppy disk drive light will come on, indicating that the computer is reading the DOS files. Several messages may appear on-screen followed by a DOS prompt, as shown in Figure 3.7.

4. You can now remove the Startup disk from drive A.

Performing a Warm Boot

A cold boot consists of booting your computer when the computer is turned off. Because the computer has not yet had a chance to warm up, this is referred to as a cold boot. Once the computer is warm, you seldom need to perform a cold boot. If the computer locks up, it is best to reboot it without turning off the power. This is called a *warm boot*.

To perform a warm boot with a hard disk, simply hold down Ctrl + Alt + Del. To perform a warm boot from a floppy disk, make sure the Startup/Support disk is in floppy disk drive A, and then press Ctrl + Alt + Del.

NOTE: In this book, whenever you need to press more than one key at a time, the keys are shown separated by plus signs. For example Ctrl + Alt + Del means hold down the first two keys while pressing the third key.

Moving On from the DOS Prompt

Although the DOS prompt, C:\> or A:\>, doesn't tell you much, it does tell you one important thing: that your computer is now ready to do some real work. In the next few chapters, you will learn how to run the DOS Shell from the prompt and perform other operations at the DOS prompt.

In This Chapter

Starting the DOS Shell

The Parts of the DOS Shell

Getting Around in the Shell

Selecting Commands from Pull-Down Menus

Using the Mouse and Keyboard

Getting On-Screen Help for Shell Procedures

Starting the DOS Shell

1. At the DOS prompt (C:> or A:>), type **dosshell**.
2. Press ⏎Enter.

Parts of the DOS Shell Screen

- *Title bar*   Lets you know that you are currently using the Shell.
- *Menu bar*   Contains the names of the pull-down menus, each of which contains a set of related commands.
- *Active disk letter*   Shows the letter of the currently active disk and the name of the current directory.
- *Disk icons*   Show you the available disk drives.
- *Directory Tree window*   Shows the directories and subdirectories on the currently active disk drive.
- *File List window*   Shows a list of files in the current directory.
- *Program List*   Shows some common programs you can run from inside the DOS Shell.
- *Command bar*   Displays keys that are commonly pressed to enter commands.

Getting Help

- To get context-sensitive help, get to the point at which you need help and press F1.
- To get additional help, press Alt+H or click on Help in the menu bar. Select the Help option you want to use.

Working in the DOS Shell

As mentioned in the preceding chapter, you will use DOS mostly to manage information that is stored on disk—that is, to run programs and to manage disks, directories, and files. With MS-DOS 6, you can perform these tasks in either of two ways. You can type commands at the DOS prompt, or you can select commands from menus in the DOS Shell. These two options are illustrated in Figure 4.1.

In the Shell, you select commands from menus.

At the DOS prompt, you type commands.

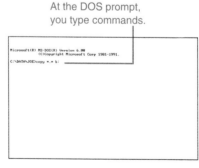

Figure 4.1

You can type commands at the DOS prompt or select commands from menus.

In this chapter, you will learn how to run the DOS Shell, move around in the Shell with both the keyboard and the mouse, change the look of the Shell, and exit the Shell. In Chapter 5, you will learn how to enter commands at the DOS prompt. Throughout this book, I will tell you how to complete each task using both methods.

Starting the DOS Shell

To start the DOS Shell, perform the following steps:

1. At the DOS prompt (for example, C:> or C> or A>), type `dosshell`.

2. Press ⏎Enter. A message box appears for a moment, indicating that Shell is reading your disk; then the DOS Shell appears, as shown in Figure 4.2.

Figure 4.2
The DOS Shell.

Menu bar   Active disk   Mouse pointer   Title bar   File List window

Active directory

Directory Tree window

Program List window

Status bar

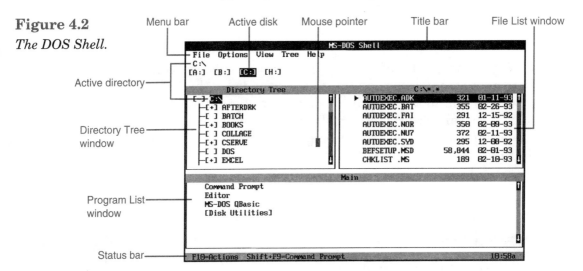

Parts of the DOS Shell

Before you begin working with the DOS Shell, you should have a general understanding of its parts. The following list introduces you to the parts of the Shell and the purpose of each part:

Title bar   At the top of the screen is the MS-DOS Shell title bar. This bar lets you know that you are currently using the Shell.

Menu bar   The menu bar contains the names of the pull-down menus. If you select a menu (as explained later), the menu opens to cover a small portion of the screen. Each menu contains a list of commands from which you can choose (see Figure 4.3).

Active disk letter   Just below the menu bar is the letter of the currently active disk. The active disk is the one at which DOS is currently looking.

Disk drive icons   Disk icons (pictures) show you the available disk drives. The active drive is highlighted. To switch drives, you can select the icon of the drive you want to activate.

Directory Tree window   The Directory Tree window shows the directories and subdirectories on the currently active drive. The active directory is highlighted. The scroll bar lets you see more of the list.

Program List   Shows some common programs that come with DOS which you may want to run from inside the DOS Shell.

File List window   Shows a list of files in the current directory. The scroll bar lets you see more of the list.

Command bar   The command bar displays keys that are commonly pressed. For example, if you want to activate the menu bar, press F10 or click on one of the menu names on the menu bar.

Mouse pointer   If you have a mouse installed on your computer, a mouse pointer will appear on-screen. You can use the mouse to point to and select drives, directories, and files and to select items from menus.

NOTE: *Click* (sometimes referred to as *click on*) means to press and release the left or right mouse button once without moving the mouse. *Double-click* means to press and release the button twice in quick succession. *Drag* means to hold down the mouse button while moving the mouse. Use the left mouse button throughout this book, unless instructed to use the right button.

Figure 4.3

The File menu pulled down from the menu bar.

File menu

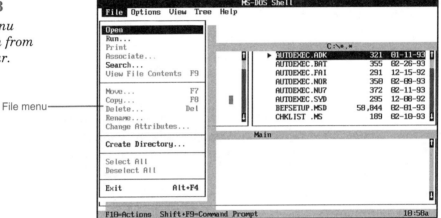

Working in the Shell

Although the DOS Shell is fairly easy to use, you need to know the basics of how to move around on the screen and enter commands. The following sections explain the basics of using the Shell with both the keyboard and the mouse.

Moving Around in the Shell

If you have a mouse, moving around in the DOS Shell is simple: you roll the mouse on your desk until the tip of the mouse pointer (on-screen) is touching the desired area of the screen; then you click the left mouse button.

If you have a keyboard, use the keys listed in Table 4.1 to move around on the screen.

Press	To Move to the
Alt or F10	Menu bar
Tab ⇄	Next screen area
⇧Shift + Tab ⇄	Previous screen area
Home	Beginning of a list or line
End	End of a list or line
Ctrl + Home	Beginning of a list
Ctrl + End	End of a list
PgDn	Next screenful of information
PgUp	Previous screenful of information
↓	Next item in a list
↑	Previous item in a list
Letter key	Next item in a list that starts with that letter

Table 4.1
Keys for Moving Around in the Shell

Selecting Commands from Menus

Selecting a command from one of the pull-down menus is a two-step process: you *pull down* the menu and then *select* the command. The two sets of Quick Steps that follow explain how to select a command using the keyboard or the mouse.

Selecting a Menu Command with the Keyboard

1. Hold down Alt and press the underlined letter in the name of the menu you want to open.

The menu is pulled down from the menu bar.

continues

continued

2. Type the underlined letter in the command you want to run.

Shell carries out the command and closes the menu.

TIP: When a menu is pulled down from the menu bar, you can move to another menu by pressing ⟵ or ⟶.

Another way to open a menu with the keyboard is to press F10 to activate the menu bar. You can then use ⟵ and ⟶ to highlight the name of the menu you want to open, and press ↵Enter to open the menu. To select a command from the menu, you can use ↑ and ↓ to highlight the command, and then press ↵Enter.

Selecting a Menu Command with the Mouse

1. Move the mouse pointer to the name of the menu you want to open, and click the left mouse button.

The menu is pulled down from the menu bar.

2. Move the mouse pointer to the command you want to run, and click the left mouse button.

Shell carries out the command and closes the menu.

If you open a menu or select a command by mistake, you can cancel it. Press Esc or click anywhere outside the menu with your mouse.

Changing Disk Drives

When you first start Shell, it activates the current disk drive and displays the directories and files on that disk. To select a different drive using the mouse, click on the disk icon for the drive to which you want to switch. To select a different drive using the keyboard, perform the following Quick Steps.

If you try to change to a drive that does not contain a disk, DOS will display an error message telling you that the drive is not ready.

Selecting a Drive with the Keyboard

1. Press Tab⇅ or ⇧Shift+Tab⇅ until the disk drive icon line is active.

   The selection cursor moves up to the disk drive icons (see Figure 4.4).

2. Use ← and → to highlight the letter of the drive to which you want to switch.

   The drive letter appears highlighted.

3. Press Spacebar or ⏎Enter.

   DOS Shell reads the disk and displays its directories and files.

TIP: A quick way to activate a disk is to hold down [Ctrl] while typing the letter that represents the disk. For example, to switch to drive A, press [Ctrl]+[A].

Figure 4.4

Activate a disk drive by selecting its icon.

Select a disk drive icon.

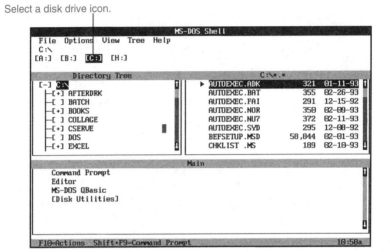

Working in the Directory Tree

The Directory Tree window displays a list of directories on the current drive. Only one directory in the list is highlighted; the names of the files stored in the selected directory appear in the File List window (see Figure 4.5).

To change directories with the mouse, click on the name of the directory to which you want to change.

To change directories with the keyboard, press [Tab↹] or [⇧Shift]+[Tab↹] until the Directory Tree window is activated (its title bar will appear highlighted). Then perform one of the following steps to select the directory:

- Use [↑] or [↓] to highlight the name of the directory.

- Type the first letter in the directory's name. This highlights the first directory whose name starts with that letter. Or use the arrow keys to highlight it.

- Press [Home] to go to the top of the tree, or [End] to go to the bottom.

If the Directory Tree is long, part of it may not appear in the window. To see more of the tree, use the scroll bar as shown in Figure 4.6, or use [PgDn] or [↓].

Active directory   Active disk drive

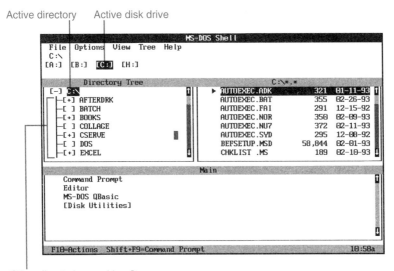

Other directories on drive C

Figure 4.5

The Directory Tree window shows a list of the directories on the current disk drive.

Click arrow to move up one directory, or hold down mouse button to scroll quickly.

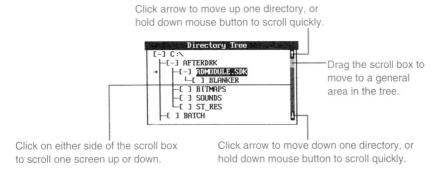

Drag the scroll box to move to a general area in the tree.

Click on either side of the scroll box to scroll one screen up or down.

Click arrow to move down one directory, or hold down mouse button to scroll quickly.

Figure 4.6

Use the scroll bar to view more of the directory tree.

Notice that some of the directories in Figure 4.5 have a plus sign (+) to the left of their names. This indicates that the directory contains at least one subdirectory that is not shown. You can expand the directory in order to view its subdirectories, by performing the following Quick Steps.

Expanding the Directory Tree

1. Select the directory you want to expand using either the keyboard or the mouse.

   The directory's name appears highlighted.

2. Press ⊞ or click on the plus sign to the left of the directory's name.

   The subdirectories sprout out from the selected directory, and a minus sign appears to the left of the expanded directory.

Once a directory is expanded, it stays expanded until you quit the Shell or collapse the directory. To collapse a directory, perform the following Quick Steps.

Collapsing the Directory Tree

1. Select the directory you want to collapse using either the keyboard or the mouse.

   The directory's name appears highlighted.

2. Press ⊟ or click on the minus sign to the left of the directory's name.

   The subdirectories retract into the selected directory, and a plus sign appears to the left of the collapsed directory.

TIP: ⊞ and ⊟ expand and collapse only the selected directory. To display all subdirectories under the selected directory, press ⊡. To display all the directories and subdirectories in the tree, press Ctrl+⊡.

Working in the File List

The File List appears to the right of the Directory Tree window and displays a list of files in the current directory (see Figure 4.7). You will select files from the list in order to view the file's contents, copy or delete the file, or move the file from one disk or directory to another. (See Chapter 8 for more details.)

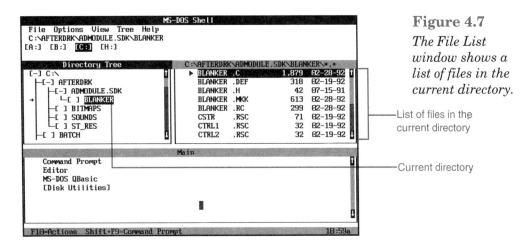

Figure 4.7
The File List window shows a list of files in the current directory.

To select a file with the mouse, click on the name of the file.

To select a file with the keyboard, press Tab ⇆ or ⇧Shift + Tab ⇆ until the File List window is activated (its title bar will appear highlighted). Then perform one of the following steps:

- Use ↑ or ↓ to highlight the name of the file.

- Type the first letter in the file's name. This highlights the first file whose name starts with that letter. Or use the arrow keys to highlight the name.

- Press Home to go to the top of the list, or End to go to the bottom.

If the file list is long, part of it may not appear in the window. To see more of the list, use the scroll bar as shown in Figure 4.8, or use PgDn or ↓.

Figure 4.8

*Use the scroll bar
to see more of the
file list.*

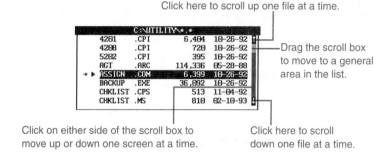

Click here to scroll up one file at a time.

Drag the scroll box
to move to a general
area in the list.

Click on either side of the scroll box to
move up or down one screen at a time.

Click here to scroll
down one file at a time.

Working with Dialog Boxes

As you work with the various DOS Shell commands, you will
encounter dialog boxes that allow you to select options and enter
information. Each dialog box contains one or more of the following
elements:

Text boxes allow you to type a specific entry (such as a file
name) in the box.

List boxes contain several items from which you can
choose.

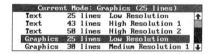

Check boxes appear to the left of some options. When you
select the option, an X appears inside the box, indicating
that the option is active. If you select the option again, it is
turned off, and the X is removed. When multiple check
boxes are displayed, you can select more than one.

[ ] Display hidden/system files

[ ] Descending order

Option buttons are similar to check boxes, but you can choose only one option button in a group of option buttons. Selecting one option button turns the other option off.

Command buttons allow you to enter a command. Most dialog boxes and windows contain at least two command buttons: a Cancel button for canceling the command, and an OK button for executing the command.

To select an item in a dialog box with the mouse, click on the item. To select an item with the keyboard, perform the following steps:

1. Press Tab↹ to move to the area of the dialog box that contains the item. See Figure 4.9.

2. Use the arrow keys to move to the specific item in the group of items.

3. Press ↵Enter.

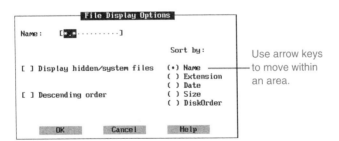

Figure 4.9

Press the Tab key to move to a different area in the dialog box.

Going to the DOS Prompt

Although you can perform most of your computer tasks through the DOS Shell, sometimes it is more convenient to work at the

DOS prompt. In such cases, you can temporarily go to the DOS prompt, perform the task, and then return to the Shell, as explained in the following Quick Steps.

CAUTION Don't run big, complicated programs like Windows from the temporary command prompt, because there may not be enough memory for the program to work correctly.

Going to the MS-DOS Command Prompt

1. Press ⇧Shift+F9.

The DOS Shell remains in memory, but the DOS command prompt appears.

2. Perform the desired task from the DOS prompt.

Techniques for working at the DOS prompt are discussed in the next chapter.

3. When you are finished, return to the DOS prompt.

4. Type exit and press ↵Enter.

You are returned to the DOS Shell.

Displaying the Program List

In Chapter 9, you will learn the details of how to set up and run other programs from the DOS Shell. However, at this point, you should learn about the Program list that appears at the bottom of

your screen. If your screen does not show the program list, perform
the following Quick Steps.

Displaying the Program List and File List

1. Press ⌈Alt⌉+⌈V⌋ or click on
View in the menu bar.

The **V**iew menu opens.

2. Press ⌈F⌋ or click on
Program/File Lists.

The Shell displays a list of
programs and program
groups, as shown in Fig-
ure 4.10.

A program group, such as Disk Utilities, contains several
programs. If you double-click on a program group icon, or highlight it and press ⌐Enter⌐, another program list will appear,
showing the programs in that group. To run a program, double-
click on it, or highlight it and press ⌐Enter⌐.

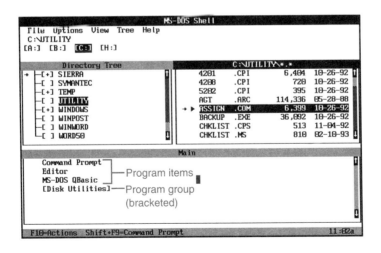

Figure 4.10
*The Program List
window displays
programs and
program groups.*

TIP: If you prefer, you can set up the DOS Shell to show only the Program List. Open the View menu and select Program List. You can also set up the screen to show only the File List: open the View menu and select Single File List.

Changing the Appearance of the Shell

When you first start the Shell, it runs in either text mode or graphics mode and in either color or black-and-white, depending on the type of monitor you have. To change the screen colors, perform the following Quick Steps.

Changing the Screen Colors

1. Press Alt + O or click on **Options** in the menu bar.	This opens the **Options** menu.
2. Press O or click on Colors.	The Color Scheme dialog box appears, as shown in Figure 4.11.
3. Use the arrow keys to highlight the desired color scheme, or click on it.	
4. Tab to the Preview button and press ↵Enter, or click on the Preview button.	The Shell repaints the screen to show how the new color scheme will look.
5. Repeat steps 3 and 4 until the screen appears as you like it.	

6. Tab to the OK button and press ⏎Enter, or click on the OK button.

The Shell closes the dialog box and appears in its new colors.

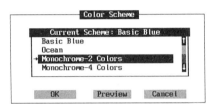

Figure 4.11

Use the Color Scheme dialog box to change the colors used to display the Shell.

In addition to changing the screen colors, you can select either of two display modes—graphics or text. *Graphics mode* displays icons for the disk drives and directories. *Text mode* uses characters, such as [], to represent the drives and directories. You can also choose to reduce the size of the type on-screen to display more directory names and file names at the same time.

NOTE: Although text mode is not as pretty as graphics mode, it does update the screen a little faster, so some users prefer it. If your monitor is capable of displaying graphics, however, you will probably want to work in graphics mode.

To change display modes, perform the following Quick Steps.

Changing from Graphics to Text Mode and Back

1. Press Alt+O or click on Options in the menu bar.

This opens the Options menu.

continues

continued

2. Press ⬚D⬚ or click on Display.	The Screen Display Mode dialog box appears, as shown in Figure 4.12.
3. Use the arrow keys to highlight the desired display mode, or click on it.	
4. Tab to the Preview button and press ⬚⏎Enter⬚, or click on the Preview button.	The Shell redraws the screen to show how the display mode will look.
5. Repeat steps 3 and 4 until the screen appears as you like it.	
6. Tab to the OK button and press ⬚⏎Enter⬚, or click on the OK button.	The Shell closes the dialog box and appears in its new display mode.

Figure 4.12

Use the Screen Display Mode dialog box to change from graphics mode to text mode and back.

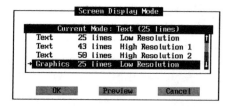

NOTE: The rest of the screens shown in this book will be in graphics mode. Set your screen to graphics mode if you want yours to look the same as you follow along.

Getting Help in the DOS Shell

When you get stuck or forget the meaning of a command or how it works, the DOS Shell provides a handy on-line help system. The help is context-sensitive, meaning the program identifies the command or function you are about to perform and provides help on it. You can also call up a help index and locate the specific information you desire.

You can get help in either of two ways: Press F1 or pull down the **H**elp menu from the menu bar, as shown in Figure 4.13. The **H**elp menu offers the following options:

Index   Displays an extensive alphabetical list of topics about which you can get help.

Keyboard   Displays help for keyboard users.

Shell Basics   Offers information about the skills you need to get started.

Commands   Displays information about Shell commands.

Procedures   Provides help about specific tasks you may want to perform.

Using Help   Teaches you how to use the on-line help system.

About Shell   Displays a dialog box that tells you the current version of DOS that you are running.

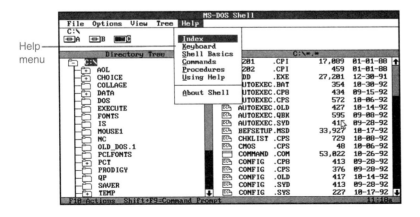

Figure 4.13
The Help menu offers various help options.

Getting Around in a Help Window

When you select an item from the Help menu or press F1, a help window appears, like the one in Figure 4.14. This window contains the following items:

Helpful information Each help window contains information that the Shell assumes you want to know. To see more information, use the scroll bar, PgDn, or ↓.

Additional help topics Most help windows contain additional help topics which are shaded or appear in a different color. To select one of these topics with the mouse, double-click on the topic. To select a topic with the keyboard, press Tab↹ to move to the next topic or ⇧Shift + Tab↹ to move to the previous topic, and then press ↵Enter.

Command buttons At the bottom of each help window are several command buttons: Close, Back, Keys, Index, and Help. To select one of these buttons, click on it with the mouse, or tab to the button and press ↵Enter.

Figure 4.14
A typical help window.

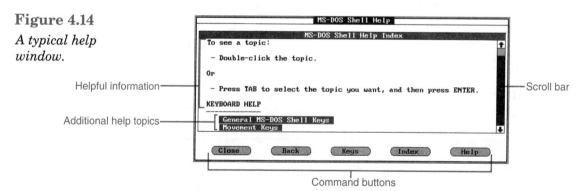

Getting Context-Sensitive Help

DOS Shell monitors everything you do with the keyboard or mouse. If you want help on a particular command, highlight it with the arrow keys, and then press F1. A help window for the highlighted command appears.

To get help for a procedure you want to perform, start performing the procedure up to the point at which you need help. Then press F1.

Exiting the DOS Shell

To exit the DOS Shell and return to the DOS prompt, perform the following Quick Steps.

Leaving the DOS Shell

1. Press Alt + F or click on File in the menu bar.

The File menu opens.

2. Press X or click on Exit.

The DOS Shell is removed from memory, and you are returned to the DOS prompt.

TIP: To leave the DOS Shell without going through the File menu, press Alt + F4.

Is That All?

In this chapter, you learned only the basics of working in the DOS Shell. In later chapters, you will learn how to use the DOS Shell to copy and move files, run programs, and perform more complex tasks. In the next chapter, you will learn the basics of working at the DOS prompt.

In This Chapter

How to Type a Command at the DOS Prompt

Parts of a DOS Command

Cancelling a DOS Command

Some Common DOS Commands

Getting Help at the DOS Prompt

Parts of a DOS Command

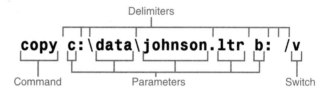

Changing Disk Drives

1. Type the letter of the desired drive followed by a colon. For example, to change to drive A, type `a:`.
2. Press `↵Enter`.

Changing Directories

1. Change to the drive that contains the desired directory.
2. Type `cd\ dirname`, where *dirname* is the name of the desired directory.
3. Press `↵Enter`.

Viewing a List of Files

1. Change to the drive and directory that contains the files you want to list.
2. Type `dir` and press `↵Enter`.

Getting Help at the DOS Prompt

1. At the DOS prompt, type `help`.
2. Press `↵Enter`.
3. Select the command for which you want help.

5

Working at the DOS Prompt

When you start your computer, one of the first things you see on-screen is a *prompt* indicating that the computer is now ready to accept a command. The prompt typically consists of a letter followed by a colon (:) and an angle bracket. It looks something like one of these:

```
C:>

C:\>

C>
```

Like the DOS Shell, the DOS prompt provides a way for you to communicate with DOS and use DOS to perform specific tasks. However, unlike the DOS Shell, the prompt requires you to know the names of the DOS commands and how to enter the commands. In this chapter, you will learn the basics of working at the DOS prompt.

Entering Commands at the DOS Prompt

If you ran DOS Shell in the preceding chapter, you have already entered a command at the DOS prompt. You typed `dosshell` and pressed ⏎Enter. That was pretty easy, as are most of the DOS commands you will encounter. However, some commands require a little more information. For example, the COPY command (used for copying files) requires that you specify the name of the file you want to copy and the location of the disk or directory to which you want to copy the files. In order to have DOS carry out the command, you need to know how to enter that information.

The following sections explain the various parts of a typical command and the order in which you must type the parts.

The Parts of a DOS Command

A typical DOS command (see Figure 5.1) consists of the following elements:

Command   This is the name of the command. It tells DOS which action you want DOS to carry out.

Delimiters   Delimiters are spaces and special characters (such as /, \, : and) that break down the command line for DOS. Think of delimiters as the spaces between words in a sentence. Without the spaces, a sentence would be difficult or impossible for you to read and understand.

Parameters   Parameters specify the objects on which you want DOS to perform the action. For example, if you tell DOS to copy a file, you must specify which file or files you want it to copy and where you want the copies placed.

Switches   Switches allow you to control how the command performs its action. For example, the DIR command shows a list of files in the current directory. If you add the /W switch (DIR /W), the listing appears in several columns across the screen, allowing more file names to appear on-screen. You can use more than one switch at a time.

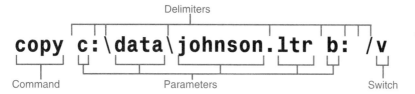

Figure 5.1
A typical DOS command.

Does Capitalization Matter?

When you type a DOS command, you can use uppercase characters, lowercase characters, or a mix of the two. DOS does not distinguish between uppercase and lowercase characters; to DOS, DIR, dir, and dIr are all the same command.

Being Grammatical in DOS

Although capitalization doesn't matter, grammar, or *syntax*, does. That is, each part of a DOS command has a specific location in the command line. If you type the part in any other location, DOS will not be able to properly execute the command.

So what is the proper syntax? Command first, then parameters, then switches, as shown in Figure 5.1.

A Brief Course in DOS Syntax

With most DOS commands, you can learn about the various parameters and switches you can use by typing the command followed by a space and the /? switch and pressing ⏎Enter. For example, to learn which parameters and switches you can use with the DISKCOPY command, type `diskcopy /?` at the DOS prompt and press ⏎Enter. You will see a screenful of information as in Figure 5.2.

Figure 5.2

DOS has a distinct way of showing you the proper way to enter a command.

What the command does   Proper syntax for the command   List of switches

Notes about the command

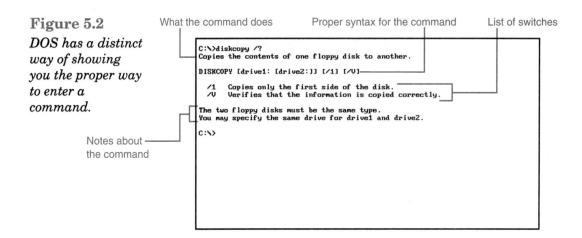

```
C:\>diskcopy /?
Copies the contents of one floppy disk to another.

DISKCOPY [drive1: [drive2:]] [/1] [/U]

  /1  Copies only the first side of the disk.
  /U  Verifies that the information is copied correctly.

The two floppy disks must be the same type.
You may specify the same drive for drive1 and drive2.

C:\>
```

This screen tells you what the command does and shows you a complete command line with all the options listed. Each parameter and switch is shown in square brackets [ ]. When you type the command, you substitute specific entries for the parameters and you type the switches—without the square brackets. For example, the following list provides some sample entries for the DISKCOPY command:

```
diskcopy a: a:

diskcopy a: b:

diskcopy a: a: /1

diskcopy b: b: /v
```

Conventions Used in This Book

In this book, I use a slightly different way for telling you how to type a DOS command. The command itself and any parameters and switches I want you to type will appear in bold, monospaced, colored print. Optional parameters and switches will appear the same way but will be italic. (With optional parameters, you may have to supply a specific entry.) For example, at some point in the book, I may tell you to type

```
copy d1:filename.ext d2:
```

where *d1* is the name of the drive you want to copy the file from, *filename* is the name of the file, *ext* is the file name extension, and *d2* is the letter of the drive to which you want to copy the file.

You will have to supply a drive letter for *d1*, a file name and extension for *filename.ext*, and a drive letter for *d2*. For example, you may type the following:

```
copy c:johnson.ltr a:
```

Editing a Command

If you make a mistake while typing a command, you can edit the command by backspacing over it and typing your correction. To replace the entire command, press Esc to delete whatever you typed, and then type the command you want to enter.

Later in this chapter, you will learn about a DOS program called DOSKey that can help you edit DOS commands.

Cancelling or Stopping a Command

No DOS command is executed until you press ⏎Enter. If you type the command and decide that you don't want to enter it, simply press Esc. If you press ⏎Enter by mistake, you may be able to stop the command by pressing Ctrl+Break or Ctrl+C, but don't count on it.

Entering Some Commonly Used DOS Commands

The easiest way to learn about DOS commands is to try entering a few at the DOS prompt. The following sections explain some of the commonly used commands and how to enter them at the DOS prompt.

Choosing a Disk Drive

To activate a disk drive in DOS, first make sure a formatted disk is in the drive to which you want to change. This disk can be a program disk you purchased, a floppy disk on which you saved files, or your hard disk. Type the drive letter followed by a colon, and press ⏎Enter. Here are two examples:

- To change to drive C, type c: and press ⏎Enter.
- To change to drive A, type a: and press ⏎Enter.

NOTE: DOS has two types of commands: internal and external. *Internal* commands are commands that DOS has at its fingertips and can execute very quickly. *External* DOS commands run actual programs that come with DOS.

Changing Directories

Before you can view a list of files in a given directory, you must change to (activate) that directory. To change to a directory in DOS, you use the CHDIR or CD command, both of which stand for Change Directory. Because CD is shorter, I will use it in my examples. The following examples explain how to use the CD command:

- To change to the root directory (the first directory on the disk), type `cd\` and press `↵Enter`.

- To change to a subdirectory of the root directory (a directory just under the root directory), type `cd\`*dirname*, where *dirname* is the name of the directory to which you want to change. Press `↵Enter`.

- To change to a subdirectory of the current directory, type `cd` *dirname*, where *dirname* is the name of the subdirectory.

- To change to a specific subdirectory, type `cd\` followed by a complete path to the subdirectory. (Remember from Chapter 3 that a path consists of the directory and subdirectories that lead to the desired directory.) For example, type `cd\`*dirname1**dirname2**dirname3* and press `↵Enter`.

> **NOTE:** When you change to a directory, the DOS prompt may or may not display the name of the current directory. If the name of the directory does not appear and you want it to appear, type `prompt $p$g` and press `↵Enter`. The PROMPT command tells DOS how to display the prompt. $p tells DOS to display the current drive and directory, and $g tells DOS to display the angle bracket >.

Viewing a Directory Tree

Although the DOS prompt does not allow you to change directories by selecting them from a directory tree (as Shell does), you can view a directory tree by using the TREE command. To view a directory tree, perform the following Quick Steps.

Viewing a Directory Tree at the DOS Prompt

1. Change to the drive whose directory tree you want to view.

   For example, type c: and press ⏎Enter.

2. Type tree and press ⏎Enter.

   The directory tree for the current drive appears, as shown in Figure 5.3.

Figure 5.3

The directory tree for the current disk drive.

Volume label and serial number of disk

Directory tree for drive C

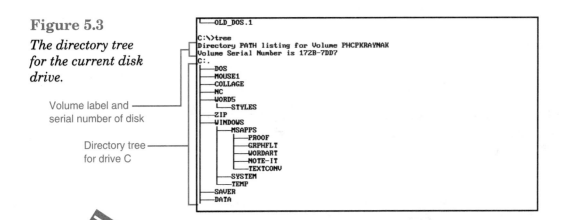

TIP: The TREE command allows you to enter two switches to change the display of the tree /f and /a: tree /f displays a list of files in each directory; tree /a uses slashes and plus signs to show the branches of the directory tree (without the /a switch, the branches appear as angled lines, which makes the display look cleaner). Adding | MORE to the end of the command, as in tree /f ¦ more, shows the tree one screenful at a time.

Viewing a List of Files

Even if you stick a label on your disk telling you what is on the disk, you won't know which files are on a disk until you view a list of the files. In the preceding chapter, you saw how the DOS Shell displayed a list of files in the File List window. At the DOS prompt, however, there is no File List window; you must enter a command to view a list of files. To view a list of files at the DOS prompt, perform the following Quick Steps.

Viewing a List of Files

1. Change to the disk drive that contains the list of files you want to view.

   For example, type `c:` and press `⏎Enter`.

2. Change to the directory that contains the files you want to view.

   For example, to view a list of files in the DOS directory, type `cd\dos` and press `⏎Enter`.

3. Type `dir` and press `⏎Enter`.

   A file list appears, as shown in Figure 5.4.

```
DEFAULT  SLT        26 10-14-92   2:41p
MWAV     INI        24 10-14-92   2:43p
MSBACKUP OVL    133328 10-26-92   6:00a
MSBACKUP HLP    314226 10-26-92   6:00a
MSBCONFG HLP     45782 10-26-92   6:00a
DBLSPACE EXE    286338 10-26-92   6:00a
DBLSPACE HLP     35342 10-26-92   6:00a
DBLSPACE INF      1113 10-26-92   6:00a
DBLSPACE SYS       217 10-26-92   6:00a
DELOLDOS EXE     17710 10-26-92   6:00a
EMM386   EXE    114782 10-26-92   6:00a
RAMDRIVE SYS      5873 10-26-92   6:00a
SMARTDRV EXE     44121 10-26-92   6:00a
COMMAND  COM     53022 10-26-92   6:00a
QBASIC   INI        48 10-14-92   4:02p
DOSBACK  LOG         0 10-14-92   3:56p
DOSSHELL INI     17169 10-30-92  12:52p
AUTOEXEC UMB       320 10-17-92   5:52p
CONFIG   UMB       227 10-17-92   5:10p
DOSBACK  TMP      5022 10-14-92   3:50p
DOSBACK  RST       600 10-14-92   3:50p
       170 file(s)     7229010 bytes
                       4192256 bytes free

C:\DOS>
```

Most of the file list has scrolled off the screen.

Figure 5.4

The DIR command displays a list of files in the current drive and directory.

Preventing the List from Scrolling off the Screen

If the file list contains too many files to fit on one screen, the list scrolls off the top of the screen. To prevent the list from scrolling off the screen, you have three options:

- Type dir /w and press ⏎Enter to display only the names of the files and to display the file names in five columns across the screen (see Figure 5.5). This display shows many more files and usually is sufficient for showing all the files in a directory, but it too can scroll off the screen.

- Type dir /p and press ⏎Enter to display only one screenful of file names at a time. Press any key to see the next screenful of names.

- Type dir ¦more and press ⏎Enter. This does the same thing as dir /p.

Figure 5.5

A list of files as displayed with the DIR /W command.

More file names fit on-screen, but part of the list is still not shown.

```
SHELL.CLR       SHELL.HLP       SHELL.MEU       DOSSHELL.HLP    QBASIC.HLP
DOSUTIL.MEU     HELP.HLP        QBASIC.EXE      DOSHELP.HLP     DOSHELP.EXE
4201.CPI        4208.CPI        5202.CPI        ASSIGN.COM      EDIT.HLP
GRAFTABL.COM    HELP.COM        EDIT.COM        JOIN.EXE        LCD.CPI
PRINTER.SYS     EXE2BIN.EXE     APPEND.EXE      CHKDSK.EXE      DISKCOMP.COM
DISKCOPY.COM    FC.EXE          FIND.EXE        LABEL.EXE       MORE.COM
RESTORE.EXE     CHKLIST.CPS     DOSHELP.CPS     SORT.EXE        DRIVER.SYS
GRAPHICS.COM    GRAPHICS.PRO    DOSSHELL.EXE    MWUNDEL.EXE     REPLACE.EXE
TREE.COM        DOSKEY.COM      SUBST.EXE       LOADFIX.COM     README.TXT
APPNOTES.TXT    UNDELETE.EXE    MWUNDEL.HLP     MWAVDOSL.DLL    MWGRAFIC.DLL
MWAVDRVL.DLL    MWAVDLG.DLL     MWAVSCAN.DLL    MWAV.EXE        MWAVABSI.DLL
MWAVTREE.DLL    MSAVW.HLP       UNGRAFIC.DLL    MWAVSOS.DLL     WNTSR.DLL
MWAVTSR.EXE     VSAFE.COM       MSAV.EXE        MSAVIRUS.LST    MSAV.HLP
CPSHELL.OVL     CHKSTATE.SYS    MEMMAKER.EXE    MWBACKUP.EXE    MWBACKUP.HLP
MEMMAKER.HLP    MEMMAKER.INF    SIZER.EXE       MSTOOLS.DLL     WNTOOLS.GRP
VFINTD.386      MWBACKF.DLL     MWBACKR.DLL     MSBACKDB.OVL    MSBACKDR.OVL
MSBACKFB.OVL    MSBACKFR.OVL    MSBCONFG.OVL    MSBACKUP.EXE    DEFAULT.SLT
MWAV.INI        MSBACKUP.OVL    MSBACKUP.HLP    MSBCONFG.HLP    DBLSPACE.EXE
DBLSPACE.HLP    DBLSPACE.INF    DBLSPACE.SYS    DELOLDOS.EXE    EMM386.EXE
RAMDRIVE.SYS    SMARTDRV.EXE    COMMAND.COM     QBASIC.INI      DOSBACK.LOG
DOSSHELL.INI    AUTOEXEC.UMB    CONFIG.UMB      DOSBACK.TMP     DOSBACK.RST
        170 file(s)     7229018 bytes
                        4161536 bytes free

C:\DOS>
```

Using Wild-Card Characters for Groups of Files

Many times, you may not want to view all the files in a directory. You may, for example, want to view only those files that have the .EXE extension or the .COM extension. To view a group of files, you can use *wild-card characters*.

A *wild-card character* is any character that takes the place of another character or a group of characters. Think of a wild-card character as a wild card in a game of poker. If the Joker is wild, you can use it in place of any card in the entire deck of cards. In DOS, you can use two wild characters: a question mark (?) and an asterisk (*). The question mark stands in for a single character. The asterisk stands in for a group of characters. The following examples show how you can use wild-card entries with the DIR command:

- Type `dir *.com` and press Enter to view a list of all files with the .COM file name extension (for example, HELP.COM, EDIT.COM, and TREE.COM).

- Type `dir ???.*` and press Enter to view a list of all files that have a file name of three letters or fewer (for example, EGA.SYS, SYS.COM, and FC.EXE).

- Type `dir s???.*` and press Enter to view a list of all files whose file name starts with S and has four letters or fewer (for example, SORT.EXT and SYS.COM).

- Type `dir *.?o?` and press Enter to view a list of all files that have a three-letter file name extension whose middle letter is O (for example, GRAPHICS.COM and DOSBACK.LOG).

Getting Help at the DOS Prompt

DOS provides a great deal of helpful information about its commands, including details about the available switches for each command, the proper way to enter the command, and plenty of examples. However, you need to know how to get this help. The following sections explain how to use the DOS Help system.

Accessing the MS-DOS Help: Command Reference

If you don't know what you want help with, the best action to take is to type **help** at the DOS prompt and press ⏎Enter. DOS displays the MS-DOS Help: Command Reference window, shown in Figure 5.6.

This window displays as many commands as will fit on-screen. To view additional commands, press PgDn, or use ↓. If you have a mouse, you can use the scroll bar at the right of the screen to display more of the list.

Figure 5.6

The MS-DOS Help: Command Reference window.

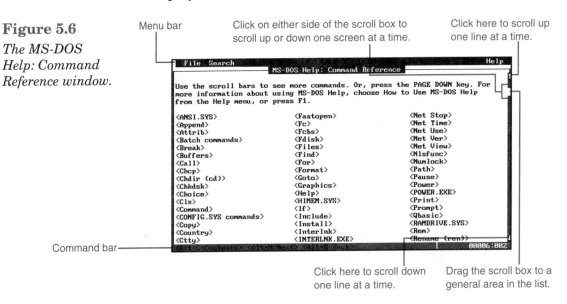

Menu bar

Click on either side of the scroll box to scroll up or down one screen at a time.

Click here to scroll up one line at a time.

Command bar

Click here to scroll down one line at a time.

Drag the scroll box to a general area in the list.

Notice that all the commands appear between angled brackets <>. DOS refers to any item that appears between angled brackets as a *jump*. You can select one to jump to a help window that displays specific information about the jump item. To view information about a command in the list, tab to the command (or press ⇧Shift+Tab⇥ to move to a previous command) and press ⏎Enter, or click on the command with your mouse. A help window will appear like the one in Figure 5.7.

Select Notes to see more information.

Select Examples to view sample entries.

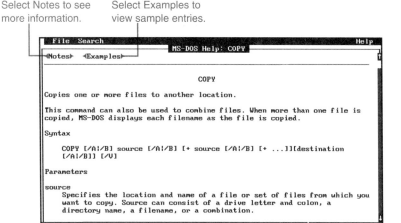

Figure 5.7

When you select a command, DOS displays information about that command.

Keep in mind that some of the information about a particular item may not fit in the help window. To view more information, use PgDn, ↓, or the scroll bar to scroll the information into view.

At the bottom of each help window are the following command buttons, which let you move quickly through the help system. To select a command button, press the key or keys associated with the button or click on the button with your mouse.

<Alt+C=Contents> Press Alt + C or click on this button to go back to the list of DOS commands.

<Alt+N=Next> Press Alt + N or click on this button to display the next help screen in this particular series of screens.

<Alt+B=Back> Press Alt + B or click on this button to move to the previous help screen. You can keep pressing this button to step back through the help screens.

Although you can find most of the information you need by selecting a command from the Command Reference list, sometimes you won't know which command to use for the task you want to perform. For example, say you want to back up the files on your hard disk. Would you know that the command to use is MSBACK? To find help for backing up files, you could have DOS search for the text "back up." The following Quick Steps lead you through the operation.

Searching for Help

1. Press Alt+S or click on Search in the menu bar.

   The Search menu opens.

2. Press F or click on Find.

   The Find dialog box appears, prompting you to specify the text for which you want to search (see Figure 5.8).

3. Type the text you want to search for in the Find What text box.

4. Press Tab⁵ to move to the Match Upper/Lowercase check box, and press Spacebar if you want to search for text that exactly matches what you typed, including upper- and lowercase characters.

   If you leave this option off, DOS will not pay attention to capitalization.

5. Press Tab⁵ to move to the Whole Word check box, and press Spacebar if you want to search only for whole words that match the words you typed.

   If you leave this option off, DOS will search for any text that matches what you typed, even if that text appears as a part of a larger word.

6. Tab to the OK button and press ⏎Enter, or click on it with your mouse.

   DOS starts searching for the text you typed and stops on the first text that matches your entry.

7. If this is the help screen you wanted, you can stop. Otherwise, press F3 to search for the next occurrence of the text that matches what you typed.

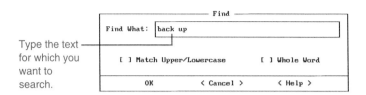

Type the text for which you want to search.

Figure 5.8
*Use the Find
dialog box to
search for a help
topic.*

When you have found the help you needed, and read or printed the help screen, you will want to exit the Help system and return to the DOS prompt. To exit the Help system, perform the following Quick Steps.

Exiting the Help System

1. Press ⌊Alt⌋+⌊F⌋ or click on File in the menu bar.

    The File menu opens.

2. Press ⌊X⌋ or click on Exit.

    This closes the Help window and returns you to the DOS prompt.

Getting Help About a Specific Command

If you know which DOS command you want help with, you can quickly go to the help screen for that command by typing `help` followed by the name of the command for which you need help. For example, type `help copy` to view information about copying files from one disk or directory to another.

Saving Time with DOSKey

DOSKey is a special DOS program that makes working at the DOS prompt much easier. Normally, when you need to edit a command, you must backspace over the characters to delete the mistyped command and then type new text. With DOSKey, you can use the arrow keys to move to the error and then type your correction. In other words, you correct only the error, not the entire command line. DOSKey also allows you to call up previously entered commands so you don't have to retype them.

To run DOSKey, type `doskey` at the DOS prompt and press ⏎Enter. A message appears on-screen indicating that DOSKey is now in memory. To edit with DOSKey, use the keys listed in Table 5.1.

Table 5.1
DOSKey Editing Keys

Press	To
← or →	Move left or right one character at a time.
Ctrl+← or Ctrl+→	Move left or right one word at a time.
Home	Move to the beginning of the command.
End	Move to the end of the command.
Esc	Erase the command.
Del	Delete the character that the cursor is on.
◆Backspace	Delete the character to the left of the cursor.
Ins	To switch from Overstrike mode to Insert mode. In Insert mode, anything you type is inserted at the cursor position. In Overstrike mode, anything you type replaces existing text.

In addition to allowing you to edit a DOS command line, DOSKey lets you recall previously entered commands at the DOS prompt. To recall a command, use the keys listed in Table 5.2.

Table 5.2
DOSKey Command Recall Keys

Press	To Recall
↑	The DOS command that you entered before the command that is displayed.
↓	The DOS command that you entered after the command that is displayed.
PgUp	The first DOS command that you entered.

Press	To Recall
PgDn	The last DOS command that you entered.
F1	The last DOS command, one character at a time.
F7	A list of DOS commands that are stored in memory.

Is That All?

DOS includes hundreds of commands that you can enter at the DOS help. Many of these commands are covered in this book; whereas others are too advanced for this book. However, now that you know how to enter a command at the DOS prompt and how to get help for a command, you can learn about any command, no matter how advanced.

Throughout this book, I will focus on entering DOS commands from the DOS Shell. If you can perform the same task from the DOS prompt, I will provide those instructions as well.

In This Chapter

Managing Disks from the DOS Shell and DOS Prompt

Changing Disk Drives

Formatting Floppy Disks

Copying Disks

Comparing Disks

Changing Disk Drives

- In the DOS Shell, click on the icon for the disk drive to which you want to change. Or hold down Ctrl while typing the letter of the drive to which you want to change.
- At the DOS prompt, type the letter of the drive to which you want to change, followed by a colon, and press ↵Enter.

Displaying the Disk Utilities in the Shell

1. Press Alt+V or click on View in the menu bar.
2. Press P or select Program List.
3. Select the Disk Utilities program group.

Formatting a Floppy Disk from the Shell

1. Select the Format program icon from the Disk Utilities.
2. Type the letter of the drive you want to use for the formatting operation, and type a colon.
3. Press ↵Enter.
4. Insert the disk you want to format into the specified drive, and press ↵Enter.

Copying Disks

1. Select the Disk Copy program icon from the Disk Utilities.
2. Type the letters of the drive(s) you want to copy from and to separated by a space. For example, type a: a: or b: b:.
3. Press ↵Enter.
4. Insert the disk you want to copy into the specified drive, and press ↵Enter.
5. Follow the on-screen instructions, and switch disks when instructed to do so.

Working with Disks

As you saw in Chapter 2, disks provide permanent storage for program files and for the files you create and save. And because DOS is a *disk* operating system, it offers several features for working with disks and working with the files stored on disk.

In this chapter, you will learn how to use the disk-related DOS features, which allow you to view the contents of a disk, prepare a disk for storing data, and copy disks. In Chapter 7, you will learn how to work with the subdivisions of a disk—directories. And in Chapter 8, you will learn how to work with individual files stored on a disk.

Changing Disk Drives

In Chapter 4, you learned how to activate a disk drive in the Shell. To review, here's how you do it: Click on the drive icon for the drive you want to activate, or hold down Ctrl while typing the letter of the drive.

In Chapter 5, you learned how to change disk drives at the DOS prompt. To review, here's how you do it: Type the drive letter, followed by a colon, and press ⏎Enter. For example, type **a:** and press ⏎Enter.

Preparing a Disk for Storing Data

Before you can store data on a disk, you must *format* the disk. Formatting divides a disk into small storage areas and creates a *file allocation table* (FAT) on the disk that acts as a map, telling your computer the location of all its storage areas. Whenever you save a file to a disk, it is saved in one or more of these storage areas. By checking the FAT, DOS can find all the parts of the file and piece them together so that you can work with the file as a single unit.

Typically, you will format a given disk only once—when it is brand-new. If you have a computer with a hard disk drive, the disk may have already been formatted by the manufacturer. (If your computer has a hard disk drive and you are using your computer now, the disk has been formatted; if it weren't, you couldn't use it.)

CAUTION   If you format a disk that contains data, that data is erased during the formatting process. Before you format a disk, make sure the disk is blank or that it contains data you will never again need.

Types of Floppy Disks and Drives

All floppy disks and disk drives are not created equal. Some disks can store information on only one side of the disk, whereas others can use both sides. Some disks can store more information than others can. The point of this is that you have to know a few things before you start formatting disks. Specifically, you must ask yourself the following questions:

- *What kind of floppy disk drives do I have?* Do you have a 5 1/4-inch drive? A 3 1/2-inch drive? What capacity is the disk drive? Is it high-density (1.2M or 1.44M) or double-density (360K or 720K)? (Remember, a high-density drive can format both high-density and double-density disks, but a double-density drive can format only double-density disks.)

- *What kind of floppy disks do I want to format?* Do you have high-density or double-density disks? Check the disks or the box in which the disks came.

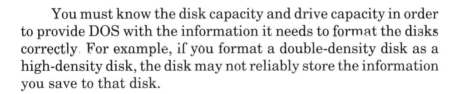

To determine the type of disks you have, look at the manufacturer's label on the disks or on the box that the disks came in. The two most common types of disks are DSDD and DSHD. DSDD stands for *double-sided, double-density*, and it is the same as *low-density* (LD)—usually 360K 5 1/4-inch disks or 720K 3 1/2-inch disks. DSHD stands for *double-sided, high-density* disks—usually 1.2M 5 1/4-inch disks or 1.44M 3 1/2-inch disks.

You must know the disk capacity and drive capacity in order to provide DOS with the information it needs to format the disks correctly. For example, if you format a double-density disk as a high-density disk, the disk may not reliably store the information you save to that disk.

Using the DOS Format Program

DOS features a separate program for formatting disks called FORMAT. You can run the program from the DOS prompt or from the DOS Shell, as explained later. However, regardless of how you run it, you must know the various parameters and switches to use with the FORMAT command in order to provide DOS with the proper instructions for formatting the disk.

If you are formatting a brand-new disk in a drive whose capacity matches the capacity of the disk (for example, a 1.2M disk in a 1.2M disk drive), you can format the disk by entering the FORMAT command followed by the letter of the drive you want to use. For example, `format b:` tells DOS to format the disk in drive B. (You must use a parameter—usually a: or b:—to specify the disk drive to use.)

However, if you wanted to perform a special formatting operation (for example, formatting a 720K disk in a 1.2M disk drive), you would need to add switches to provide DOS with more detailed instructions. In that example, you would have to enter the following command:

```
format b: /f:720
```

You can use other switches, as listed in Table 6.1, to provide additional formatting instructions.

Table 6.1
Commonly Used DOS Formatting Switches

Switch	Example	What It Does
/V:label	**format b: /v:*business***	Lets you name the disk (give the disk a volume name). If you do not use the /V switch, DOS will prompt you to enter a name after the disk is formatted.
/Q	**format a: /q**	Uses Quick Format for a previously formatted disk. Normally the Format program checks for defects on a disk. This switch tells Format not to check for defects.
/F:size	**format b: /f:*360***	Lets you format a lower-capacity disk in a higher-capacity drive.
/S	**format a: /s**	Makes a disk bootable. That is, you will be able to use the disk to start your computer.
/4	**format a: /4**	Formats a 5 1/4-inch double-density disk in a 5 1/4-inch 1.2M disk drive.

NOTE: If you choose to enter a volume name, it can be up to 11 characters and can include spaces. You cannot use tabs or any of the following characters:

```
 *  ?  /  \  |  .  ,  ;  :  +  =  [  ]  (  )  &  ^  <  >  "
```

When formatting a disk from the DOS Shell, you omit the FORMAT command, because you select it from a menu. All you need to type is the letter of the disk drive and any switches you want to use. The following Quick Steps lead you through the process of formatting from the Shell.

QUICK STEPS

Formatting from the DOS Shell

1. Press Alt+V or click on View in the menu bar.

   The **View** menu opens.

2. Press P or select Program List.

   The Shell displays a list of programs and program groups.

3. Highlight the Disk Utilities program group and press ↵Enter, or double-click on the group with your mouse.

   This displays a list of the DOS utility programs, including the Format program. (See Figure 6.1.)

4. Highlight the Format program icon and press ↵Enter, or double-click on it with your mouse.

   The Format dialog box appears, prompting you to specify the disk drive you want to use. (See Figure 6.2.)

5. Type the letter of the drive you want to use for the formatting operation, and type a colon.

continues

continued

6. To add a switch from Table 6.1, press `Spacebar` and then type the switch you want to use.

To use more than one switch, separate the switches with a space.

7. Press `↵Enter`.

You are moved to the DOS prompt, and a message appears, telling you to insert a new disk in the drive.

8. Insert the disk you want to format into the specified drive, and press `↵Enter`.

DOS starts formatting the disk and displays a message showing you the progress. At the end of the operation, DOS prompts you to enter a volume name for the disk.

9. Type a volume name (up to 11 characters) and press `↵Enter`, or press `↵Enter` without typing a volume name.

DOS displays information about the newly formatted disk and asks if you want to format another disk.

10. To format another disk of the same type, press `Y` and `↵Enter` and go back to step 8. Otherwise, press `N` and `↵Enter`.

11. Press any key to return to the DOS Shell.

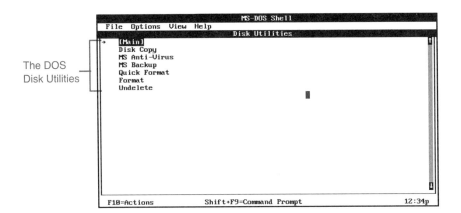

The DOS
Disk Utilities

Figure 6.1
*To run the Format
program from
DOS Shell, select
the Format icon.*

Enter parameters
and switches here.

Figure 6.2
*The Format dialog
box prompts you to
enter parameters
and switches.*

NOTE: If the Format program shows that some of the
sectors on the disk you just formatted are bad, the disk
may still be usable. When the Format program finds bad
sectors on a disk, it marks the sectors as bad so that your
computer will not try to store data on those sectors. The
disk won't have as much free space on it, but at least you
won't have to throw the whole thing away. However, you
should avoid using a disk with sector errors to hold hard
disk backup data or to store a backup copy of another disk.

Unformatting a Disk

If you accidentally format a disk that contains data, all may not
be lost. As long as you don't store any data on the disk, you may
be able to get your data back by unformatting a disk.

CAUTION   If you unformat a disk that contains data, you may lose that data. So make sure you unformat only accidentally formatted disks.

To unformat a disk, perform the following Quick Steps.

QUICK STEPS

Unformatting a Disk from the Shell

1. Press ⎡Alt⎤+⎡F⎤ or click on **F**ile in the menu bar.

The File menu opens.

2. Press ⎡R⎤ or click on **R**un.

The Run dialog box appears.

3. Type `unformat` followed by the letter of the drive you want to unformat and a colon. For example, type `unformat b:`.

4. Press ⎡↵Enter⎤.

The DOS prompt appears, and a message tells you to insert the disk you want to rebuild into the specified drive.

5. Insert the disk you want to unformat into the specified drive, and press ⎡↵Enter⎤.

Unformat checks the disk and then displays a message asking if you want to continue.

6. To proceed with the unformat operation, press ⎡Y⎤; otherwise, press ⎡N⎤ to cancel the operation.

If you pressed ⎡Y⎤, DOS unformats the disk and lets you know when the operation is complete.

7. Press any key to return to the Shell.

To unformat a disk at the DOS prompt, simply type `unformat` followed by the drive letter and a colon, and press ⏎Enter.

Renaming a Disk

Your computer considers disks as "volumes" and allows you to name the volumes for record-keeping purposes. You can name a disk when you format it, or you can name or rename a disk later, without formatting the disk.

To view a disk's volume label from the Shell, first make sure the disk is in one of the disk drives. Then open the **File** menu, select **R**un, and type `vol` followed by the drive letter and a colon (for example, `vol b:`). Press ⏎Enter. At the DOS prompt, you can view a volume label simply by entering the VOL command at the prompt. A volume label is displayed in Figure 6.3.

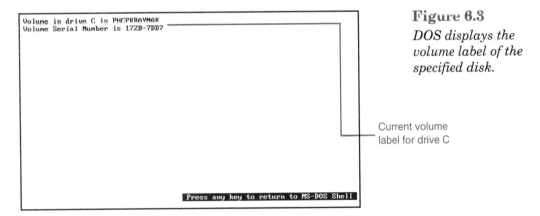

Figure 6.3
DOS displays the volume label of the specified disk.

Current volume label for drive C

To rename a disk, you use the LABEL command either from the Shell or at the DOS prompt. The following steps tell you how to change the volume name of a disk:

1. Make sure the disk you want to name is in one of the disk drives. If you want to change the name of a hard disk, it is already in the drive.

2. If you are in the Shell, open the File menu and choose Run, or go to the DOS prompt.

3. Type LABEL and the appropriate disk drive (for example: LABEL B:).

4. Press ⏎Enter. DOS displays a message showing you the current name of the disk and prompting you to enter a new name.

5. Type a new label for the disk (up to 11 characters), and press ⏎Enter. (Use upper- or lowercase characters; DOS will convert the name into all uppercase characters.)

Copying Disks

Even if your computer is equipped with a hard disk, you'll still need to make copies of floppy disks occasionally. For example, you may need to make a clone of a data disk for distribution to the branch offices in your company, or you may need to make backup copies of a new program you purchased, to protect the originals from damage.

DOS provides a program, called Disk Copy, that allows you to copy disks using one drive or two. If you have two disk drives of the same drive and capacity (for example, two 5 1/4-inch high-density drives), Disk Copy can copy one disk to the other without stopping. If you have only one disk drive of a given size and type, Disk Copy will require you to swap disks into and out of the drive during the copy operation.

Before you begin, make sure you have a blank disk of the same size and capacity of the original disk you want to copy. The blank disk does not need to be formatted. Also, write-protect the original disk to prevent it from getting damaged during the copying process (see Chapter 2). The following Quick Steps give the procedure for copying a floppy disk from the DOS Shell using one drive:.

Copying Disks with One Disk Drive

1. Press Alt+V or click on View in the menu bar.

The **V**iew menu opens.

2. Press P or select Program List.

The Shell displays a list of programs and program groups.

3. Highlight the Disk Utilities program group and press ↵Enter, or double-click on the group with your mouse.

This displays a list of the DOS utility programs, including the Disk Copy program.

4. Highlight the Disk Copy program icon and press ↵Enter, or double-click on it with your mouse.

The Disk Copy dialog box appears, prompting you to specify the disk drives you want to use. (See Figure 6.4.)

5. Type the letters of the drive(s) you want to copy from and to separated by a space. For example, type a: a: or b: b:.

6. Type a space and one of the following switches, if desired: /1 to copy only one side of the disk, or /V to have DOS verify that the disk was properly copied.

To use more than one switch, separate the switches with a space.

7. Press ↵Enter.

You are moved to the DOS prompt, and a message appears, telling you to insert the source disk (the original disk you want to copy) into the specified disk drive.

continues

continued

8. Insert the disk you want to copy into the specified drive, and press `⏎Enter`.

DOS starts copying the original disk into memory. When it has read as much of the disk as possible into memory, a message appears, telling you to insert the destination disk into the drive.

9. Remove the original disk from the drive, insert the destination disk into the drive, and press `⏎Enter`.

DOS copies the data it read from the source disk to the destination disk. DOS displays a message when it needs more information from the source disk.

10. Remove the destination disk from the drive, insert the source disk into the drive, and press `⏎Enter`.

Again, DOS reads as much information as your computer's memory can hold, and asks you to swap disks. Go back to step 9, and continue swapping disks until the copy operation is complete. At the end of the operation, DOS displays a prompt asking if you want to copy another disk.

11. To copy another disk, press `Y` and go back to step 8. Otherwise, press `N`.

12. Press any key to return to the DOS Shell.

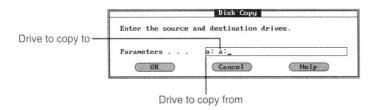

Drive to copy to ─

Drive to copy from

Figure 6.4
*The Disk Copy
dialog box asks
you to specify the
drives you want to
use.*

To copy a disk at the DOS prompt, type the following command:

diskcopy *d1: d2:*

where *d1:* is the drive you want to copy from and *d2:* is the drive you want to copy to (you can use the same drive for both disks). Press [⏎Enter]. Follow the on-screen instructions, and swap disks when prompted.

If you have two disk drives of the same size and capacity, you can copy disks more quickly. When prompted to specify the letters of the drives you want to use, type different letters for the source and destination disks (for example, type **a: b:** or **b: a:**). DOS will then copy the information from one disk to the other without prompting you to swap disks.

Comparing Disks

If you ran Disk Copy with the /V switch, DOS made sure that the copy operation went smoothly, and you can feel confident that the copy matches the original. However, if you did not use the /V switch, or if you want to double-check the disk, you can use the DOS Disk Compare program. To run Disk Compare from the Shell, perform the following steps.

Comparing Disks

1. In the Shell, press <kbd>Alt</kbd>+<kbd>F</kbd> or click on **F**ile in the menu bar.

The **F**ile menu opens.

2. Press <kbd>R</kbd> or select **R**un.

The Run dialog box appears.

3. Type `diskcomp` *d1: d2:*, where *d1* and *d2* are the letters of the disk drives you are going to use. (You can use the same drive for both disks.)

4. Press <kbd>⏎Enter</kbd>.

A message appears, telling you to insert the first disk in the drive.

5. Insert the first disk into the specified drive, and press any key.

DOS reads as much of the disk as possible into memory, and then displays a message telling you to insert the second disk.

6. Remove the first disk from the drive, insert the second disk, and press any key.

DOS compares the data it read from the source disk with data on this disk. DOS displays a message when it needs more information from the source disk.

7. Follow the on-screen prompts until the compare operation is complete.

At the end of the process, DOS displays a message indicating whether or not the disks matched and asking if you want to compare another set of disks.

8. To compare two more disks, press Y and go back to step 5. Otherwise, press N.

9. Press any key to return to the DOS Shell.

 To compare disks at the DOS prompt, type the following command:

```
diskcomp d1: d2:
```

where *d1:* and *d2:* are the drives you want to use for the compare operation (you can use the same drive for both disks). Press ↵Enter. Follow the on-screen instructions, and swap disks when prompted.

Is That All?

In this chapter, you learned how to activate a disk drive, format a disk to prepare it for data storage, copy disks, compare disks, and name and rename disks. With the procedures you learned in this chapter, you will be able to perform most of your daily disk maintenance.

In the next chapter, you will learn how to organize a disk by using directories.

In This Chapter

Using Directories to Keep Your Files Organized

Guidelines for Creating Directories

Making a New Directory

Renaming a Directory

Deleting an Empty Directory

Directory Guidelines

- Don't store all your files in the root directory.
- Make the directory tree no more than three directories deep.
- Consider using a \DATA directory for the files you create.
- Use descriptive names for your directories.
- Install applications in the suggested directories.
- Delete empty directories.

Making a Directory in the Shell

1. Change to the directory under which you want the new directory created.
2. Press Alt+F or click on File in the menu bar.
3. Press E or click on Create Directory.
4. Type a name for the directory.
5. Click on the OK button, or tab to it and press ↵Enter.

Making a Directory at the DOS Prompt

1. Change to the drive and directory under which you want the new directory created.
2. Type md *dirname*, where *dirname* is the name for the new directory.
3. Press ↵Enter.

Renaming a Directory in the Shell

1. Change to the directory whose name you want to change.
2. Press Alt+F or click on File in the menu bar.
3. Press N or click on Rename.
4. Type a new name for the directory.
5. Click on the OK button, or tab to it and press ↵Enter.

7

Organizing Your Disk with Directories

In Chapter 2, you learned that you can store related files in separate directories on a hard disk. In this chapter, you will learn how to create directories on a disk, change to a directory that contains the files with which you want to work, and rename and delete directories.

NOTE: Your hard disk contains at least two directories: the root directory and the \DOS directory. The root directory contains the files that your computer needs to get started. The \DOS directory, created when you installed DOS, branches off from the root directory and contains the DOS program files.

Changing to a Directory

In Chapter 4, you learned how to change to an existing directory in the DOS Shell. To review, here's how you do it: Use the scroll bar or <kbd>PgUp</kbd> and <kbd>PgDn</kbd> until the directory is displayed, and then click on the directory; or use the arrow keys to highlight the name of the directory.

In Chapter 5, you learned how to change directories at the DOS prompt. To review, here's how you do it: Type `cd\` followed by the name of the directory or the path to the directory and press <kbd>↵Enter</kbd>. For example, type `cd \dos` and press <kbd>↵Enter</kbd>.

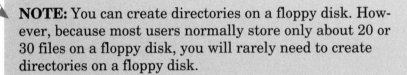

NOTE: You can create directories on a floppy disk. However, because most users normally store only about 20 or 30 files on a floppy disk, you will rarely need to create directories on a floppy disk.

Adding Directories

Before you can store files in a directory, you must create the directory you want to use. Some applications allow you to create a directory from within the program; you can then use the new directory for the files you create in that program. However, most applications require that you create the directory outside the program—that is, by using DOS.

In the following sections, you will learn some strategies for creating directories and subdirectories and the procedure for creating a directory in the DOS Shell and at the DOS prompt.

Planning Ahead

With directories, DOS is flexible; DOS allows you to create directories, subdirectories, sub-subdirectories, and sub-sub-subdirectories as deep as you want to go. But the idea behind directories is that they are supposed to help you find files, not hide them or lose them. With that in mind, here are some guidelines to follow for creating directories:

- *Keep the root directory clean.* To avoid creating new directories, many first-time computer users store all their files in the root directory. The problem with this is that the files you create get mixed in with the program files, making it difficult to find files.

- *Make the directory tree shallow.* As a general rule, go no deeper than three subdirectories (for example, c:\universe\solarsys\planet). As you go deeper in a tree, the path statement gets longer and longer. Keep in mind that whenever you want to get a file, you have to type the entire path statement to specify the file's location.

- *Consider using a \DATA directory for the files you create.* In Chapter 10, you will learn how to back up the files on your hard disk to protect your programs and data. By using a \DATA directory for all the files you create, you can back up these files separately each day. Once you have the \DATA directory, you can create subdirectories for your various projects: C:\DATA\ACME, C:\DATA\GMSALES, C:\DATA\GRAPES, and so on.

- *Use descriptive names.* When naming a directory, use a name that clearly describes the files that the directory will contain.

- *Install applications in the suggested directories.* Most programs suggest that you install the program in a specific directory. For example, the game program Math Blaster suggests that you install the program in the \MATH directory. Use the suggested directory unless you have another group of files stored in a directory of the same name.

- *Delete any empty directories.*   Empty directories clutter your disk and make your directory tree appear more complicated than it is. Delete unused directories to keep your tree clean.

Creating a Directory

You can create a directory from within the DOS Shell or at the DOS prompt. The following Quick Steps explain how to create a directory from the Shell.

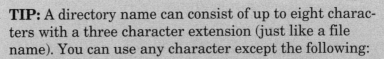

TIP: A directory name can consist of up to eight characters with a three character extension (just like a file name). You can use any character except the following:

" . / \ [ ] : * < > ¦ + ; , ?

Although you can add an extension to a directory name, it is a good idea to leave off the extension. Many programs will not display the extension, and the extension makes working with directories at the DOS prompt more difficult.

Creating a Directory in the DOS Shell

1. Change to the directory under which you want the new directory to appear.

See Figure 7.1.

2. Press Alt + F or click on File in the menu bar.

The File menu opens.

3. Press E or click on Create Directory.

The Create Directory dialog box appears, as shown in Figure 7.2.

4. Type a name for the directory.

5. Click on the OK button, or tab to it and press ⏎Enter.

The name of the new directory appears under the highlighted directory.

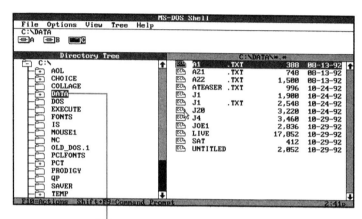

Figure 7.1

The new directory will be created under the current directory.

Select the directory under which you want the new subdirectory to appear.

Figure 7.2

The Create Directory dialog box asks you to type a name for the directory.

Type a name for the new directory.

NOTE: If you create a directory and it does not appear in the directory tree, you may have to expand the tree as explained in Chapter 4. If the directory is still not displayed, try refreshing the tree: press F5 or choose Refresh from the View menu. This tells DOS to reread and redisplay the tree.

C> To make a directory at the DOS prompt, you must use the MKDIR or MD command, both of which stand for Make Directory. Because MD is shorter, we will use it in our example. To make a directory, perform the following steps:

1. Change to the drive and directory under which you want the new directory to appear. If you want the new directory under the root directory, type `cd\` and press `↵Enter`.

2. Type `md` `dirname`, where *dirname* is the name for the new directory.

3. Press `↵Enter`. DOS creates the new directory under the current directory. To change to the new directory, enter `cd` `dirname`, where *dirname* is the name of the new directory.

Renaming a Directory

There may be times when you need to change a directory's name—to make it more descriptive or to avoid name conflicts with other directories. You can rename a directory only from within the DOS Shell; you cannot rename a directory at the DOS prompt. To rename a directory, perform the following Quick Steps.

Renaming a Directory in the Shell

1. Change to the directory whose name you want to change.

2. Press `Alt`+`F` or click on File in the menu bar.　　The **F**ile menu opens.

3. Press N or click on
Rename.

The Rename Directory dia-
log box appears. (See Figure 7.3.)

4. Type a new name for the
directory.

As you type, the name ap-
pears in the New name
text box.

5. Click on the OK button,
or tab to it and press
⏎Enter.

You are returned to the
Shell and the directory's
new name appears in the
Directory List.

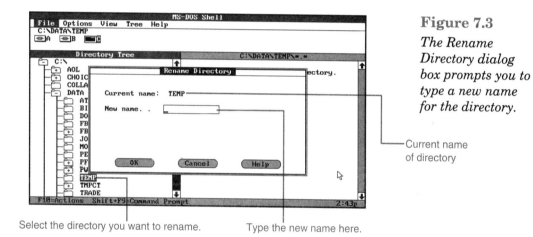

Figure 7.3

*The Rename
Directory dialog
box prompts you to
type a new name
for the directory.*

Current name
of directory

Select the directory you want to rename.

Type the new name here.

CAUTION

Many programs, including DOS, always look to
a particular directory to find their files. If you
change a directory's name, the program may not be able to
find its files, and may not run properly.

Removing a Directory

A hard disk is like a valuable piece of real estate; you don't want to use it as a garbage dump. If you create a directory and decide not to use it, or if you delete all the files in a directory and no longer need the directory, you should remove the directory.

CAUTION   DOS will not allow you to remove a directory that contains files or subdirectories. To remove the directory, you must first delete all its files and subdirectories or move the files to another directory or disk. For instructions on deleting and moving files, refer to Chapter 8.

Once you've emptied a directory, you can delete it from the Shell or remove it at the DOS prompt. The following Quick Steps explain how to delete a directory from the Shell.

Deleting a Directory from the Shell

1. In the Directory List, change to the directory you want to delete.

The directory appears highlighted.

2. Press ⎡Alt⎤+⎡F⎤ or click on File in the menu bar.

The File menu opens.

3. Press ⎡D⎤ or click on **D**elete.

The Delete Directory Confirmation dialog box appears, as shown in Figure 7.4.

4. Press ⎡↵Enter⎤ or click on the Yes button to confirm the deletion.

DOS deletes the directory from disk.

TIP: You can bypass the **F**ile menu and delete a directory quickly by highlighting the directory and pressing ⌈Del⌋. When the confirmation dialog box appears, press ⌈⏎Enter⌋ to confirm.

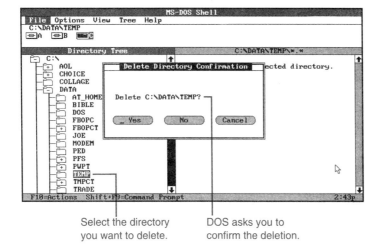

Select the directory
you want to delete.

DOS asks you to
confirm the deletion.

Figure 7.4

The Delete Directory Confirmation dialog box warns that you are about to delete a directory.

C> To remove a directory at the DOS prompt, you must use the RMDIR or RD command, both of which stand for Remove Directory. Because RD is shorter, we will use it in our example. To remove a directory, perform the following steps:

1. Change to the directory that is just above the directory you want to remove. If you want to remove a directory that is just under the root directory, type **cd** and press ⌈⏎Enter⌋.

2. Type **rd** *dirname*, where *dirname* is the name of the directory you want to remove.

3. Press ⌈⏎Enter⌋. DOS removes the directory.

DELTREE, New to DOS 6

One of the things that users have always hated about DOS is that they had to manually delete all the files in a directory before the directory could be removed. Well, not anymore.

The DELTREE command is a powerful one, because it lets you remove directories and subdirectories and delete their files in one step.

CAUTION   Use extreme caution with DELTREE. It makes it very easy to do a lot of damage. Make sure you really want to delete every file and subdirectory under a directory before using DELTREE.

To use DELTREE from the DOS prompt, follow these quick steps:

Deleting Directories with DELTREE

1. Change to the directory immediately above the one you want to delete.

   For example, to remove C:\BOOKS, change to C:\. To remove C:\BOOKS\DATA, change to C:\BOOKS.

2. Type DELTREE, a space, and the directory name to be removed, and press ⏎Enter.

   DOS asks you if you are sure you want to remove the directory.

3. Press Y for Yes.

   The directory and all its files and subdirectories are deleted.

DELTREE wipes out all subdirectories as well as files. For example, if you had 3 subdirectories under C:\BOOKS, `DELTREE C:\BOOKS` would wipe them all out.

CAUTION

Practice, Practice, Practice

Before you move on to the next chapter (about managing files), use the DOS Shell to create a new directory called \TEMP or \TEST. Change to the directory, rename it, and then delete it. Only by feeling comfortable with directories will you be able to master them.

In the next chapter, you will learn how to work with the files that are stored on disk and in directories.

In This Chapter

Changing Shell's File List Display

Selecting Files in the Shell

Copying and Moving Files

Renaming and Deleting Files

Viewing and Printing Files

Locating Misplaced Files

Selecting One File in the Shell

1. Change to the drive and directory that contains the file.
2. Tab to the File List window.
3. Use the ↑ and ↓ keys to highlight the file, or click on the file with your mouse.

Selecting Neighboring Files in the Shell

- With the mouse, click on the first file name in the group of files you want to select, and then hold down ⇧Shift while clicking on the last file in the group.
- With the keyboard, use the arrow keys to highlight the first file in the group, and then hold down ⇧Shift while pressing ↑ or ↓ to select additional files.

Copying Files in the Shell

1. Select the files you want to copy.
2. Open the File menu and select Copy, or press F8.
3. Type the path to the drive and directory where you want the files copied.
4. Select OK.

Deleting Files in the Shell

1. Select the files you want to delete.
2. Open the File menu and select Delete, or press Del.
3. Press ↵Enter or click on the OK button to continue.
4. Press ↵Enter or click on the Yes button to delete the file in question. If you selected more than one file, repeat this step until you have deleted all the selected files.

Managing Your Files

Hopefully, all the talk in Chapters 6 and 7 about disks and directories did not blur your focus on what really matters—files. Without files, there would be no need for disks or directories in which to store them.

In this chapter, you will learn how to manage files on disks. You will learn how to copy files from one disk or directory to another, move files, delete and undelete files, rename files, and even search for files you've misplaced.

NOTE: Although you can perform most file management tasks at the DOS prompt, the Shell provides a superior work area for file management. As you will see, you can use the Shell to drag files from one drive or directory to another quickly and easily.

Changing the Way Files Are Listed in the Shell

The DOS Shell has two windows for showing files and directories. In the Directory List window, Shell displays a list of directories on the current disk. In the File List window, Shell displays a list of the files that are in the selected directory. Unless you specify otherwise, these files are listed alphabetically from A to Z.

To work with files more efficiently, you can change the way Shell displays the files. For example, you can split the display to show the contents of two disks or directories on-screen at the same time. You can then move files from one disk or directory to another simply by moving them on-screen. You can also choose to display only a particular group of files (for example, only files that have the .EXE extension).

The following sections explain two common ways to change the Shell's display.

Setting the File Display Options

The file display options allow you to change the way file names are displayed in the File List window. You can change the display in the following two ways:

- *Filter the list*   When you filter the list, you tell the Shell to display only those file names that match an entry you type. For example, you can type `*.doc` to have the Shell display only those file names that have the .DOC extension. The asterisk is a wild-card character that stands for any group of characters. (For more information on using wild cards, see "Using Wild-Card Characters for Groups of Files" in Chapter 5.)

- *Sort the list*   When you sort a list, you change the order in which the files are listed. For example, you can sort the list alphabetically in ascending order (from A to Z) or in descending order (from Z to A); or you can sort the list by extension so that all files with the .DOC extension appear together in the file list.

The following Quick Steps lead you through the process of setting the file display options to both filter and sort the file list.

Filtering and Sorting the File List

1. Press `Alt`+`O` or click on Options in the menu bar.

The **O**ptions menu opens.

2. Press `F` or click on File Display Options.

The File Display Options dialog box appears, as shown in Figure 8.1.

3. To filter the file list, type a wild-card entry in the Name text box.

Refer to Chapter 5 for instructions on how to use wild-card characters.

4. To display the names of hidden and system files, select Display hidden/ system files.

Normally DOS hides the names of hidden and system files to prevent them from being accidentally deleted or changed.

5. To sort the file names in descending order (10, 9, 8 or Z, Y, X) instead of ascending order (1, 2, 3 or A, B, C), select Descending order.

6. Choose one of the following Sort by options: Name, Extension, Date, Size, or Disk Order.

The Sort by options tell DOS which feature of a file to look at when sorting the files: their names or extensions, the dates they were created, the sizes of the files, or the order in which the files were stored on disk.

continues

continued

7. Tab to the OK button and press ⎵Enter, or click on the OK button with your mouse.

Shell filters and sorts the file list according to your instructions.

Figure 8.1

Use the File Display Options dialog box to filter and sort the file list.

Select this option to display hidden files.

Select this option to sort the list in descending order.

Type an entry here to filter the list.

Select a Sort by option to sort the File List.

In Chapter 5, you learned how to display a list of file names at the DOS prompt: you change to the drive and directory whose file list you want to view and then enter the DIR command. You also learned how to use wild-card characters to filter the list; for example, if you enter `dir *.com`, DOS displays only those file names that have the .COM extension.

To sort the list, add the `/O:attributes` switch to the command (O stands for Order). In place of *attributes*, type one or more of the following codes:

N	Alphabetically by name
-N	Reverse alphabetical order by name
E	Alphabetically by extension
-E	Reverse alphabetical order by extension
D	By date and time, earliest first
-D	By date and time, latest first
S	By size, smallest first

-S	By size, largest first
G	List directories first
-G	List files first, then directories

For example, type `dir *.exe /o:gn` to display only those files with the .EXE extension, to display directory names first, and to display the file names in alphabetical order.

Opening More Windows

Although Shell's **S**ingle File List display beats working at the DOS prompt, it allows you to work with only one disk or directory at a time. To display a file list for more than one disk or directory, you must change to the Dual File Lists display as instructed in the following Quick Steps.

Displaying Two File Lists

1. Press `Alt`+`V` or click on **V**iew in the menu bar.

   The **V**iew menu opens.

2. Press `D` or click on **D**ual File Lists.

   You are returned to the Shell, and two file lists appear on-screen, as shown in Figure 8.2.

You can change drives or directories in either list independently of the other list. For example, you can use one list to display the files on drive C, and the other list to display the files on drive A. To return to the Single List display, open the **V**iew menu, and choose **S**ingle File List.

Figure 8.2

The Dual File Lists display shows two file lists.

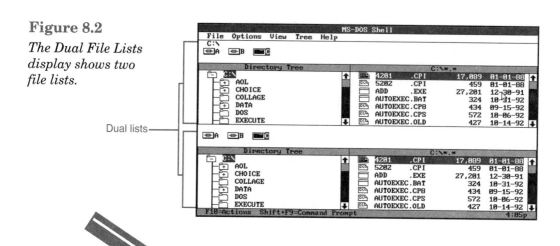

Dual lists

Figure 8.3

You can display a list of all files outside of their directory boundaries.

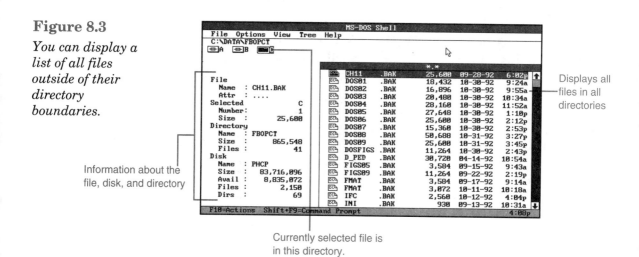

Information about the file, disk, and directory

Currently selected file is in this directory.

Displays all files in all directories

> **NOTE:** In addition to the **D**ual File Lists display option, the **V**iew menu contains the **A**ll Files option. This option displays all the files on the current disk (including hidden and system files) and does not group the files by directory (see Figure 8.3). This option is useful for working with groups of files that have the same extension but are stored in different directories.

Selecting Files

Before you can copy, move, rename, or delete files in the DOS Shell, you must select the file or files on which you want to act. The following sections provide instructions on how to select individual files and groups of files in the DOS Shell using both the keyboard and mouse.

> **C>** To select files at the DOS prompt, you specify the file or files on which you want to act when you enter the command. To act on a group of files, use wild-card characters, as you did with the DIR command.

Selecting Individual Files

You can select an individual file from the File List window using either the keyboard or the mouse. Change to the drive and directory where the file is located, and then perform either of the following steps:

- Using the keyboard, tab to the File List window and use ↑ and ↓ to highlight the name of the file.

- With the mouse, move the tip of the mouse pointer over the name of the file and click the left mouse button.

Selecting and Deselecting All Files in a Directory

To select all the files in the current directory, perform the following Quick Steps.

Selecting All Files

1. Change to the drive and directory that contains the files you want to select.

2. Press [Alt]+[F] or click on File in the menu bar.

   The File menu opens.

3. Press [S] or click on Select All.

   Shell highlights all the file names in the current directory to show that they are selected.

TIP: To select all the files with the keyboard, tab to the file list and press [Ctrl]+[/]. To deselect all selected files, choose Deselect All from the File menu, or press [Ctrl]+[\].

Selecting a Group of Neighboring Files

The DOS Shell allows you to select a group of neighboring files. The procedure consists of selecting the first or last file in the group and then *extending* the selection up or down to the other files. Perform the following Quick Steps to select neighboring files using the mouse.

Selecting Neighboring Files with a Mouse

1. Click on the first file name in the group of files you want to select.

   The selected file appears highlighted.

2. Hold down ⇧Shift while clicking on the last file name in the group of files.

   The first and last file names and all file names between them appear highlighted.

To select neighboring files with the keyboard, highlight the first file and then hold down ⇧Shift while pressing ↓. Continue holding down ⇧Shift and pressing ↓ until all the desired file names are highlighted.

Selecting a Group of Non-Neighboring Files

There may be times when the files you want to work with are not next to each other in the file list. The following sets of Quick Steps explain the procedures for selecting non-neighboring files with both the mouse and the keyboard.

Selecting Non-Neighboring Files with the Mouse

1. Click on the first file you want to select.

   The selected file appears highlighted.

2. Hold down Ctrl while clicking on each additional file you want to select.

   Each file you click on appears highlighted.

continues

continued

3. To unselect a file, hold down Ctrl and click on it again.

The file no longer appears highlighted.

QUICK STEPS

Selecting Non-Neighboring Files with the Keyboard

1. Use the arrow keys to highlight the first file you want to select.

2. Press ⇧Shift+F8.

This puts you in Add mode. ADD appears in the status bar at the bottom of the screen.

3. Use the arrow keys to highlight the next file you want to select, and then press Spacebar.

The selected file appears highlighted.

4. Repeat step 3 for any additional files you want to select.

5. Press ⇧Shift+F8 to turn off Add mode.

ADD disappears from the status bar.

TIP: If you want to select more files than not, first select all the files, and then unselect the few you don't want selected. To unselect a file, hold down Ctrl while clicking on the file's name or turn on Add mode and use Spacebar.

Selecting Files in Different Directories

So far, you have selected a file or group of files in only one directory. However, the DOS Shell will allow you to select files that are in different directories. This is called *selecting across directories*. To select across directories, perform the following Quick Steps.

Selecting Files Across Directories

1. Press `Alt`+`O` or click on **O**ptions in the menu bar.

2. Choose Select **A**cross Directories.

This turns the option on until you select the option to turn it off again. If you open the **O**ptions menu, you will see a dot next to Select Across Directories, indicating it is on.

3. Select the files you want to work with in the first directory.

4. Change to the next directory and select the files with which you want to work.

The files you selected in step 3 remain selected when you switch directories.

5. Repeat step 4 until you have selected all the files with which you want to work.

Copying Files

One of the most common file management tasks is to copy files from one disk or directory to another. For example, you may copy files from your hard disk at work to a floppy disk and then copy the files from the floppy disk to your hard disk at home. Shell lets you copy files to any disk or directory quickly and easily.

Shell handles file copying differently depending on whether you are copying files within a single disk and directory or to a different disk and/or directory. The following sections describe each procedure separately.

Copying to the Same Directory and Disk

Copying a file to the same disk and directory is useful if you want to edit a file to see if you can improve it. If editing the copy makes it worse, you can then use the original, unchanged file.

Because no two files in the same directory can have the same file name, copying a file to the same directory requires that you type a new, unique name for the file. Perform the following Quick Steps to copy a file.

Copying a File to the Same Directory and Disk

1. Select the file you want to copy as explained earlier in this chapter.

   The name of the file appears highlighted.

2. Open the File menu and select Copy, or press F8.

   The dialog box in Figure 8.4 appears, prompting you to specify a destination for the copy.

3. Type a different name and/or extension for the file.

When you start typing, the destination entry disappears and what you type appears in its place.

4. Select OK.

This copies the file to the same directory under the new name.

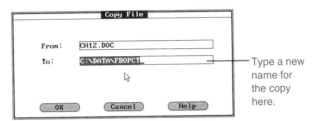

Type a new name for the copy here.

Figure 8.4

Type a name for the copy.

 At the DOS prompt, you can create a copy of a single file by changing to the drive and directory that contains the file and typing

```
copy file1.ext file2.ext
```

where *file1.ext* is the name of the file you want to copy, and *file2.ext* is the name of the copy.

In addition, you can copy a group of files to the same drive or directory (which you cannot do in the Shell). To copy a group of files, use the COPY command with wild-card characters. For example, type `copy *.doc *.bak` to create a copy of all the files that have the .DOC extension. The copies will have the same file name as the original files but will have the .BAK extension.

Copying Files to a Different Subdirectory or Disk

Copying files to a different subdirectory or disk involves the same basic procedures as those outlined previously, except you don't need to provide a new name for the copies. The following Quick Steps explain how to copy files to a different subdirectory or disk.

Copying Files to a Different Subdirectory or Disk

1. Select the files you want to copy as explained earlier.	The names of the selected files appear highlighted.
2. Open the File menu and select Copy, or press [F8].	The Copy File dialog box appears. In the From text box, the names of the selected files appear. In the To text box is the path to the current directory.
3. Type the path to the drive and directory where you want the files copied.	As you start typing, the entry in the To text box disappears and what you type appears in its place.
4. Select OK.	DOS copies the selected files to the specified drive and directory.

 To copy files from one drive and/or directory to another at the DOS prompt, perform the following steps:

1. Change to the drive and directory that contains the files you want to copy.

2. Type `copy file1.ext d2:\path2`, where *file1.ext* is the name of the file you want to copy, and *d2:\path2* is the path to the directory where you want the file copied.

3. Press ⏎Enter. DOS copies the file.

You can copy a group of files by using wild-card characters. For example, to copy all files with the .DOC extension from C:\DATA to drive A, change to the C:\DATA directory and enter `copy *.doc a:`.

Fast File Copying with a Mouse

If you have a mouse, you can quickly copy one or more files in the Shell by dragging them from disk to disk or directory to directory. Copying files using a mouse is best done with the Dual File Lists display, as explained earlier in this chapter. Use the following Quick Steps to copy files with a mouse.

Copying Files with a Mouse

1. In one file list, select the files you want to copy.

   The names of the selected files appear highlighted.

2. In the other list, select the drive where you want the files copied, and make sure the desired directory is displayed.

   You will drag the selected files to a disk or directory icon, so the icon for the desired disk or directory must appear on-screen.

continues

continued

3. Point to any one of the files you selected, hold down Ctrl and the left mouse button, and start dragging the mouse toward the icon for the drive or directory where you want the files copied.

As you drag the mouse, the mouse pointer changes into a circle with a line through it. This icon indicates that the files cannot be copied where the mouse pointer is currently positioned.

4. Drag the mouse pointer over the icon of the disk or directory where you want the files copied.

The mouse pointer changes into a stack of three files, indicating that the files can be copied to the drive and directory where the pointer is positioned (see Figure 8.5).

5. Release the mouse button.

A Confirm Mouse Operation dialog box appears.

6. Select the OK button to confirm the Copy operation.

The selected files are copied to the specified drive and directory.

Figure 8.5

Copying files in the Dual File Lists display using the mouse.

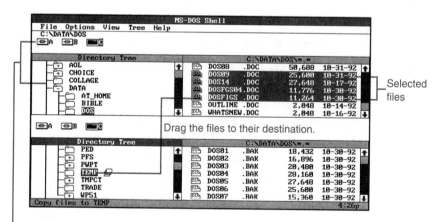

Selected files

Drag the files to their destination.

You can also drag the files to a drive icon or a directory icon in one of these lists.

Name Conflicts

If you try to copy a file to a disk or directory that already contains a file with the same name, Shell displays the Replace File Confirmation dialog box, shown in Figure 8.6. You can then choose Yes to replace the file, No to skip this file, or Cancel to cancel the Copy operation.

Figure 8.6
DOS will warn you if you are about to replace an existing file.

NOTE: Unless you choose otherwise, DOS will display a confirmation warning whenever you move or copy files with the mouse and whenever you are about to delete or replace a file. To turn confirmation warnings off, open the Options menu and select Confirmation. Select any of the Confirmation options: Confirm on Delete, Confirm on Replace, or Confirm on Mouse Operation, to turn the option off, and then select the OK button.

Moving Files

Moving a file is similar to copying a file, except that the original file is erased and only the copy remains. The following Quick Steps summarize this procedure.

Moving a File to a Different Subdirectory or Disk

1. If you haven't done so already, select the disk and directory that holds the file(s) you want to move.

2. Select the files to move in the File List window.

   The selected files appear highlighted.

3. Open the File menu and select Move, or press F7.

   The Move File dialog box appears, asking you to specify the drive and directory where you want the files moved (see Figure 8.7).

4. Type the path to the drive and directory where you want the files moved.

   As you start typing, the entry in the To text box disappears and what you type appears in its place.

5. Select OK.

   DOS moves the selected files to the specified drive and directory.

Figure 8.7

The Move File dialog box prompts you to specify where you want the files moved.

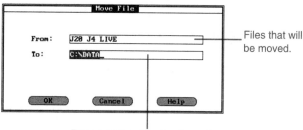

Files that will be moved.

Type a path to the directory where you want the files moved.

If you have a mouse, you can quickly move one or more files by dragging them from one disk or directory to another. The procedure for moving files differs depending on whether you are moving files to a different directory on the same disk or to a different disk. To move files to a different directory on the same disk, perform the following steps.

Moving Files to a Different Directory on the Same Disk

1. Display the list of files you want to copy in the File List window, and make sure the directory you want to copy the files to appears in the Directory List window.

   You may have to turn on the Dual File Lists display in order to view the files and destination directory at the same time.

2. Select the files you want to move.

   The selected files appear highlighted.

3. Move the mouse pointer to one of the selected files, and hold down the left mouse button.

4. Drag the mouse pointer over the directory where you want the files moved (see Figure 8.8), and release the mouse button.

   If the Confirm on Mouse Operation option is on, a confirmation warning will appear.

5. If a confirmation warning appears, select the OK button to confirm the move.

   The files are moved from the current directory to the specified directory.

Figure 8.8

Drag the mouse pointer over the directory where you want the files moved.

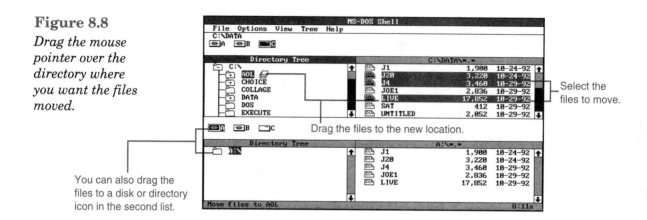

Select the files to move.

Drag the files to the new location.

You can also drag the files to a disk or directory icon in the second list.

To move files from one disk to another, you must hold down
Alt while dragging the files.

Renaming Files

You may need to rename a file or a group of files, perhaps to make the names more descriptive or to avoid name conflicts with other files. To rename files, perform the following Quick Steps.

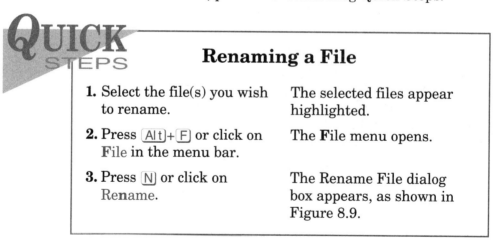

Renaming a File

1. Select the file(s) you wish to rename.

   The selected files appear highlighted.

2. Press Alt+F or click on File in the menu bar.

   The **File** menu opens.

3. Press N or click on Rename.

   The Rename File dialog box appears, as shown in Figure 8.9.

4. Type a new name for the file, and select OK.

DOS renames the file. If you selected more than one file to rename, the Rename File dialog box prompts you to rename the next file.

5. Repeat step 4 until you have renamed all the selected files.

Current file name

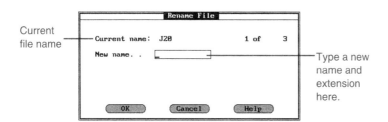

Type a new name and extension here.

Figure 8.9

The Rename File dialog box.

 To rename a single file at the DOS prompt, perform the following steps:

1. Change to the drive and directory that contains the file you want to rename.

2. Type `ren` *file1.ext file2.ext*, where *file1.ext* is the name of the file you want to rename, and *file2.ext* is the new name for the file.

3. Press `⏎Enter`. DOS renames the file.

You can rename a group of files by using wild-card characters. For example, to change the file name extension for a group of files from .DOC to .TXT, change to the drive and directory where those files are stored and enter `ren *.doc *.txt`.

Deleting Files

You should delete files you no longer need so that they don't take up precious disk space. However, before you delete a file, make sure you no longer need it. Although DOS can help you recover accidentally deleted files (as you will see later), you should delete files with caution. The following Quick Steps explain how to delete unneeded files from disk.

Deleting a File in the Shell

1. Select the file(s) you want to delete.

The selected files appear highlighted.

2. Open the File menu and select Delete, or press Del.

The Delete File dialog box appears, as in Figure 8.10, showing the names of all the selected files.

3. Press ↵Enter or click on the OK button to continue.

The Delete File Confirmation dialog box appears, prompting you to confirm the deletion of the first selected file.

4. Press ↵Enter or click on the Yes button to delete the file in question.

If you selected more than one file, repeat this step until you have deleted all the selected files.

CAUTION

If you delete a file or group of files by mistake, don't panic. Don't turn off your computer. And don't copy or move files. Skip ahead to the next section, "Undeleting Files," to find out what to do.

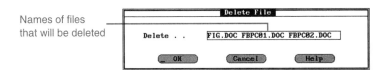

Names of files
that will be deleted

Figure 8.10
*The Delete File
dialog box shows
the names of the
files that will be
deleted.*

To delete a single file at the DOS prompt, perform the following steps:

1. Change to the drive and directory that contains the file you want to delete.

2. Type `del filename.ext`, where *filename.ext* is the name of the file you want to delete.

3. Press `Enter`. DOS deletes the file.

You can delete a group of files by using wild-card characters. For example, to delete all files that have the .BAK extension, change to the drive and directory where those files are stored and type `del *.bak`.

Undeleting Files

When you delete a file, DOS doesn't actually delete the file. DOS deletes the first character of the file name and allows the space used by that file to be used by the next file you save to disk. As long as you don't save another file to disk, you can get back the file you deleted. Here are three good rules to follow when you've accidently erased a file:

- Don't panic.
- Don't turn off your computer.
- Don't save or copy any files to disk or install any programs.

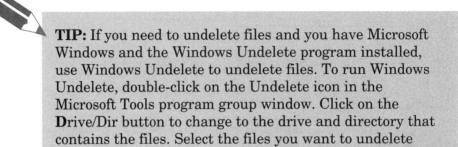

TIP: If you need to undelete files and you have Microsoft Windows and the Windows Undelete program installed, use Windows Undelete to undelete files. To run Windows Undelete, double-click on the Undelete icon in the Microsoft Tools program group window. Click on the **D**rive/Dir button to change to the drive and directory that contains the files. Select the files you want to undelete from the list, and then click on the **U**ndelete button. It's as simple as that.

Running Undelete

You can undelete files from the Shell or at the DOS prompt. However, it is safer to undelete files at the DOS prompt. If the files you want to undelete are vitally important, skip ahead to the procedure for undeleting files at the DOS prompt.

To undelete files from the Shell, it is best to have your screen show both a File List window and a Program List window, as shown in Figure 8.11. If yours isn't like this already, open the View menu and select Program/File Lists. Then, choose the Disk Utilities icon to display the DOS Disk Utilities programs.

Figure 8.11

To run Undelete from Shell, display a File List window and a Program List window.

Program List with the Disk Utilities displayed

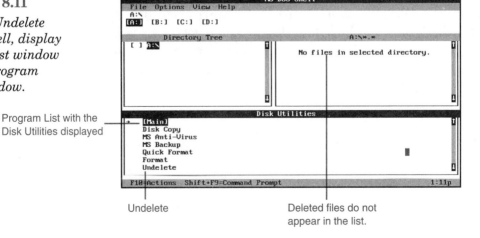

Undelete

Deleted files do not appear in the list.

Once the File List and Program List windows are displayed, use the following Quick Steps to undelete files.

Undeleting Files from the Shell

1. Change to the drive and directory that contains the accidentally deleted files.

2. Highlight Undelete in the Program List window and press ⏎Enter, or double-click on Undelete.

The Undelete dialog box appears, as shown in Figure 8.12. The /LIST switch tells DOS to list the files that may be undeleted, but not to undelete them.

3. Press ⬅Backspace to delete the /LIST switch, and then click on the OK button, or tab to it and press ⏎Enter.

You are sent to the DOS prompt, and DOS displays the name of the first file that can be undeleted. You are asked if you want to undelete this file. (See Figure 8.13.)

4. To undelete the file, press Y, or press N to skip this file.

If you pressed Y, DOS prompts you to type the first letter of the file's name.

5. Type the first letter of the file's name (if you can re-member it), or type any character.

DOS undeletes the file. If another file can be undeleted, DOS displays a prompt asking if you want to undelete the file.

continues

---

continued

6. If you are asked if you want to undelete another file, return to step 4; otherwise, go on to step 7.

Once you have undeleted or skipped the last file, a message appears telling you to press any key to return to the Shell.

7. Press any key to return to the DOS Shell.

You are returned to the DOS Shell.

8. If the names of the undeleted files do not appear in the File List window, tab to the Directory List window and press ⌊F5⌋.

This makes DOS reread the directory listing of files.

NOTE: Undelete may not allow you to type the correct first character of the file's name if a file with the same name is in the current directory. Instead, type any character, and then rename the files later.

Figure 8.12

The Undelete dialog box allows you to enter parameters and switches for the Undelete command.

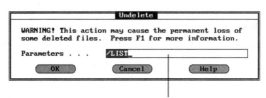

Backspace over the /LIST switch to delete it.

Undelete will act on drive A. Type the Undelete command and press Enter.

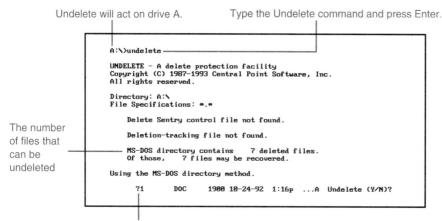

```
A:\>undelete

UNDELETE - A delete protection facility
Copyright (C) 1987-1993 Central Point Software, Inc.
All rights reserved.

Directory: A:\
File Specifications: *.*

    Delete Sentry control file not found.

    Deletion-tracking file not found.

    MS-DOS directory contains    7 deleted files.
    Of those,    7 files may be recovered.

Using the MS-DOS directory method.

    ?1      DOC      1900 10-24-92  1:16p  ...A  Undelete (Y/N)?
```

The number of files that can be undeleted

First file that can be undeleted

Figure 8.13
DOS asks if you want to undelete this file.

To undelete files at the DOS prompt, perform the following steps:

1. Change to the drive and directory that contains the files you want to undelete.

2. Type `undelete` and press `⏎Enter`. DOS displays the name of the first file that can be undeleted and asks if you want to undelete the file.

3. To undelete the file, press `Y`.

4. Type the first letter of the file's name or any character.

5. If you are asked if you want to undelete another file, return to step 3.

When undeleting files, you can add either of two switches to the UNDELETE command to control the way it works: /LIST and /ALL. The /LIST switch tells DOS to display a list of all the files that can be undeleted, but does not allow DOS to undelete the files. The /ALL switch tells DOS to undelete all files without asking for your confirmation. DOS supplies the number sign (#) or a letter for the first character in each file's name. You can also use wild-card characters to specify groups of files you want to undelete. Following are two examples:

`undelete *.doc /all`   Tells DOS to undelete all files that have the .DOC extension without asking for your confirmation.

`undelete *.bak /list`   Tells DOS to list all recoverable files that have the .BAK extension.

If you are using the switches in the Shell, type them in the Undelete dialog box and omit the UNDELETE command.

Enhancing File Recovery

In the preceding section, you learned that when you delete a file, DOS does not actually erase the contents of the file. You can get the file back simply by running Undelete and typing the first character of the file's name. However, DOS comes with two programs that further protect deleted files:

Delete Tracker   Stores the full names of all deleted files. If you run Undelete to undelete files protected with Delete Tracker, you don't have to supply the first character of the deleted file's name. You simply answer Yes or No when Undelete asks if you want to undelete the file.

Delete Sentry   Offers more protection than Delete Tracker, but requires more disk space. This program stores a copy of each deleted file in a separate, hidden directory (named \SENTRY) on each disk that it protects. This gives you an excellent chance of recovering any deleted file.

Both Delete Tracker and Delete Sentry are memory-resident programs (they stay in your computer's memory while you work with other programs). Whenever you delete a file, Delete Tracker or Delete Sentry keeps a record of it, allowing you to undelete it.

TIP: Because Delete Sentry stores a copy of each deleted file, you can recover a file even if you delete it and then save a file onto the same area of the disk that contained the deleted file. With Delete Tracker, such a file would be lost.

Running Delete Tracker

To run Delete Tracker open the Shell's **F**ile menu and select **R**un or go to the DOS prompt. Then enter the following command:

```
undelete /td-nnn
```

where /*t* is the switch that turns Delete Tracker on, *d* is the letter of the drive on which you want Delete Tracker to store undelete information, and *nnn* is the maximum number of deleted files you want to keep track of (1–999). For example,

```
undelete /tc-300
```

tells Delete Tracker to save file name entries for up to 300 deleted files on drive C. If you do not specify a number of entries, Delete Tracker will use a default number based on disk capacity (for example, 25 entries for a 360K disk, 75 entries for a 1.2M disk, and 303 entries for a 32M hard disk).

Running Delete Sentry

To run Delete Sentry open the Shell's **F**ile menu and select **R**un or go to the DOS prompt. Then enter the following command:

```
undelete /s:d
```

where /*s* is the switch that turns Delete Sentry on, and *d* is the letter of the drive you want Delete Sentry to protect. For example,

```
undelete /s:c
```

tells Delete Sentry to protect the files on drive C. If you do not specify a drive, Delete Sentry will protect the current drive.

Running Delete Tracker or Delete Sentry at Startup

Although DOS allows you to run Delete Sentry or Delete Tracker after you boot your computer, it is better to set up either program to run at startup. By running the program when you first start your computer, you can be assured that your files are protected for your entire work session.

To run either of these programs at startup, type the command for running the program at the end of your AUTOEXEC.BAT file. This file contains a series of commands that DOS automatically runs whenever you start your computer. The procedure for editing your AUTOEXEC.BAT file is explained in Chapter 15.

Viewing a File's Contents

Sometimes, you may want to view the contents of a file before doing anything to the file. For example, if you think you will no longer need a file, but you are not sure what that file contains, you can view the file before deleting it. Perform the following Quick Steps to view a file from the Shell.

Viewing a File

1. Select the file you want to view from the File List window.

The selected file appears highlighted.

2. Open the File menu and select View File Contents, or press F9.

The contents of the file appear on-screen, as shown in Figure 8.14.

3. To change the display from ASCII to Hexadecimal code or vice versa, press F9, or open the Display menu and select the desired format.

ASCII (pronounced "ASK-Kee") displays normal alphabetic characters, whereas hexadecimal displays the hexadecimal equivalents of characters, which are unintelligible to anyone but programmers.

4. To return to the File List Window, press Esc.

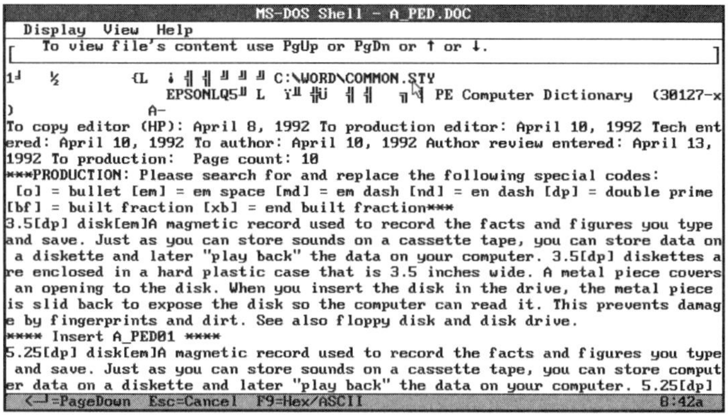

Figure 8.14

When you choose to view a file, its contents appear on-screen.

C> To view a file's contents at the DOS prompt, you use the TYPE command. For example, to view a file named LETTER.TXT, you would change to the drive and directory where the file is stored and enter `type letter.txt`. To prevent the text from scrolling off the screen, add the ¦MORE switch; for example, enter `type letter.txt ¦more`. With the ¦MORE switch, the file is displayed one screen at a time; you can press any key to view the next screenful of information.

Printing a File

If you need a quick paper printout of a file's contents, you can print the file from the Shell or at the DOS prompt.

NOTE: If you've formatted a document (by adding indents or making some text bold, for instance), that formatting will not appear on the printout. Still, the PRINT command serves well to make quick copies of text and binary documents.

Before you can print a file, you must run the DOS PRINT.EXE program from the DOS prompt to activate DOS's printing capabilities. Type `print` at the DOS prompt and press ⏎Enter. DOS displays a message asking you to specify the printer port (the port to which your printer is connected). Press ⏎Enter to accept [PRN], the default (LPT1), or type an entry if you know that your printer is connected to a different port (for example, LPT2 or COM2).

Once PRINT.EXE is running in memory, you can use the following Quick Steps to print a file from the Shell.

QUICK STEPS

Printing a File from the Shell

1. In the File List window, select the file you want to print.

   The selected file appears highlighted.

2. Open the File menu and select Print.

   DOS starts printing the file.

C> To print a file from the DOS prompt, first run the PRINT.EXE program, as explained earlier. Then change to the drive and directory that contains the file you want to print, type `print` *`filename.ext`* (where *filename.ext* is the name of the file you want to print), and press ⏎Enter.

Changing File Attributes

Every file has certain *attributes*—special characteristics that tell your computer and DOS how to treat the file. These attributes are

Read only   Indicates whether the file can be both read and written to (read only off) or just read (read only on).

Hidden   Indicates whether the file is visible (hidden off) in a normal DOS directory or invisible (hidden on). Note that Shell can list hidden files. (Refer to the section called "Setting the File Display Options" earlier in this chapter.)

System   Indicates whether the file is reserved for system use (system on) or regular application use (system off).

Archive   Indicates if the file has not been recently backed up using any of several types of disk backup programs, including FastBack and DOS Backup. When archive is on, the file is new or has been edited and should be backed up in the next backup session. When archive is off, the file has already been backed up and needn't be backed up again.

You can change the attributes at any time to change the way the file is treated. To change a file's attributes, perform the following Quick Steps.

Changing a File's Attributes

1. Select the file(s) whose attributes you want to change.

   The selected files appear highlighted.

2. Open the **F**ile menu and select Change Attributes.

   If you selected more than one file in step 1, a dialog box appears asking if you want to change the attributes for one file at a time or all files at once. If you selected only one file, skip to step 4.

3. Choose 1. Change selected files one at a time or 2. Change all selected files at same time.

   The Change Attributes dialog box appears, as shown in Figure 8.15.

continues

continued

4. To turn an attribute on or off, click on the attribute, or highlight it and press Spacebar.

When an attribute is on, an arrow appears to the left of the attribute.

5. Select the OK button to proceed with the change.

DOS changes the attributes for the selected files as specified.

Figure 8.15

The Change Attributes dialog box lets you turn attributes on or off for the selected files.

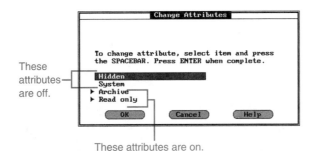

These attributes are off.

These attributes are on.

 To change file attributes at the DOS prompt, use the ATTRIB command with the following switches: +H, -H, +S, -S, +R, -R, +A, -A. H is for Hidden, S is for System, R is for Read Only, and A is for Archive. The plus sign tells DOS to turn the attribute on; the minus sign turns the attribute off. For example, to hide all files that have the .EXE extension, change to the drive that contains those files, type `attrib +h *.exe`, and press ⏎Enter.

Locating Files

Throughout this chapter, I have assumed that you know where all your files were located. However, this is not always the case. Even the most experienced, most organized computer user often mis-places a file or forgets the name of a file. In such cases, DOS can help locate the file. To search for a file from the DOS Shell, perform the following Quick Steps.

Locating Files by Name

1. Change to the drive that contains the file you want to find.

If you are unsure of which drive contains the file, you will have to search each drive.

2. Open the File menu, and select Search.

The Search File dialog box appears, as shown in Figure 8.16.

3. Type the name of the lost file or type a wild-card entry.

You can use the wild-card characters * and ?. For example, to find all files with the .DOC extension, type *.doc. Use * in place of a group of characters or ? in place of single characters.

4. To have DOS search the entire disk drive for the specified files, make sure there is an X in the Search entire disk check box.

If the Search entire disk option is off, DOS will search only in the current directory.

5. Select the OK button.

DOS searches for the names of the files that match your search instructions and displays a list of files that match your entry.

6. Press Esc to return to the Shell.

Figure 8.16

The Search File dialog box prompts you to specify the files for which you are searching.

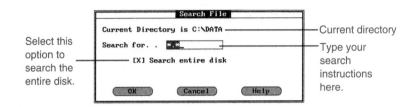

Select this option to search the entire disk.

Is That All?

In this chapter, you learned how to copy, move, rename, delete, undelete, and locate files, and how to perform other file management tasks. In the next chapter, you will learn how to manage your programs from the Shell.

In This Chapter

Running Programs from the Shell

Opening Document Files

Running Programs from the Program List

Adding Programs to the Program List

Running Several Programs at the Same Time

Running a Program with the Run Command

1. Open the File menu and select Run.
2. Type the command required to run the program.
3. Select the OK button to execute the command.

Running a Program with the Open Command

1. Change to the drive and directory that contains the program you want to run.
2. In the File List window, select the program or batch file that initiates the program (a file that has the .COM, .EXE, or .BAT extension).
3. Open the File menu and select Open.

Running a Program from the Program List

1. If the Program List is not displayed, open the View menu and select Program List or Program/File Lists.
2. If the program you want to run is in a program group, highlight the program group item and press ⏎Enter, or double-click on the group with your mouse.
3. Highlight the program item you want to run and press ⏎Enter, or double-click on it with your mouse.
4. If a dialog box appears, type the desired parameters and switches, and select OK.
5. To return to the Shell, quit the program as you normally would, and then press any key at the DOS prompt.

Running Programs from the DOS Shell

Imagine the convenience of running a program simply by selecting the program from a list. Or how about launching the program and retrieving a document by selecting the document file from the file list? Or how about running several programs at the same time and switching from program to program with the press of a key? In this chapter, you will learn how to do all these things and more from the Shell.

TIP: If you want to make Shell your permanent program launcher, you should have it run automatically when you start your computer. If Shell is not set up to run automatically, add the DOSSHELL command to your AUTOEXEC.BAT file, as explained in Chapter 15.

How to Run Programs from Shell

Shell offers various methods for running programs. The following list provides an overview of these methods. Each method is explained in detail later in this chapter.

- The **R**un command on the **F**ile menu lets you run a program as you would from the DOS prompt. When you select this command, a dialog box opens, allowing you to enter the DOS command required to run the program.

- The **O**pen command on the **F**ile menu lets you run a program by selecting the program's executable file from the File List window. (The executable file is the file that starts the program.) If you select a data file instead of a program file, this command runs the associated program (assuming you created an association) and then loads the data file into the program.

- The Program List contains a list of programs that you can run by selecting a program from the menu. The DOS installation program added several programs to the menu automatically, but you can add a program to the menu if it's not listed or edit the program's command line to change the way it runs.

Using the Run Command

The **R**un command displays the Run dialog box, which allows you to enter a command the same way you would enter the command at the DOS prompt. To use the **R**un command, perform the following Quick Steps.

Running a Program with the Run Command

1. Open the **File** menu and select **R**un.

The Run dialog box appears, as shown in Figure 9.1.

2. Type the command required to run the program. If the program file is not in the current directory, type the path to the directory before the command.

For example, if Microsoft Word is stored in the C:\WORD5 directory, you can type `c:\word5\word` to run the program. If you normally type parameters and switches after the command, you can type them here as well.

3. Select the OK button to execute the command.

Assuming the command is correct, Shell runs the program.

4. To return to the Shell, exit the program as you normally would and then press any key when you get to the DOS prompt.

You are returned to the DOS Shell.

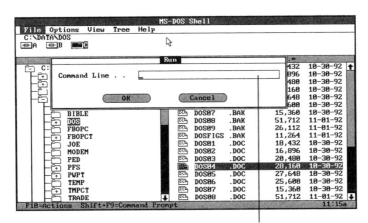

Type the command to run the program.

Figure 9.1

The Run dialog box prompts you to type the command required to run the program.

Using the Open Command

The **O**pen command provides a more powerful tool for running programs. You simply select the file that executes the program from the File List window and then "open" the file. The following Quick Steps give this procedure.

Running a Program with the Open Command

1. Change to the drive and directory that contains the program you want to run.

2. In the File List window, select the program or batch file that initiates the program (a file that has the .COM, .EXE, or .BAT extension).

   The selected file appears highlighted.

3. Open the **F**ile menu and select **O**pen.

   Shell runs the program.

4. To return to the Shell, exit the program as you normally would and then press any key when you get to the DOS prompt.

TIP: To bypass the **F**ile menu and enter the **O**pen command directly, try one of the following shortcuts:

- Highlight the name of the program or batch file in the file list and press ⏎Enter.

- If you're using a mouse, double-click on the desired program or batch file.

Although the **O**pen command is designed to open programs and batch files, you can also use it to start a program and load a document at the same time. However, Shell won't let you open a nonprogram or nonbatch file (for example, a .TXT document file created by a word processor) unless you've "associated" the document type with one of your programs. Shell monitors the file extensions of documents, so when you open a document, Shell finds the program that is associated with the document, starts the program, and loads the document. See the section in this chapter entitled "Associating Document Files with Programs" for instructions on how to associate data files with programs.

Running Programs from the Program List

The Program List allows you to run programs from the Shell simply by selecting the program item from a list. By selecting a program item, you tell Shell to carry out a series of commands that are assigned to that program item. The following sections explain how to display the Program List and how to add items to the Program List.

Running a Program

Before you can run a program from the Program List, you must display the menu by performing the following steps:

1. Press $\boxed{Alt}$+$\boxed{V}$ or click on View in the menu bar.

2. Select Program List or Program/File List. If you selected Program List, the Program List appears, as shown in Figure 9.2.

Figure 9.2

The Program List displays program items and program groups.

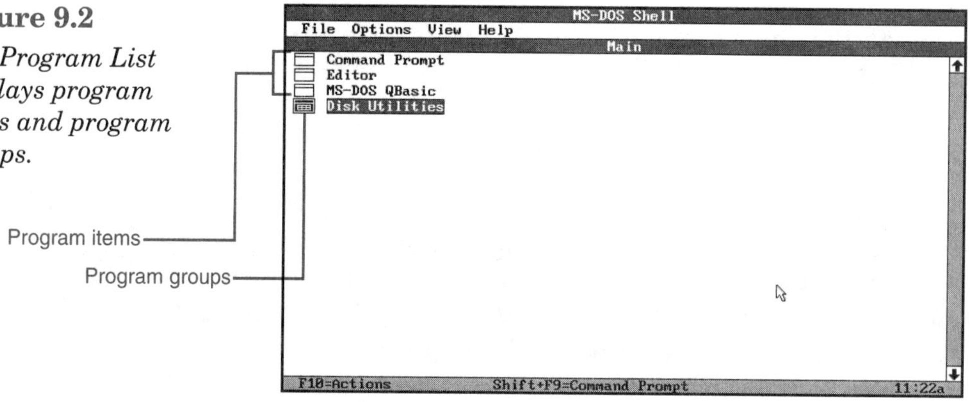

Program items ──────

Program groups ──────

```
                              MS-DOS Shell
    File  Options  View  Help
                                 Main
    ☐ Command Prompt                                                      ↑
    ☐ Editor
    ☐ MS-DOS QBasic
    ▣ Disk Utilities



                                              ↳



    F10=Actions          Shift+F9=Command Prompt              11:22a  ↓
```

As you can see, the Program List already contains several entries (called *program objects*), which can be classified as the following:

Program items   Program items represent individual programs, for example the Command Prompt, the Editor, and MS-DOS Basic. If you select a program item, Shell runs the program.

Program groups   A program group represents two or more related programs, for example Disk Utilities. If you select a program group, a submenu appears, as shown in Figure 9.3. This submenu can contain additional program items and/or program groups.

Once the Program List is displayed, you can run a program from the menu by performing the following Quick Steps.

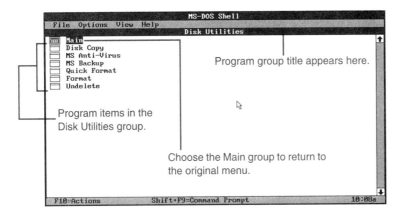

Program group title appears here.

Program items in the Disk Utilities group.

Choose the Main group to return to the original menu.

Figure 9.3

Selecting a program group opens a submenu containing additional program items and/or groups.

Running a Program from the Program List

1. If the program you want to run is in a program group, highlight the program group item and press ⏎Enter, or double-click on the group with your mouse.

   This displays a list of the program items in the group.

2. Highlight the program item you want to run and press ⏎Enter, or double-click on it with your mouse.

   A dialog box may appear, prompting you to type parameters or switches for the command.

3. If a dialog box appears, type the desired parameters and switches, and select OK.

   The Shell runs the selected program.

4. To return to the Shell, quit the program as you normally would, and then press any key at the DOS prompt.

Adding Programs to a Program List

You can add programs or program groups to the Program List at any time. The following Quick Steps lead you through the process of adding a program group.

Adding a Program Group

1. If needed, open the Program group in which you want the group's name to appear.

You can add a program group to the Main Program group or to one of its subbgroups.

2. Open the File menu and select New.

The New Program Object dialog box appears, as in Figure 9.4, asking if you want to add a program group or program item.

3. Select Program Group, and press ⏎Enter or click on the OK button.

The Add Group dialog box appears, as in Figure 9.5.

4. Type a title for the group (up to 23 characters) in the Title text box, and press Tab⇥.

The cursor moves to the next text box, Help Text.

5. (Optional) To add explanatory text to the program group, type your text (up to 255 characters) in the Help Text box, and press Tab⇥.

This help text will appear if you highlight the program group and press F1. To start a new line, do not press Enter; instead, type ^m where you want the line broken.

6. (Optional) To protect the group with a password, type a password (up to 20 characters).

If you add a password, you'll have to enter it whenever you want to access the program group.

7. Select OK to add the group to the menu.

You are returned to the DOS Shell, and the new group appears on the Program List.

If you password-protect a program group and then later forget the password, you can delete the group (as explained later in this lesson) and then recreate it.

CAUTION

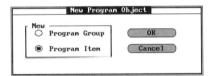

Figure 9.4

The New Program Object dialog box asks if you want to create a program group or item.

Figure 9.5

The Add Group dialog box lets you create a new program group.

You can add a program item to the Main program group or to a group you created. The following Quick Steps explain the procedure.

Adding a Program
Item to a Group

1. Highlight the program group in which you want the program listed and press ⏎Enter, or double-click on the group.

A submenu appears, showing the programs that are already in the group, if any.

2. Open the File menu and select New.

The New Program Object dialog box appears, as in Figure 9.4, asking if you want to add a program group or program item.

3. Select Program Item, and press ⏎Enter or click on the OK button.

The Add Program dialog box appears, as in Figure 9.6.

4. Type a title for the program (up to 23 characters) in the Program Title text box, and press Tab⇥.

The cursor moves to the Commands text box.

5. In the Commands text box, type the path to the directory that contains this program's program files, followed by the name of the file that runs the program. Press Tab⇥.

For example, if you had WordPerfect in a directory called WP51 on drive C, you would type `c:\wp51\wp.exe`. You can type up to 255 characters, and you can add parameters and switches.

6. (Optional) In the Startup Directory box, enter a path to the directory that contains the files you created using the program. Press Tab⇥.

For example, if you store WordPerfect document files in C:\WP51\FILES, type `c:\wp51\files`. This directory will be made current when you run the program.

7. (Optional) In the Application Shortcut Key box, hold down ⸂Shift⸃, ⸂Ctrl⸃, or ⸂Alt⸃, and type a letter. For example, ⸂Ctrl⸃+⸂W⸃.

This key combination will let you quickly switch to the program once it is running. (See the caution below to determine which keys you cannot use.)

8. (Optional) To return directly to the Shell without pausing when you exit the program, tab to the Pause after exit option and press ⸂Spacebar⸃.

Many times, it is useful to keep this option on so you can read any exit messages that appear before you return to the Shell.

9. (Optional) To protect the item with a password, type a password (up to 20 characters).

If you add a password, you'll have to enter it whenever you want to run the program from the Program List.

10. Select OK to accept the information you just entered.

The name of the new program item appears on the Program List.

CAUTION

In step 7, do not use any of the following shortcut key combinations:

⸂Ctrl⸃+⸂C⸃, ⸂Ctrl⸃+⸂M⸃ , ⸂Ctrl⸃+⸂I⸃, ⸂Ctrl⸃+⸂H⸃, ⸂Ctrl⸃+⸂[⸃, ⸂Ctrl⸃+⸂5⸃ (on the numeric keypad)

⸂Shift⸃+⸂Ctrl⸃+⸂M⸃, ⸂Shift⸃+⸂Ctrl⸃+⸂I⸃, ⸂Shift⸃+⸂Ctrl⸃+⸂H⸃, ⸂Shift⸃+⸂Ctrl⸃+⸂[⸃, ⸂Shift⸃+⸂Ctrl⸃+⸂5⸃ (on the numeric keypad)

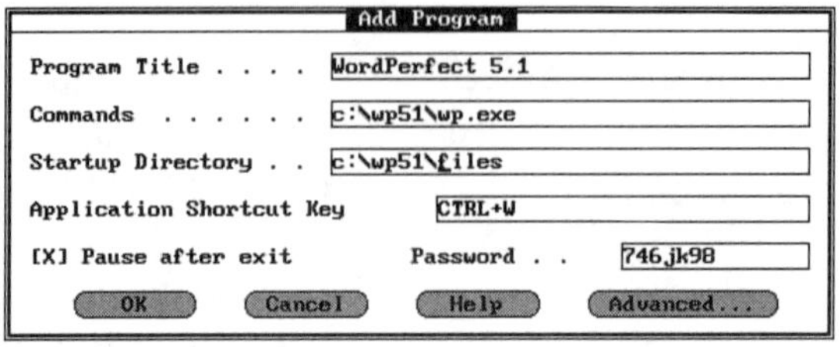

Figure 9.6

*The Add Program
dialog box requests
information about
the program.*

Figure 9.6

*The Add Program
dialog box requests
information about
the program.*

Editing a Program Group or Item

If you add a program item to the Program List and it doesn't run as expected, or if you'd like to change a program group or item in any way, you can edit it. To do so, highlight the program group or item, open the File menu, and select Properties. This displays the Program Item Properties (see Figure 9.7) or Program Group Properties dialog box, where you can enter your changes.

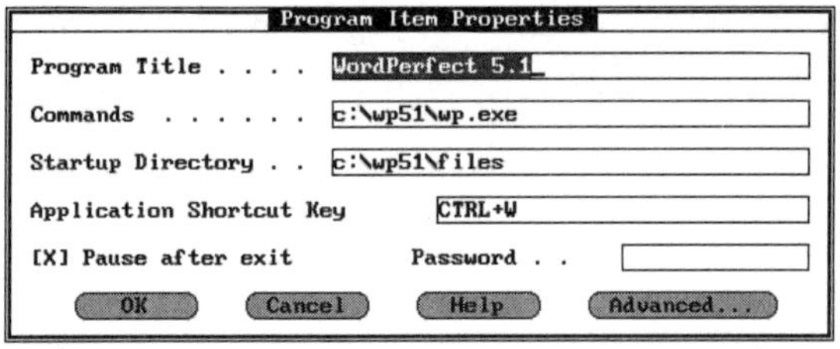

Figure 9.7

*The Program Item
Properties dialog
box lets you edit
the instructions for
a program item.*

Using Advanced Program Options

At the bottom of the Add Program dialog box (Figure 9.6) or the Program Item Properties dialog box (Figure 9.7) is a button labeled Advanced. If you select this button, you'll see the Advanced dialog box, shown in Figure 9.8. This dialog box lets you enter advanced instructions about how you want the program to run:

Help Text   You can type up to 255 characters in this box to have help text appear when you or another user highlights this program item and press F1.

Conventional Memory   KB Required   If a program requires a minimum amount of conventional memory to run,
you can type that amount (in kilobytes) in this box. If the
specified amount of conventional memory is not available
when you try to run the program, DOS will display an
Insufficient memory message. If you leave this box empty,
DOS uses 128 kilobytes as the default.

XMS Memory   KB Required   KB Limit   If you have a
program that uses extended memory, you can specify the
minimum and maximum amounts of extended memory
you want to be available for the program.

Video Mode   If you have a text-based program, such as a
basic word processor, set the video mode to Text. This
speeds up task-swapping operations. If you have a graphics program (one that displays pictures and icons on-
screen), set the video mode to Graphics, so the graphic
elements will be displayed.

Reserve Shortcut Keys   These are key combinations that
Shell uses for task swapping. If one or more of these key
combinations conflict with keys you use to perform essential operations within the program you are running, you
can block Shell's use of the key.

Prevent Program Switch   If you activate task swapping,
as explained later in this chapter, you can switch between
active programs and keep a program active when you
return to Shell. To prevent task swapping for a program,
select Prevent Program Switch to put an X in the check
box.

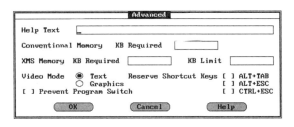

Figure 9.8

*The Advanced
dialog box lets you
customize a
program's
operation.*

Creating Custom Dialog Boxes for Your Programs

You may recall from Chapter 6 that when you choose to format a disk from the Shell, a dialog box appears, asking you to specify which floppy disk drive you want to use. You can create similar dialog boxes for your own programs.

To create a custom dialog box, perform the following Quick Steps.

Quick Steps — Creating a Custom Dialog Box

1. Highlight the program item for which you want to create the dialog box.

2. Open the File menu, and select Properties.

    The Program Item Properties dialog box appears, as in Figure 9.7.

3. Move down to the Commands text box, and press End to move to the end of the command.

    You need to be at the end of the command to type the parameter that displays the dialog box.

4. Press Spacebar, and then type %1.

    You can type additional % switches to create more than one dialog box. For example, you can type %1 %2 %3 to create three dialog boxes.

5. Press ↵Enter to accept your changes.

    The Program Item Properties dialog box appears, as shown in Figure 9.9, prompting you to type the information that you want to appear in your dialog box.

6. In the Window Title text box, type the title you want to use for the dialog box.

This title will appear at the top of the dialog box.

7. Tab to the Program Information text box, and type a brief description of the program or any other information.

This information will appear at the top of the box, just below the title.

8. Tab to the Prompt Message text box, and type a message that tells the user what parameters or switches to enter.

For example, you might ask the user to type the name of the files to open.

9. Tab to the Default Parameters text box, and type any parameters that the user can accept simply by pressing ⏎Enter.

These parameters will appear in the text box of this dialog box whenever the user chooses to run the program. The user can then delete the parameters or press ⏎Enter to accept them.

10. Press ⏎Enter to accept the information you typed.

You are returned to the Shell.

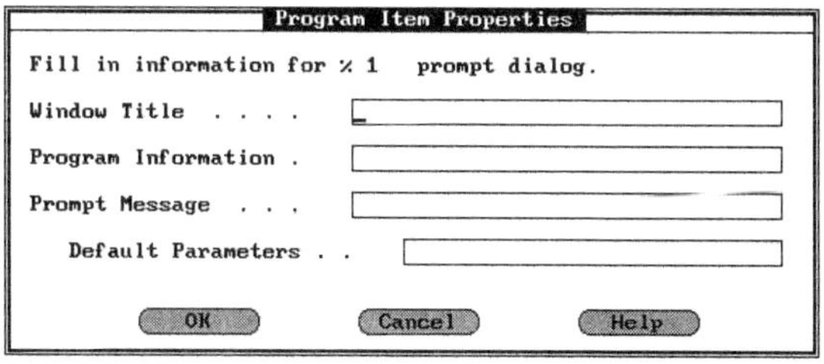

```
┌──────────Program Item Properties──────────┐
│ Fill in information for % 1   prompt dialog.│
│                                             │
│ Window Title  . . . .  [                  ] │
│                                             │
│ Program Information .  [                  ] │
│                                             │
│ Prompt Message  . . .  [                  ] │
│                                             │
│   Default Parameters . .  [              ]  │
│                                             │
│      ( OK )        ( Cancel )      ( Help ) │
└─────────────────────────────────────────────┘
```

Figure 9.9

Use this dialog box to create a custom dialog box for a program.

Deleting a Program from a Program List

If a Program List contains programs that you never run from the Shell, you may want to delete their names from the menu. To delete a program, perform the following Quick Steps.

Deleting a Program Item from the Menu

1. Display the menu that contains the program item you want to delete.

2. Select the program item you want to delete.

   The program item appears highlighted.

3. Open the File menu and select Delete, or press ⌐Del⌐.

   The Delete Item dialog box appears, asking you to confirm the deletion.

4. Press ⌐Enter⌐ or select OK to confirm the deletion.

You can delete a program group by deleting all the program items in the group and then performing the steps above.

Moving a Program in a Program List

If you don't like the position of one of the programs on the menu, you can move the program group or item in the list. To do so, perform the following Quick Steps.

Reordering the Program List

1. Highlight the program group or item you want to move.

2. Open the File menu and select Reorder.

   A message appears at the bottom of the screen telling you what to do next.

3. Highlight the position where you want the selected program group or item moved and press ↵Enter, or double-click on the position with your mouse.

   The program group or item appears above the selected item, and the items below it move down.

Associating Document Files with Programs

One of the most useful features of Shell is that you can run a program by selecting (from the File List window) a data file that you created using the program. However, in order for this to work, you must first *associate* the data file with the program in which it was created. For example, you can associate a data file having the extension .DOC with the Microsoft Word program. With a single command, you can then run Word and load a selected document file into the program.

You can associate data files and programs in either of two ways: by associating the data file with the program or the program with the data file(s). To associate a data file with a program, perform the following Quick Steps.

Associating a Data File with a Program

1. In the file list, select a data file that has the file name extension you want to associate with a program.

DOS will use the file's extension to figure out which program to run.

2. Open the File menu and select Associate.

The Associate File dialog box appears (see Figure 9.10), prompting you to specify the program with which you want to associate this type of data file.

3. Type the path to the directory that contains the program followed by the name of the file that runs the program.

For example, to associate the data file with WordPerfect, you might type c:\wp51\wp.exe.

4. Press ↵Enter or select OK.

The association is made.

Figure 9.10

The Associate File dialog box prompts you to specify the file that runs the program.

File names with this extension will be associated to the specified program.

Type the program's path and executable program file name here.

You can also associate a program with one or more types of data files. To create this association, perform the following Quick Steps.

Associating a Program with One or More Data Files

1. In the file list, select the program file that runs the program.

For example, if you want to associate WordPerfect with a type of data file, select the WP.EXE program file.

2. Open the File menu and select Associate.

The Associate File dialog box appears, prompting you to specify the file name extension you want to associate with this program.

3. Type one or more file name extensions separated by spaces. (Do not type the period that comes before the file name extension.)

For example, you can type `DOC WPF TXT` to associate all files that have the .DOC, .WPF, or .TXT extensions.

4. Press ⏎Enter or select OK.

The association is made.

Once a file is associated with a particular program, you can run the program and load the document file with a single command:

1. Highlight the document file you want to load.

2. Open the File menu and select Open. Shell runs the program and loads the selected document file into it.

TIP: A quicker way to open an associated data file is to double-click on it in the file list or highlight it and press ⏎Enter.

Running Several Programs at the Same Time

Throughout this chapter, I have focused on running a single program from the Shell. However, Shell offers a way to keep two or more programs running at the same time. You can then switch from program to program with the press of a key.

Before you can run two or more programs, however, you must turn on Shell's Task Swapper option: Open the Options menu and select Enable Task Swapper. When Task Swapper is on, the Program List displays two columns: the Program List on the left and the Active Task List on the right (see Figure 9.11). The Active Task List shows the names of any programs that are currently running.

Figure 9.11

When you enable the Task Swapper, the Program List splits in two.

Active Task List ————

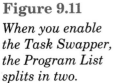

To run more than one program, perform the following steps:

1. Run the first program using one of the methods discussed earlier in this chapter.

2. Press Ctrl+Esc to return to the Shell.

3. Run the next program and press Ctrl+Esc to return to the Shell. You now have two programs in the Active Task List (see Figure 9.12).

4. Repeat step 3 to run additional programs.

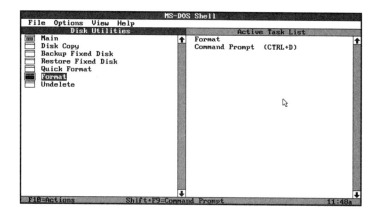

Figure 9.12

When you run a program, it is added to the Active Task List.

Switching Between Programs

To switch from one active program to another, use the methods listed in Table 9.1.

To	Do This
Go back to the Shell	Press Ctrl+Esc.
Go to another program from Shell	Select the program from the Active Task List.
Cycle forward through the active programs	Press Alt+Tab.
Cycle back through the active programs	Press ⇧Shift+Alt+Tab.
Go to the next program	Press Alt+Esc.
Go to the previous program	Press ⇧Shift+Alt+Esc.
Go to a program with an application shortcut key	Press the shortcut key combination you assigned to the program.

Table 9.1
Active Task Swapping Methods

Quitting a Program

The best way to quit an active program is to go to the program and then use the procedure you would normally perform to exit the program. This ensures that any data file on which you may have been working gets saved to disk before you exit the program.

However, if you cannot get to the program in order to quit it (that is, if the program stops responding to Shell commands), you can quit the program by deleting it from the Active Task List. Highlight the program's name in the Active Task List, and then open the **F**ile menu and select **D**elete or press ⌐Del⌐. A warning will appear telling you to quit the program before deleting it. Select the OK button to override the warning.

> **FYI**
> **IDEAS**
>
> Now that you know how to add programs to the Program List, add all the programs you commonly use to the menu, and make sure you assign each program a shortcut key combination. When you start your day, run each program you commonly use from the Shell. Then, whenever you need to use a program, press the shortcut key to go to it. As you get used to working in this way, you will never want to go back to running each program separately.

Is That All?

In this chapter, you learned various methods for running your programs from the DOS Shell. You learned how to create program groups and items that allow you to run your programs by selecting them from a menu. You learned how to associate data files with programs in order to run the program and open the data file with a single command. And you learned how to automate your work by using the Task Swapper.

In the next chapter, we will shift gears and look at how you can protect your data and program files by creating backups.

In This Chapter

Understanding Backups

Backup Strategies

Configuring Microsoft Backup for Your Computer

Backing Up All the Files on a Disk

Backing Up Selected Files on a Disk

Starting Microsoft Backup for the First Time

1. Type msbackup at the DOS prompt, and press ↵Enter.

2. Follow the on-screen instructions to set up the backup program for your computer.

Backing Up All the Files on Your Hard Disk

1. At the DOS prompt, type msbackup and press ↵Enter.

2. Press Alt+B or click on the Backup button.

3. In the Backup From list, double-click on the disk(s) you want to back up, or highlight each disk, and press Spacebar.

4. Select the Backup To button, select the drive and type of disk you're using from the list, and select the OK button.

5. Select Start Backup.

6. Follow the on-screen instructions to complete the backup operation.

Running Backup for Windows

1. Look for a program group window called Microsoft Tools. If you see the window, click anywhere on it to bring it to the front. If you don't see the window, click on Window in the Program Manager menu bar, and then click on Microsoft Tools.

2. Double-click on the Backup icon.

3. If this is the first time you have run the program, follow the on-screen instructions to set up Backup for your system.

4. Click on the Backup button to perform a backup.

Backing Up Files on Your Hard Disk

The most valuable part of your computer is the data and program files that are stored on your hard disk. These files may include business and personal letters, your diary, your checkbook register, art you've created, business contacts, your resume, and perhaps your favorite recipes. In addition, the disk stores the programs you installed and configured and maybe even some time-saving macros.

What would you do if you lost all those files? If you turned on your computer one day, and a message appeared telling you that drive C had bit the dust? Or you changed to a directory to get a file and found the directory empty—not even a crumb of a file left behind?

If you had updated backup files (on a set of floppy disks or a backup tape), the answer would be easy; you could use the backups to restore your files to your hard disk. In this chapter, you will learn how to back up the files on your hard disk and restore files in the event that any of your files get damaged or destroyed.

NOTE: Why use a special program for backing up files? In Chapter 8, you learned how to copy files from one disk to another. You may be wondering, then, "Why not just copy files from your hard disk to floppies?" The answer is that backup files take less time to create and take up less space on disk. During a backup, the backup program compresses the files before storing them on disk, so you can often store backup files on a third of the disks it would take to store copies.

Establishing a Backup Strategy

Backups are worthless if you don't have a backup strategy—a plan that ensures the backup copies are up-to-date. For best results, you should back up all your files at least once a week, and back up any files that change during the day at the end of the day.

In the next few sections, you will learn about the various types of backups you can perform with Microsoft Backup. By looking at the various types of backups, you will be able to develop a practical and effective backup strategy that fits the way you work.

Backup Types and Why They Matter

Microsoft Backup offers three types of backups: full, incremental, and differential. To understand the different types, you must understand how archive attributes work.

What's an *archive attribute?* It's a code attached to each file. Whenever you create or edit a file, the archive attribute is turned on, indicating that the file has not been backed up. When the file is backed up (by any backup program), the archive attribute is turned off. The backup program then knows which files were changed or created since the last backup. This becomes important in deciding which backup method to use: Full, Incremental, or Differential.

Backing Up All Files with a Full Backup

A full backup backs up all the files on the hard disk, or the files and subdirectories you tell the program to back up. During a full backup, Microsoft Backup ignores the setting of the archive attribute. Backup backs up all files and turns their archive attributes off.

> **TIP:** You can do a full backup without backing up all files. The term "full backup" simply means that DOS will back up all selected files regardless of their archive attribute status. Later in this chapter, you'll learn how to select individual files for backup.

You should perform at least one full backup to back up all the files on your hard disk. You can then perform incremental or differential backups daily to back up any files that have changed.

The Pros and Cons of Incremental Backups

An incremental backup backs up only those files that have changed since the last backup; that is, any files that have their archive attribute turned on. When the backup is complete, the backup program turns the archive attributes off for the backed-up files. Incremental disks are added to the full backup disks, so you end up with a single set of backup disks. If you ever have to restore your files, you will have to use both your full and your incremental backup disks.

If you want to save all the changes a file goes through, create incremental backups. With each incremental backup, a copy of the most recent version of the file is saved. If you want to look at a version of the file you created a week ago, simply restore that version to a different directory and open it.

The problem with incremental backups is that you may end up with a big set of backup disks, consisting of several renditions of a file. If you end up with too many backup disks, consider creating another full backup and start incrementing it anew.

The Pros and Cons of Differential Backups

A differential backup backs up all files that were changed or added to the disk since the last full backup. When the files are backed up, the backup program does not turn their archive attributes off. Differential backups give you two sets of backup disks: a set for the full backup and a set for any added or changed files.

If you rarely install new programs on your hard disk, and you do not keep track of the various renditions of a file, differential backups may be right for you. You can create a full backup that stores all your program and data files, and then perform a differential backup on a daily basis to protect all files that were added to the hard disk since the full backup.

There are two problems with differential backups. First, a differential backup does not store all the renditions of your data files—only the most recent version is saved. Second, if you add many files to your hard disk since the last full backup, a differential backup can become time-consuming. If the differential backup gets too time-consuming, it may be a good time to create a new full backup and start over.

FYI
IDEAS

What's my backup strategy? I don't like to mess around with incremental and differential backups. I have a full backup of all the programs on my hard disk. Every couple months, or whenever I install a new program on the hard disk, I back up all my programs again.

As for my data files, which change daily, I store all of them in a directory called \DATA. I store the files for each of my books in a separate directory under the DATA directory. Each day, I back up all the files in the DATA directory and its subdirectories, except files with the .BAK extension (backup files created by Microsoft Word). This usually takes about four disks and 5 to 10 minutes.

Setting Up Microsoft Backup for Your System

When you first run Microsoft Backup, the program leads you through a setup process that configures the backup program for your system. Before you begin, get two blank floppy disks of the same type to create a test backup (the disks do not have to be formatted).

NOTE: What about backup for windows? If you installed Backup for Windows, and you want to use it rather than the DOS version, skip to the end of the chapter (to the "Running Backup for Windows" section) to figure out how to get the program up and running. Although most of this chapter deals specifically with the DOS version, the steps in the Windows version are nearly identical; only the screen appearance varies.

To configure the backup program for your system, perform the following steps:

1. From the DOS prompt, type `msbackup` and press ⏎Enter.

   OR

   From the Shell's main program window, select Disk Utilities and then select MS Backup.

2. Read the dialog box, and select Start Configuration. Microsoft Backup tests your mouse and video driver and displays the Video and Mouse Configuration dialog box, as shown in Figure 10.1.

Figure 10.1

The Video and Mouse Configuration dialog box.

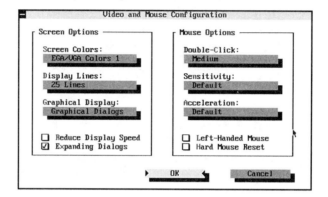

3. To change a setting, click on the setting's button, or hold down [Alt] while typing the highlighted letter in the button's name. A dialog box will appear (for example, if you select Graphical Display, you will see Figure 10.2). Select a setting, and then select OK.

Figure 10.2

If you choose to change a setting, another dialog box will appear asking you to enter your change.

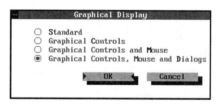

4. To accept the Video and Mouse Configuration settings, select the OK button. The Floppy Drive Change Line Test dialog box appears.

5. Remove any disks from your floppy disk drives, and select the Start Test button. Your floppy drives grind briefly, and the Backup Devices dialog box appears, as shown in Figure 10.3.

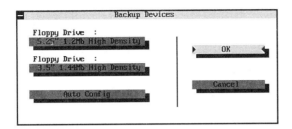

Figure 10.3

The Backup Devices dialog box prompts you to specify the backup devices your system has.

6. If the drive types displayed are correct, select the OK button. Otherwise, click on a drive button, and select the correct drive type.

7. Select the OK button to start the backup test. Microsoft Backup performs some diagnostic tests, and then displays the Floppy Disk Compatibility Test dialog box.

8. Select Start Test. Microsoft Backup automatically works through several dialog boxes to select a set of files to back up. A dialog box appears telling you that the program is now pausing so you can select a drive to back up to.

9. Press ⏎Enter to select Continue. The Backup To dialog box appears, as shown in Figure 10.4.

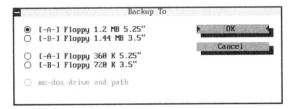

Figure 10.4

The Backup To dialog box prompts you to specify the drive you want to use for the backup test.

10. Select the drive and disk type to which you want to back up the test files, then select OK. You're instructed to insert a floppy disk into the specified drive.

11. Insert a floppy disk into the specified drive, close the drive door (if necessary), and press ⏎Enter to select Continue. Backup starts backing up the test files to the floppy disk (see Figure 10.5).

NOTE: If you get a message telling you that the disk contains data, change disks and select Retry, or select Overwrite to replace any data on the disk with the backup test files.

Figure 10.5

Microsoft Backup displays the progress of the backup operation.

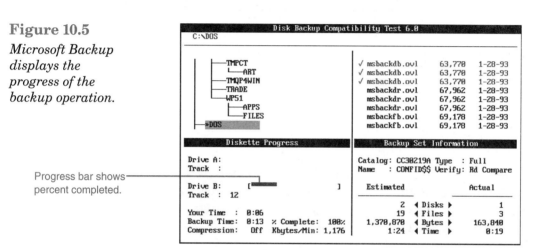

Progress bar shows percent completed.

12. When Backup instructs you to insert the next floppy disk, remove the first disk from the floppy drive, insert the second disk, and press ⏎Enter. When the Backup is done, you'll see the Backup Complete dialog box.

13. Select the OK button to continue. Backup works through a series of dialog boxes to select the compare operation, and you are instructed to insert the first backup floppy into the floppy drive.

14. Insert the first floppy disk into the specified drive, close the drive door (if necessary), and press ⏎Enter to continue. Backup starts comparing the backed-up files to the originals. Backup displays a prompt when it needs the next disk.

15. Remove the first disk from the floppy drive, insert the second disk, and press ⏎Enter. When Backup is done comparing the test files, it displays the Compare Complete dialog box, as shown in Figure 10.6.

Figure 10.6

The Compare Complete dialog box shows whether or not the backup files match the originals.

16. Press ⏎Enter), or click on the OK button. The Compatibility Test dialog box appears, showing whether the backup test was successful.

17. Press ⏎Enter), or click on the OK button. The Configure dialog box appears, allowing you to enter any changes to the configuration settings.

18. Change any of the configuration settings you want, and select the Save button to save your settings. The Backup menu appears, as in Figure 10.7. You will use this menu to back up, compare, and restore files.

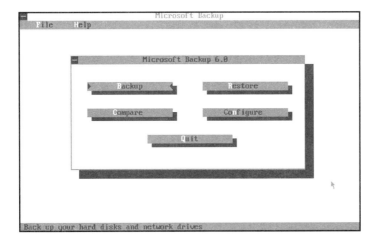

Figure 10.7

Whenever you start Backup, you will see the Backup menu.

NOTE: If your computer can't pass the test at any speed, make sure all memory-resident programs are unloaded from memory, and then retest your computer:

1. Start Microsoft Backup as explained earlier to display the Backup menu.

2. Select Configure.

3. Select Compatibility Test.

4. Select Start Test.

Running Microsoft Backup

Now that Microsoft Backup is set up, whenever you run it, you'll see the screen shown in Figure 10.7. To run Microsoft Backup, perform the following steps:

1. From the DOS prompt, type `msbackup` and press ⏎Enter.

   OR

   From the Shell's main program window, select Disk Utilities, and then select MS Backup.

2. Press Alt+B or click on the **B**ackup button. The Microsoft Backup screen appears, as shown in Figure 10.8.

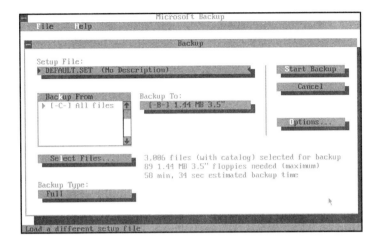

Figure 10.8

When you choose the Backup button, the Microsoft Backup screen appears.

Selecting the Drive You Want to Back Up

Before your itchy trigger finger clicks on the **S**tart Backup button, check to make sure you have selected the disk drive you want to back up. In the Backup From box, double-click (or right-click) on each disk drive you want to back up, or highlight the drive and press (Spacebar).

When you select a drive in this way, All files appears next to the selected drive, indicating that all files will be backed up. If you select a drive and All Files does not appear, try selecting the drive again. (Later in this chapter, you will learn how to back up a select group of files.)

Selecting a Drive for Storing the Backups

While you're at it, check the Backup To box to make sure you have selected the correct disk drive for storing the backed-up files. If the drive you want to use is not displayed, press (Alt)+(A) or click on the Backup To button. A list of available disk drives appears.

Click on the drive you want to use, or highlight it, and press
(Spacebar). Then select the OK button. If you selected one of the floppy
disk drives, you are done. If you selected MS-DOS Drive and Path,
a box appears under the Backup To option. In this box, type the
letter of the drive you want to use for the backups. You can type
the letter of a backup tape drive, a Bernoulli drive, a removable
hard disk cartridge, a hard disk drive, or a network drive.

> **NOTE:** What's an MS-DOS drive? An MS-DOS drive is
> basically any drive that is not a floppy disk drive. In other
> words, if you have a special backup tape drive or a
> Bernoulli box that you want to use for storing your back-
> ups, you must select the MS-DOS Drive and Path option
> to use it.

If you are backing up files to a set of floppy disks, look at the
bottom of the dialog box to see how many disks you will need for
the backup. Obtain the suggested number of blank disks, or disks
that contain information you will never need. The backup operation will overwrite anything on the disks.

Selecting a Backup Type

Before you begin your backup, make sure you have selected the
correct backup type: Full, Incremental, or Differential. The first
time you back up, you should select Full to back up all the files on
the disk. To change the backup type, press (Alt)+(Y), or click on the
button under Backup Type. Select the desired backup type, and
then select OK.

Selecting Additional
Backup Options

Even though you can start your backup right now, you'll probably
want to set additional options before you begin. To set additional

options, press Alt+O, or click on the Options button. The Disk
Backup Options dialog box appears, as shown in Figure 10.9.

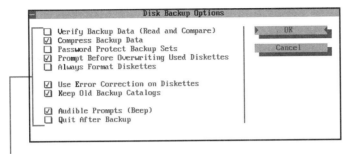

Select an option to turn it on or off.

Figure 10.9

*The Disk Backup
Options dialog box.*

Here is a list of the available options:

Verify Backup Data (Read and Compare)   When this
option is selected, the backup program checks to make
sure the backed-up files match the originals.

Compress Backup Data   Compression reduces the size of
the backup copies so they will consume less disk space
than the original files.

Password Protect Backup Sets   This option lets you add a
password to the backed-up files to prevent prying eyes
from restoring sensitive data.

Prom**p**t Before Overwriting Used Disks   When this option
is selected, the backup program will notify you if you try to
back up files to a floppy disk that already has files on it.

Always Format Diskettes   Normally, the backup program
formats disks only when necessary. With this option
selected, the program will format new disks or reformat
any used disks. This ensures that you are backing up to
freshly formatted disks, but it takes additional time.

Use **E**rror Correction on Diskettes   When this option is
on, the backup program uses about 10 percent of the
floppy disk's space to store information that will help you
recover files even if the floppy disk is damaged. In general,

it is better to turn on the Verify option. If you turn the Verify option off, however, you should turn Error Correction on.

Keep Old Backup Catalogs   When you create a backup, the backup program stores a list of the backed-up files and directories in a *catalog* on the hard disk. If you perform the same type of backup again, the program replaces the old catalog with the new one. If you want to keep the old catalogs for future reference, select this option.

Audible Prompts (Beep)   This option tells the program to beep to get your attention. With this option turned on, the computer will sound a beep whenever you need to insert the next disk during a backup.

Quit After Backup   This option tells the program to automatically quit after the backup is complete.

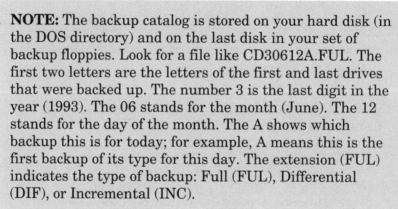

NOTE: The backup catalog is stored on your hard disk (in the DOS directory) and on the last disk in your set of backup floppies. Look for a file like CD30612A.FUL. The first two letters are the letters of the first and last drives that were backed up. The number 3 is the last digit in the year (1993). The 06 stands for the month (June). The 12 stands for the day of the month. The A shows which backup this is for today; for example, A means this is the first backup of its type for this day. The extension (FUL) indicates the type of backup: Full (FUL), Differential (DIF), or Incremental (INC).

Backing Up All Files on a Hard Disk

With the Microsoft Backup program configured and the desired options selected, you can now back up your hard disk. If this is the first time you've backed up the drive, you should use the full backup method and back up everything on the disk.

During the backup process, Microsoft Backup will prompt you to insert Disk Number *xx* into the drive. Write this number on the diskette so that you can readily identify it. If and when you need to restore the hard disk with previously backed-up data, you'll be prompted to insert one or more of these numbered diskettes into the drive.

The following Quick Steps summarize what you've learned so far. Follow this simple procedure to back up your entire hard disk.

Performing a Full Backup

1. At the DOS prompt, type `msbackup`, and press ⏎Enter.

   The opening backup screen appears.

2. Press Alt+B or click on the **B**ackup button.

   The Microsoft Backup screen appears.

3. In the Bac**k**up From list, double-click (or right-click) on the disk(s) you want to back up, or highlight each disk and press Spacebar.

4. Select the Backup To button.

   A list of the available backup drives appears.

5. Select the drive and type of disk you're using from the list, and select the OK button.

   The selected destination appears on-screen.

   If you chose the MS-DOS Drive and Path option, type a path to the drive under the Backup To button.

continues

continued

6. Select **S**tart Backup.

If you chose the MS-DOS Drive and Path option, the backup operation starts. If you are backing up to floppy disks, a message appears to insert a disk into the floppy drive.

7. If applicable, insert a disk, and select **C**ontinue.

If Microsoft Backup thinks the disk contains information, a warning message will be displayed.

8. If a warning message appears, select **O**verwrite to override the warning, or switch disks and select **R**etry.

The backup process begins, and the progress is displayed.

9. If applicable, switch disks when prompted.

As you remove a backup disk, write a number on it to keep the disks in order. When the backup is complete, a dialog box appears, showing the number of disks used and other information.

10. When the Backup Complete dialog box appears, choose **O**K, and then choose **Q**uit to exit the program.

If you backed up your files to floppy disks, you may be wondering where you should store the disks. There are two schools of thought on this subject. Some folks like to store the disks near the computer. That way, if anything happens to the files on the hard disk, the backups are in a convenient location. Other people believe you should store the backups away from the computer—at home if your computer is at work, or at work if your computer is at home. My recommendation is to carry your backup disks back and forth between work and home. If you work at home, try a neighbor's house.

Backing Up Modified Files

Now that you have a backup copy of all the files on your hard disk, you can perform daily, incremental backups to copy only those files that have changed since the full backup. The following Quick Steps explain how to perform an incremental backup.

Performing an Incremental Backup

1. At the DOS prompt, type msbackup and press ⏎Enter.

   The opening backup screen appears.

2. Press Alt+B or click on the Backup button.

   The Microsoft Backup screen appears.

3. In the Backup From list, double-click (or right-click) on the disk(s) you want to back up, or highlight each disk and press Spacebar.

   Make sure All files appears next to each disk you want to back up.

4. Press Alt+Y or click on the Backup Type button.

   A list of backup methods appears.

5. Select Incremental, and then select OK.

continues

continued

6. Select the Backup To button.

A list of the available backup drives appears.

7. Select the drive and type of disk you're using from the list, and select the OK button.

The selected option appears on-screen.

If you chose the MS-DOS Drive and Path option, type a path to the drive under the Backup To button.

8. Select Start Backup.

If you chose the MS-DOS Drive and Path option, the backup operation starts. If you are backing up to floppy disks, a message tells you to insert a disk into the floppy drive.

9. If applicable, insert a disk, and select Continue.

If Microsoft Backup thinks the disk contains information, a warning message appears.

10. If a warning message appears, select Overwrite to override the warning, or switch disks and select Retry.

The backup process begins, and the progress is displayed.

11. If applicable, switch disks when prompted.

As you remove a backup disk, write a number on it to keep the disks in order. When the backup is complete, a dialog box appears, showing the number of disks used and other information.

12. When the Backup Complete dialog box appears, choose OK, and then choose Quit to exit the program.

Backing Up Selected Directories and Files

You don't have to back up all the files on your hard disk, or even all the files that have changed. For example, you may have two or three directories that contain the data files you created. Because the files in these directories change more often than program files change, you may want to back up your data files daily and back up your program files once a month or whenever you add or modify a program.

To select the files you want to back up, start Microsoft Backup, select the Backup button, and then choose the Select Files button. The Select Backup Files screen appears, as shown in Figure 10.10.

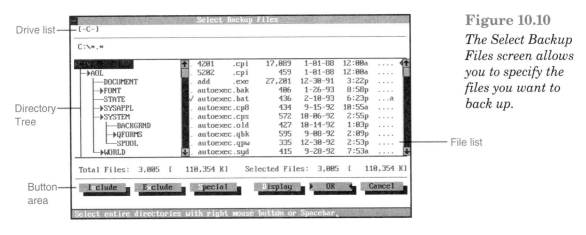

Figure 10.10

The Select Backup Files screen allows you to specify the files you want to back up.

Resist the temptation to start selecting disks, directories, and files from the directory tree and file list. Any selections you make here will override other selections you may make using the Include and Exclude buttons, as you will see in the next two sections. For now, just look at the screen and note that it is divided into four areas: the drive list, the directory tree, the file list, and the buttons. Use the Tab key to move from area to area.

Selecting a Drive to Back Up

If you have only one hard drive (C), you don't have to worry about selecting a different drive. If you have two or more drives, however, you may want to back up files on various drives. To change drives, click on the drive letter you want to change to, or tab to the drive list, use the arrow keys to highlight the drive letter, and then press (Spacebar).

Including and Excluding Groups of Files

A quick way to include or exclude groups of files is to use the Include and Exclude buttons at the bottom of the screen. Press Alt)+N) or click on Include to display the dialog box shown in Figure 10.11. Notice that, initially, the dialog box is set to include all files on the selected disk.

Figure 10.11

The Include Files dialog box lets you specify which files you want to back up.

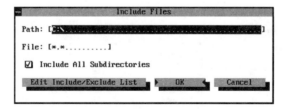

Including a Group of Files

If you want to back up files in a single directory and any of its subdirectories, edit the **Path** entry. For example, to back up only those files in C:\DATA, you would type `c:\data` as the **P**ath entry. Edit the **F**ile entry, if you want to specify a group of files to back up. For example, to back up only those files that have the *.DOC extension, type `*.doc` as the **F**ile entry. To include subdirectories of the selected directory, make sure there is a check mark in the Include All **S**ubdirectories check box. Choose the OK button to enter your selections.

Excluding a Group of Files

You can perform a similar series of steps to exclude groups of files. Select the Exclude button to display the Exclude Files dialog box (it looks just like the Include Files dialog box). Change the **P**ath entry to exclude files in a given directory. Change the **F**ile entry to exclude a group of files. To exclude subdirectories of the selected directory, make sure there is a check mark in the Exclude All **S**ubdirectories check box. Select the OK button to enter your selections.

Editing the Include/Exclude List

You may have noticed that both the Include Files and Exclude Files dialog boxes have an **E**dit Include/Exclude List button. Click on this button, or press Alt+E to display the dialog box shown in Figure 10.12. This dialog box lets you enter several include or exclude statements to specify which files you want to include and exclude in the backup.

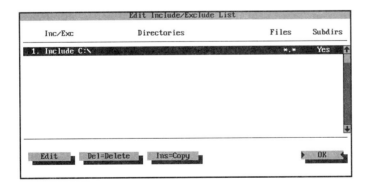

Figure 10.12

You can edit the Include/Exclude list to specify the files you want to include and exclude in the backup.

Normally, the list starts with a statement that includes all the files on the selected disk. To add a statement, highlight an existing statement, and then click on the Copy button or press Alt+C. Highlight the new statement, and then click on the Edit button, or press Ins. This opens a dialog box like the one in Figure 10.11. Change any of the entries to specify a group of files you want to include or exclude in the backup. Then, choose the OK button.

CAUTION   When editing the Include/Exclude list, keep in mind that the include and exclude statements will be executed in the specified sequence. If you have an exclude statement that excludes all files that end in .BAK, and follow it with an include statement that includes all files, the second statement will override the first one, and all files will be included (even those with the .BAK extension).

Choosing Directories from the Tree

Instead of (or in addition to) using the Include/Exclude list to specify the files and directories you want to back up, you can select directories from the directory tree. When you select a directory, all files in the directory are selected, regardless of the specifications in the Include/Exclude list. To select a directory, perform one of the following steps:

- Double-click on the directory.

- Right-click on the directory.

- Highlight the directory and press Spacebar.

If you have a mouse, you can select a group of directories. Move the mouse pointer over the first directory you want to select, hold down the right mouse button, and drag the mouse pointer over additional directories.

If you make a mistake and select a directory you don't mean to include, highlight the directory, and press (Spacebar), or right-click on it again.

> **TIP:** If you want to back up most of the directories on the hard disk, select all the directories and then deselect those that you want to exclude. An easy way to do this is to go back to the Microsoft Backup screen, and right-click on the drive in the Backup From list (to select all files). Then, choose the Select Files button, and choose any directories you want to exclude (by right-clicking on them, or high-lighting them and pressing (Spacebar)).

Selecting and Deselecting Files

You can select or deselect individual files the same way you select or deselect directories. To select a file, do one of the following:

- Double-click on the file.

- Right-click on the file.

- Highlight the file, and press (Spacebar).

If you're using a mouse, you can select several files at once by dragging over them. Position the mouse pointer on the first file you want, press and hold the right mouse button, and drag the mouse pointer to the last file in the series. Release the mouse button.

A check mark appears next to the name of each file that will be included in the backup. If you see a little dot next to a file name, the file will be excluded from the backup because of some other selection you made. For example, if you performed a full backup and are now performing an incremental backup, check marks will appear next to the names of any files that have changed since the full backup; other files will be marked with a dot, meaning they have already been backed up.

TIP: To make file selection easier, you can change the display to list the files in a specific order. In the Select Backup Files dialog box, press ⌈Alt⌋+⌈D⌋, or click on the Display button. Use the dialog box that appears to sort the files by date, name, extension, size, or file attribute. You can also group specific files together in the list.

Excluding Special Groups of Files

At the bottom of the Select Backup Files screen is a button labeled **S**pecial. Select this button to display the Special Selections dialog box. You can use this box to *exclude* specific groups of files:

Apply Date Range   This option lets you exclude any files created *outside* a specific date range. Select this option to turn it on, and then enter dates in the **F**rom and **T**o fields.

Exclude Copy Protected Files   Selecting this option prevents any copy protected files from being backed up.

Exclude **R**ead Only Files   Selecting this option prevents any read only files from being backed up. Some files, such as files that your computer needs to function properly, are marked as read only to prevent them from being changed.

Exclude **S**ystem Files   Selecting this option prevents any of your computer's system files from getting backed up. System files include several files that come with DOS.

Exclude **H**idden Files   To exclude hidden files from the backup, select this option. Some files are hidden to prevent them from appearing in directory listings.

After making your selections, choose the OK button to accept them. This returns you to the Select Backup Files dialog box.

Accepting Your File Selections

When you are done with the Select Backup Files dialog box, click on the OK button, or tab to it, and press ⏎Enter. You are returned to the Microsoft Backup screen, and your selections are put into action.

Saving Your File Selections

Setting the backup options and selected directories and files to include in a backup can be time-consuming. To save time, save your settings and selections in a setup file. For example, you can create one setup file for your monthly (full) backup and another setup file for your daily (incremental) backups. Once all your settings are entered, perform the following Quick Steps to create a setup file.

Saving the Current Setup

1. Press Alt+F or click on File in the menu bar, and select Save Setup As.

   A dialog box appears, prompting you to type a name for the setup file.

2. Type a name for the setup file. (Don't use an extension; .SET will automatically be added.)

   The setup file is named.

3. If desired, press Alt+C or tab to the Description field, and type a description for the setup file.

   For example, type `Full Backup`.

4. Press Alt+S or click on the Save button.

   Microsoft Backup saves the file selection settings in the new setup file.

> **TIP:** If you want your file selections to be in effect whenever you start Microsoft Backup, save them in the DEFAULT.SET file.

The saved settings include the Backup From entry, specifications about the drive and backup media you're using, the Compress option you selected, the directories and files you want included and excluded, and any other options you may have chosen. The following Quick Steps tell how to use the setup files you create.

Using a Setup File for Backup Settings

1. Be sure that you don't need to save any options you've changed during the current session with Microsoft Backup.

   This prevents you from losing any important setting you made in the current session.

2. Press Alt+P or click on the box under Setup File.

   This displays the Setup Files dialog box, which contains the names of the setup files you created.

3. In the Setup Files list, right-click on the setup file you want to use, or highlight it, and press Spacebar.

4. Press Alt+O or click on the Open button.

   The selected setup file is opened and its settings are now in effect. You can start the backup as you normally would.

Running Backup for Windows

If you use Microsoft Windows, you may want to run Backup for Windows instead of the DOS version. With the Windows version, you can perform a backup in the background while you work in another program. If you are backing up to floppy disks, the backup program will interrupt you when you need to insert the next disk.

How do you run Backup for Windows? The following steps lead you through the process:

1. Look for a program group window called Microsoft Tools. If you see the window, click anywhere on it to bring it to the front. If you don't see the window, click on Window in the Program Manager menu bar, and then click on Microsoft Tools.

2. Double-click on the Backup icon. This starts Backup for Windows. The first time you run it, you must set it up for your system. The setup process is similar to the setup for the DOS version, as explained earlier in this chapter.

3. Once you have set up the program, click on the Backup button to perform a backup. The Microsoft Backup screen appears, as shown in Figure 10.13.

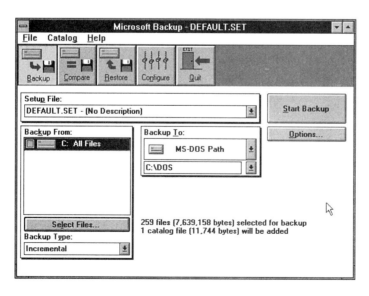

Figure 10.13
Although Backup for Windows looks different, it has the same elements as the DOS version.

NOTE: If you created setup files in Microsoft Backup for DOS, you won't be able to use them in Backup for Windows. You will have to create new setup files for the Windows version.

Backups: Past, Present, and Future

Now that you are finished with this chapter, rethink your backup strategy, and then commit to it. Make sure you have at least one full backup of all the files on your hard disk. And then make sure you perform an incremental or differential backup on a regular basis. Stick to it, and when you lose a file (I guarantee you will eventually lose one), you will be prepared.

And what happens when you discover that a file has been sucked into a mysterious black hole? That's the subject of the next chapter.

In This Chapter

Comparing Your Backup Files to the Originals

Using the Backup Files to Restore Lost or Damaged Files

Restoring All the Files in the Backup

Restoring Only Selected Files

Setting the Restore Options to Prevent Overwriting Existing Files

Setting the Restore Options

1. Type msbackup at the DOS prompt, and press ⏎Enter.
2. Select Restore.
3. Select Options.
4. Select an option to turn it on or off. A check mark next to the option means it is on. Make sure the Verify Restore Data option and the Prompt Before Overwriting Existing Files options are on.

Restoring Backup Files to Your Hard Disk

1. Type msbackup at the DOS prompt, and press ⏎Enter.
2. Select Restore.
3. Press Alt+K or click on the Backup Set Catalog button.
4. Select the catalog you want to use, and then select Load.
5. Make sure the Restore From setting is correct.
6. In the Restore Files list, right-click on a drive to select all the files for the Restore operation. All files appears next to the drive.
7. Select Start Restore.
8. Follow the on-screen prompts until the restoration is complete.

Comparing and Restoring Backup Files

In this chapter, you will learn two things. First, you will learn how to compare your backup files against the originals to ensure that the backup copies are the same as the originals. Second, you will learn how to restore lost or damaged files from the backup disks to your hard disk.

Comparing Backup Files to the Originals

In the previous chapter, you backed up the files on your hard disk to a set of floppy disks or some other backup device. But how do you know that the backup copies match the original files? How can you be sure that one of the backup files is not stored on a defective area of one of the backup disks? The answer is that you can't be sure until you compare the backup files to the originals. Microsoft Backup offers a Compare feature that compares the files for you.

To start Compare, perform the following steps:

1. Type `msbackup`, and press ⏎Enter.

2. Choose Compare. The Compare screen appears, as shown in Figure 11.1.

Figure 11.1

The Compare screen allows you to control the compare operation.

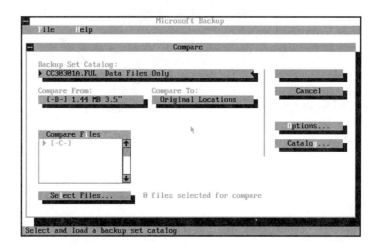

Choosing a Backup Set Catalog

In the upper left of the Compare dialog box is a Backup Set Catalog button. Do you need to worry about it? Maybe not. If you just performed a backup, and you want to compare the newly backed-up files to the originals, you don't have to select a backup catalog; the catalog for the most recent backup is already selected. You can safely skip ahead to the next section.

However, if you want to compare files from a previous backup, you must select the appropriate catalog. So, what's a backup catalog? When you create a backup, the backup program stores a list of the backed-up files and directories in a *catalog* on the hard disk.

The program saves two types of catalogs: a *master* catalog and an *individual* catalog. The master catalog contains information about the full backup created with a given setup file. The master catalog also contains information about any incremental or differential backups that were performed using that same setup file. The master catalog is useful if you want to restore a previous version of a file.

NOTE: The file name for the master catalog is the same as the name of the setup file, but ends in the extension .CAT. For example, if you create a full backup using a setup file called DATA.SET, a master catalog will be created with the name DATA.CAT.

Individual catalogs contain information about a single backup and are useful for restoring the most recent version of a file. Each individual catalog has a distinctive name, such as CD30612A.FUL. The first two letters are the letters of the first and last drives that were backed up (if only one drive was backed up, the first two letters are the same). The number 3 is the last digit in the year (1993). The 06 stands for the month (June). The 12 stands for the day of the month. The A shows which backup this is for today; for example, A means this is the first backup of its type for this day. The extension (FUL) indicates the type of backup: Full (FUL), Differential (DIF), or Incremental (INC).

To select a backup catalog, perform the following steps:

1. Press Alt + K or click on the Backup Set Catalog button. The Backup Set Catalog dialog box appears, as shown in Figure 11.2.

2. Right-click on the catalog you want to use, or highlight it, and press the Spacebar.

3. Press Alt + L or click on the Load button. The selected catalog is loaded.

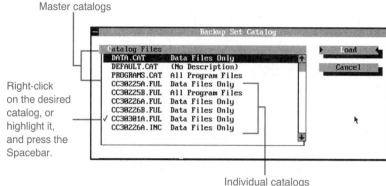

Master catalogs

Figure 11.2

Select a backup catalog from the list.

Right-click on the desired catalog, or highlight it, and press the Spacebar.

Individual catalogs

CAUTION

If the catalog you need is not on your hard disk or is damaged, you can load the catalog from the last floppy disk in your backup set. In the Compare dialog box, press Alt+G, or click on the Catalog button. Select Retrieve. Select the floppy drive (A or B) that you used for the backup, or select MS-DOS, press Tab, and type the drive and directory where you stored the backup files. Select OK. Insert the last disk of the backup set in the specified drive, and select Continue. Follow the on-screen instructions to retrieve the catalog from the floppy disk to your hard disk. (The Rebuild option allows you to rebuild a catalog if both the catalog on the hard disk and the floppy disk is damaged, although this rarely happens.)

Choosing a Compare Source and Destination

Before you start the compare operation, make sure the correct drives are listed in the Compare From and Compare To boxes. The Compare From box shows the drive where Compare will look for the backup files. The Compare To box shows the drive where Compare will look for the original files: the original drive and directory or a different drive or directory.

To change the Compar**e** From entry, press Alt+E, or click on the Compare From button. Select the floppy drive, and type of disk you used for the backup, or select MS-DOS Drive and Path, press Tab↹, and type a path to the drive and directory where the backup files are stored. Select OK.

Normally, you will want to compare the backup files to the files on the drive and directory that contained the original files. However, if you moved the files to a different drive and directory, you can compare the backups to the files in the new location by changing the **C**ompare To entry. To change the **C**ompare To entry, press Alt+C or click on the Compare To button. Select **O**riginal Locations, **O**ther **D**rives, or **O**ther **D**irectories. Select OK.

Selecting the Files to Compare

Usually, you will compare *all* the files in a given backup to the originals. To do that, right-click on the drive(s) whose files you want to compare in the Compare **F**iles list, or highlight the drive, and press Spacebar. When you select a drive, All files appears next to it. You can now skip ahead to the next section, "Starting the Compare Operation."

> **NOTE:** All files in this case does not mean all files on the disk; it means all files in this backup. For example, if you are comparing files in an incremental backup that backed up only seven files, all files means seven files.

If you want to compare only select files, press Alt+L, or click on the Select Files button. This opens the Select Compare Files screen, as shown in Figure 11.3.

Check marks indicate selected files that will
be included in the Compare operation.

Figure 11.3

*You can select
directories and
files to exclude
them from the
Compare
operation.*

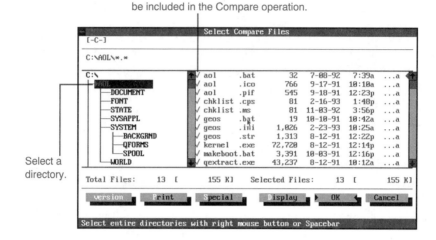

Select a
directory.

The Select Compare Files screen does not allow you to select files or directories that were not included in the backup. However, you can use this screen to exclude files from the compare operation. To do so, right-click on the directory or file you want to exclude, or highlight it, and press (Spacebar).

At the bottom of the Select Files screen are several buttons that allow you to perform additional tasks:

Version   If you selected a master catalog, and the catalog has information about more than one version of a file, you can click on this button to compare a backup file to an earlier version of the file.

Print   Choose the Print button to print the catalog.

Special   The Special button allows you to exclude certain groups of files from the compare operation. For example, you can exclude files that were created outside a specified date range.

Display   Select the Display button to sort the file list. For example, you can sort the file list by extension so all files that have the .DOC extension will appear together in the list.

When you are done selecting the files you want to compare and other compare options, click on the OK button, or tab to it, and press (↵Enter). You are returned to the Compare Files screen.

Starting the Compare Operation

Once you have specified which files you want to compare, press Alt+S, or click on Start Compare. A dialog box will appear, telling you to insert the first disk of the backup set in the floppy drive. Insert the disk, and press Alt+C, or click on Continue. Follow the on-screen instructions, inserting the backup floppy disks when advised.

The following Quick Steps summarize the compare operation.

Comparing Backup Files to the Originals

1. Type msbackup at the DOS prompt, and press ↵Enter.	Starts Microsoft Backup.
2. Press Alt+C, or click on the Compare button.	The Compare Files screen appears.
3. Press Alt+K, or click on the Backup Set Catalog button.	The Backup Set Catalog dialog box appears.
4. Right-click on the catalog you want to use, or highlight it, and press Spacebar.	A check mark appears to the left of the selected catalog.
5. Press Alt+L, or click on the Load button.	The selected catalog is loaded.
6. Select Compare From, choose the drive that contains the backup files, and select OK.	This specifies which drive was used to store the backup files.

continues

continued

7. In the Compare Files list, right-click on the drive(s) you want to compare, or highlight each drive, and press the `Spacebar`.	`All files` appears to the right of the selected drive.
8. Press `Alt`+`S` or click on the Start Compare button.	A dialog box appears, prompting you to insert the first floppy disk of the backup set in the specified drive.
9. Insert the required disk, and select Continue.	Microsoft Backup starts the compare operation.

Restoring Files to Your Hard Disk

Should anything ever happen to the data on your hard disk, you can recover it with the backup disks you made with Microsoft Backup. You can restore the entire contents of the hard disk, or only the subdirectories and files you lost.

CAUTION   Your backup files are only as good as they are recent. If you backed up a file last week and then made extensive changes to it this week, when you restore the file, you will get last week's file. Before you restore a deleted file, try undeleting it first, as explained in Chapter 8.

Setting the Restore Options

Before you start restoring files, you should check the Restore options to make sure the settings are the ones you want to use. These settings allow you to tell the Restore program to check with you before creating a directory or a file and before overwriting existing files on the hard disk with the backup copy.

To set the options, first start Restore. Type msbackup at the DOS prompt, press ↵Enter), and then select the **R**estore button. To set the Restore options, press Alt)+ O), or click on the **O**ptions button. The Disk Restore Options dialog box appears, as shown in Figure 11.4, offering the following options:

Verify Restore Data (Read and Compare)   Make sure there is a check mark in the check box next to this option. When this option is on, Restore checks the restored file against the backup file to make sure the two files are identical.

Prompt Before Creating **D**irectories   If you want Restore to check with you before creating a directory, select this option to turn it on. (I leave it off.)

Prompt Before **C**reating Files   If you want Restore to check with you before creating a file, select this option to turn it on. (I leave this one off, too.)

Prompt Before Overwriting **E**xisting Files   Turn this option on. This ensures that Restore will display an Alert box before replacing an existing file on your hard disk with the backup copy.

Restore Empty Directories   If you want a directory restored even if it does not contain any files, turn this option on. (I turn this option on, but it's no big deal.)

Audible Prompts (Beep)   If you don't like being beeped at when you are restoring files, make sure this option is turned off. You will still see the prompts on-screen, but you won't have to listen to the beep.

Quit After Restore   Turn this option on if you want Restore to automatically quit after the restoration is complete.

Once you have entered your settings, select OK to return to the Restore screen.

Figure 11.4

Use the Disk Restore Options dialog box to enter your preferences.

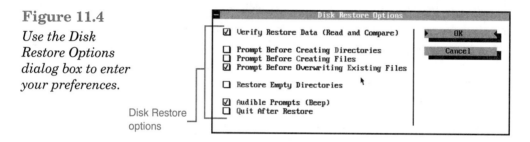

Disk Restore options

Restoring All the Files on Your Hard Disk

What should you do if you manage to wipe out all the files on your hard disk? Well, the last thing you should do is restore all the files from your backups. You may be able to get the files back by performing some other operation. For example, if you accidentally formatted your hard disk, you can unformat it to get everything back.

However, if you tried everything and nothing seems to work, you may have to perform a full restoration. But first, assuming everything on your hard disk was lost (including DOS), reinstall DOS as if you were installing it on a new computer. (Refer to the section called "Installing DOS on a New Computer's Hard Disk" in Chapter 3.) Once DOS is installed, perform the following steps to restore the remaining files:

1. Type msbackup at the DOS prompt, and press ⏎Enter. Because you are running Microsoft Backup for the first time (you just installed it), you will have to reconfigure it, as explained at the beginning of Chapter 10.

2. Select Restore. The Restore screen appears, shown in Figure 11.5.

3. Press Alt + G, or click on the Catalog button.

4. Select Retrieve.

5. Select the floppy drive (A or B) that you used for the backup, or select MS-DOS, press Tab↹, and type the drive and directory where you stored the backup files.

6. Select OK.

7. Insert the last disk of the backup set in the specified drive, and select Continue. Follow the on-screen instructions to retrieve the catalog from the floppy disk (or other backup device) to your hard disk.

8. Select the Restore From button. This opens a dialog box that allows you to select the drive and type of disk on which the backup files are stored.

9. Select the type of disks that contain the backup files you want to restore.

10. Replace the last disk of the backup set with the first disk of the set.

11. Select Start Restore. Microsoft Backup starts restoring the files from the floppy disk to the hard disk. The progress is displayed as in Figure 11.6.

12. If Restore finds a file on the hard disk whose name matches one of the backup files, you'll see an Alert box that offers the following options:

    Overwrite replaces the hard disk file with the backup file.

    Do **N**ot Restore skips this file and proceeds to the next file in the backup.

    Cancel Restore quits the Restore program and returns you to the Microsoft Backup opening screen.

13. If the Warning box appears, enter your selection.

14. Follow the on-screen prompts, and swap disks when told to do so.

As soon as possible, you should check the files on the hard disk to make sure the restoration was a success. To check program files, run the program, and make sure all its features are working properly. To check data files, open the files in the programs you used to create them. If you make another backup of the hard disk, use a new set of diskettes, and keep the original backup until you are sure that all files on your hard disk are intact.

Figure 11.5
The Restore screen.

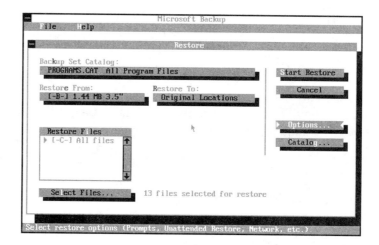

Figure 11.6
Microsoft Backup displays the progress of the restoration.

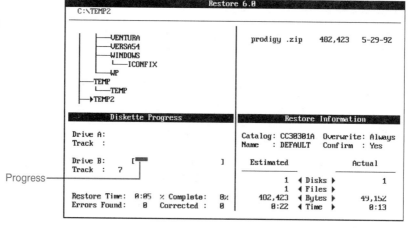

> **TIP:** If your hard disk is partitioned into several drives (for example C, D, E, F), you can use the **R**estore To button to restore the files to a different drive. You can also restore the files to a hard disk on another computer, assuming Microsoft Backup is installed on the other computer. Just make sure you don't overwrite files of the same name on the other computer.

Restoring Selected Files to Your Hard Disk

Partial restoration lets you restore only selected files or subdirectories. Use this procedure if only some of the files on your hard disk have become corrupted or erased. (Before using Restore, try to undelete files using the Undelete command, as discussed in Chapter 8.) For partial restoration of hard disk data, perform the following Quick Steps.

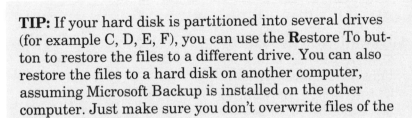

Performing a Partial Restoration

1. Type `msbackup` at the DOS prompt, and press ⏎Enter.

   The Microsoft Backup opening screen appears.

2. Select Restore.

   The Restore screen appears.

3. Press Alt + K or click on the Backup Set Catalog button.

   The Backup Set Catalog dialog box appears, prompting you to specify the backup catalog you want to use.

continues

continued

4. Right-click on the catalog you want to use, or highlight it, and press [Spacebar]. (If the catalog you want to use is not listed, press [Esc], select Catalog, and use the Retrieve option to retrieve the catalog from the last disk in the backup set.)

5. Press [Alt]+[L], or click on the Load button.

The selected catalog is loaded.

6. Press [Alt]+[E], or click on the Restore From button.

A list of drives appears.

7. Select the drive that contains the backup files you want to restore, and select OK.

You are returned to the Restore screen.

8. If you want to restore the files to a drive or directory other than the original, press [Alt]+[R], or click on the Restore To button. Select Other Drives to restore to a different drive, or select Other Directories to restore the files to a different directory. Select OK.

9. In the Restore Files list, right-click on a drive to select or unselect all the files for the Restore operation.

(You can select all files and then deselect the files you want to exclude, or deselect all files and then select only the files you want to restore.)

10. Press Alt+L, or click on the Select Files button.

This opens the Select Files screen, shown in Figure 11.7.

11. To select or unselect a directory in the tree, right-click on it, or highlight it, and press Spacebar.

An arrow appears to the left of each selected directory.

12. Press Tab, or click in the file list. To select or deselect a file in the list, right-click on it, or highlight it and press Spacebar.

A check mark appears to the left of each selected file.

13. Repeat steps 11 and 12 until you've selected all the directories and files you want to restore. Select OK when you're done.

You are returned to the Restore screen.

14. Select Start Restore.

Microsoft Backup starts restoring the files from the floppy disk to the hard disk. If Restore finds a file on the hard disk whose name matches one of the backup files, you'll see an Alert box.

continues

---

continued

15. If an Alert box appears, enter your selection, and then select OK.

The restoration continues.

16. Follow the on-screen prompts, and swap disks when told to do so.

At the end of the restoration, the Restore Complete dialog box appears.

17. Select OK.

You are returned to the Microsoft Backup opening screen.

Figure 11.7

The Select Files screen allows you to exclude certain files from the restoration.

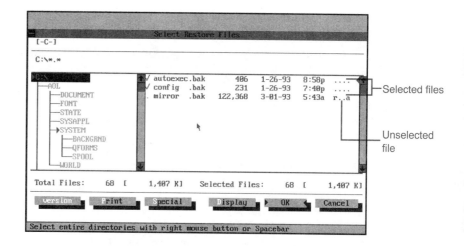

As soon as possible, you should check the integrity of the program and data files to make sure the restoration was a success. If you make another backup of the hard disk, use a new set of diskettes, and keep the original backup until you are sure that all files on your hard disk are intact.

It's All in the Catalog

Once you have mastered the notion of the backup catalog and you have the Restore options set so the program will not do anything without your okay, restoring files is easy. You select the catalog you want to use, specify where the backup files are stored, and then select Start Restore. The Restore program takes care of the rest.

However, if you don't have a feel for catalogs, go back to the beginning of this chapter and work through the section on catalogs until you have mastered the concept. Try loading a catalog, try getting a catalog from the last floppy disk in the set, and try using master catalogs. Once you feel comfortable with catalogs you can move on to Chapter 12 and whip your hard disk into shape.

TIP: If the catalog file is lost or damaged, you can still use the disks. You must go through a rather long and tedious process called Rebuilding a Catalog. See your DOS documentation for details.

Summing It Up

In this chapter and the previous one, you waded through some pretty complex material, but gained some important skills. Backing up your files regularly will ensure that no matter what atrocities fate may visit upon your computer, your data will be safe.

In This Chapter

Reclaiming Lost Pieces of Files with CHKDSK

Improving the Speed of Your Hard Disk by Defragmenting Its Files

Increasing the Storage Space on Your Hard Disk with DoubleSpace

Managing Disks That Were Compressed with DoubleSpace

Increasing Storage Space on Floppy Disks

Cleaning Up Lost Pieces of Files with CHKDSK

1. Change to the drive whose file pieces you want to reclaim.
2. Type chkdsk /f, and press ⏎Enter.
3. Press Y to reclaim the lost file pieces or N to delete them (these file pieces are rarely useful).

Defragmenting Files on a Disk

1. Type defrag at the DOS prompt, and press ⏎Enter.
2. Click on the letter of the disk you want to defragment, or use the arrow keys to highlight it.
3. Select OK.
4. Click on Optimize, or press ⏎Enter.

Creating More Disk Space with DoubleSpace

1. Exit all programs, including DOS Shell and Windows.
2. Type dblspace, and press ⏎Enter.
3. Read the screen, and press ⏎Enter to continue.
4. Press ⏎Enter to accept the Express Setup option.
5. Press C for Continue.
6. Wait until DoubleSpace displays a message telling you that the compression is complete, and then press ⏎Enter to exit.

Optimizing Your Hard Disk

Your computer's hard disk is a lot like a silverware drawer. The more you use it, the more cluttered and disorganized it gets. If you haven't tidied up your hard disk lately, it is likely that the disk contains several pieces of files that it doesn't know what to do with. In addition, parts of files are probably scattered all over the disk, making it difficult for your computer to read and use the files. You may even be running out of precious disk space.

In this chapter, you will learn how to use the DOS disk management utilities to give your hard disk the tune-up it needs.

CAUTION

Be safe; back up your hard disk before you use any of the disk management utilities in this chapter. Although these programs are easy to use and rarely cause data loss, updating your backup files is a good safety measure.

Reclaiming Pieces of Files with CHKDSK

If you reset or warm boot your computer in the middle of something, you sometimes get bits and pieces of unnamed files saved
to your hard disk. Although you won't be able to use these
unnamed files, they take up valuable disk space and can bog down
the disk. To get rid of these pieces, you first have to find them and
give them names by running CHKDSK (which stands for Check
Disk).

CAUTION   Do not run CHKDSK when other programs are
running. CHKDSK might identify any program
files being used and any data files as "lost" pieces and try
to correct the problem. This could result in lost files.

Also, do not run CHKDSK on a disk that has been compressed with DoubleSpace. On compressed disks, run the
DoubleSpace version of CHKDSK, as explained in "Maintaining a Compressed Disk" later in this chapter.

To run CHKDSK, type `chkdsk /f` at the `C:\>` prompt, and
press `Enter`. If DOS finds any lost file pieces, DOS displays a
message like this:

```
15 lost allocation units found in 3 chains.
Convert lost chains to files? (Y/N)
```

You can then press `Y` to save the file pieces or press `N` to have
DOS delete them.

If you want to save the pieces and check to see if they contain
any important data, type Y. DOS saves the file pieces in the root
directory of the current hard disk in a series of files named
FILEnnnn.CHK. You can then open the files in whatever editing
program you use to view their contents.

TIP: Personally, I've never met a .CHK file that was good for anything, so I press $\boxed{\text{N}}$ whenever asked if I want to convert the lost chains to files. If you already saved the lost chains, you can delete them by typing

```
del \file*.chk
```

and pressing $\boxed{\text{←Enter}}$. You can now move on to more important things.

Eliminating File Fragmentation with Defrag

When you first copy or save files to your hard disk, all parts of each file are stored in neighboring areas of the disk. To open a file, the computer moves the read/write head on the disk drive to the place where the file starts, and then it reads the file from beginning to end.

If you delete a file from the disk, a space is left where no data is stored. This space is then free to store the next file you save or copy to disk. But say you copy a file that is too big for that space— what happens then? Your computer stores a part of the file in that space and then stores any remaining parts of the file in the next free space.

As you delete and save files, they get more and more *fragmented*; that is, their parts get scattered over the disk, as shown in Figure 12.1. If your computer needs to open or use one of these fragmented files, the disk drive's read/write heads must skip around from place to place on the disk to read each section of the file. This slows down your computer and makes it more likely that you will lose a file or a portion of it.

Figure 12.1

As you save and delete files from a disk, the files get fragmented.

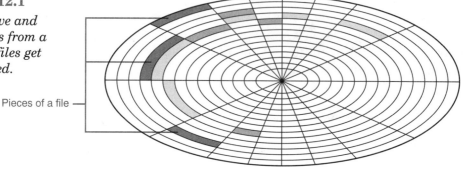

Pieces of a file ──

To decrease fragmentation, you should run DOS's Defrag program on a regular basis. This program tests your disk for fragmentation, recommends whether or not you need to Defrag the disk, and then performs the defragmentation to place the parts of each file on neighboring areas of the disk.

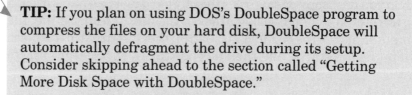

TIP: If you plan on using DOS's DoubleSpace program to compress the files on your hard disk, DoubleSpace will automatically defragment the drive during its setup. Consider skipping ahead to the section called "Getting More Disk Space with DoubleSpace."

Starting Defrag

As Defrag works, it reads parts of a file off the hard disk into memory, clears a space on the disk for the file, and then writes all the parts of the file to disk in neighboring areas. Because parts of files are getting shuffled back and forth between memory and disk, there is a slight chance that data can get jumbled, so before you run Defrag, take the following precautions:

- Do not run Defrag on a disk that has been compressed with DoubleSpace. On compressed disks, run the DoubleSpace version of Defragment, as explained in "Maintaining a Compressed Disk" later in this chapter.

- Unload any memory-resident programs from memory. Memory-resident programs could interfere with the proper operation of Defrag and cause considerable data damage.

- If you want to undelete accidentally deleted files, do it now. Running Defrag will probably overwrite any deleted files.

- Do not run Defrag from another program, such as the DOS Shell or Windows. These programs are memory-resident programs, and they can interfere with Defrag.

- To really play it safe, back up your hard disk before running Defrag. If anything should happen to the data, you can restore it using the backed-up version.

- Although you can run Defrag on a floppy disk, few users ever do, because files generally don't get as fragmented on floppy disks.

TIP: If you are not sure whether any memory-resident programs that might interfere with Defrag are running, reboot your computer from a bootable floppy disk instead of from your hard disk. This is known as a *clean boot*; it prevents any programs from running automatically at startup.

Don't try to run Defrag from the DOS Shell, because the Shell is a memory-resident program that might interfere with the defragmentation process. If you are in Shell, open the File menu, and select Exit to return to the DOS prompt. To run Defrag, perform the following Quick Steps.

Defragmenting a Disk Drive

1. Type `defrag` at the DOS prompt, and press ⏎Enter.

   The Defrag screen appears, as shown in Figure 12.2, prompting you to select the disk you want to defragment.

2. Click on the desired disk letter, or use the arrow keys to highlight it. Select OK.

   Defrag analyzes the disk and displays the Recommendation dialog box.

3. Read the dialog box to determine the percent of the disk that is not defragmented and to determine the recommended defragmentation option.

4. To defragment the disk with the recommended defragmentation method, click on Optimize, or press ⏎Enter. To change the optimization method or other options, click on Configure, or tab to Configure, press ⏎Enter, and skip to the next section, "Configuring Defrag."

   Defrag starts to defragment the specified disk.

If you chose Optimize, Defrag starts optimizing the disk. You will see two letters appear on-screen: r and W. The r means Defrag is reading data from disk. The W means Defrag is writing data to disk. When Defrag is done, the Finished Condensing dialog box appears; press ⏎Enter to choose OK. You are then asked if you want to condense another disk. Select Another Drive to defragment another disk, or Configure to change the Defrag options, or Exit DEFRAG to quit.

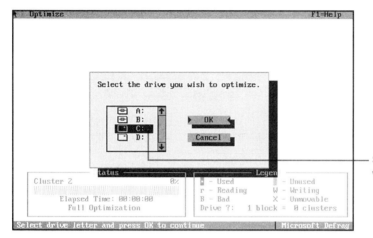

Figure 12.2
When you start Defrag, it prompts you to specify which disk you want to defragment.

Select the disk you want to defragment.

Configuring Defrag

If you chose Configure in step 4 in the preceding steps, the Optimize menu appears, as shown in Figure 12.3, offering the following options:

Begin Optimization   Starts the optimization process using the current settings.

Drive   Allows you to select a different disk to optimize.

Optimization Method   Selecting this option displays a dialog box that offers two choices—Full and Unfragment Files Only. Full optimization moves all the parts of each file to neighboring locations on the disk and moves the files to the beginning of the disk. This leaves all the empty space at the end of the disk, so when you save files in the future, those files will not get fragmented. Unfragment Files Only stores all the parts of each file together, but does not move empty space to the end of the disk.

File Sort   This option allows you to tell Defrag to sort the file names on disk. By sorting the file names, you make it easier for your computer to find certain groups of files, and might increase the speed of your computer slightly. You can sort by name, extension, date and time, or file size. You can also sort in ascending order (A, B, C, and so on) or descending order (Z, Y, X, and so on). (Sorting only works when you perform a full optimization.)

Map Legend   This option displays a key that helps you interpret the disk map that's displayed.

About Defrag   This is a fairly useless option that displays general information about the Defrag program.

e**X**it   Choose this option to quit Defrag.

When you are done entering your preferences, select the Begin Optimize option or press ⟨Alt⟩+⟨B⟩ to start optimizing the selected disk.

Figure 12.3

The Optimize menu allows you to change the Defrag settings.

The Optimize menu

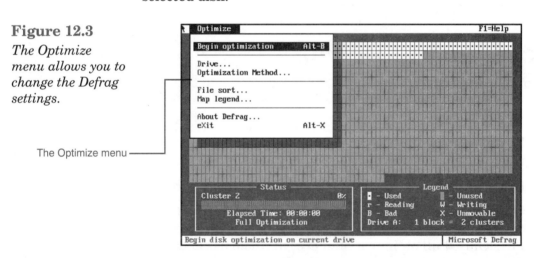

Getting More Disk Space with DoubleSpace

DoubleSpace is a new DOS program that compresses the files on a disk so that they take up less room. Think of it as a trash compactor that can restore trash to its original form automatically. DoubleSpace can increase the free space on your disk roughly 50 to 100 percent. Once DoubleSpace is installed, it works in the background to automatically compress and uncompress the files as you use them, so you really don't have to do much. Even the setup operation is easy, as you'll see later.

So, what's the down side of this new space-saving feature? First, it slows down your computer slightly, and I do mean slightly. Every time your computer needs a file, DoubleSpace has to uncompress it. However, DoubleSpace performs its magic so quickly that you may not notice a difference.

Second, you may have old versions of utility programs (such as PC Tools or The Norton Utilities) that have features you should not use on a compressed drive. Before running one of these programs on a compressed disk, check with the manufacturer's technical support department. If there's a conflict with a utility program, you'll need to upgrade your utility program or figure out some other way to save disk space.

NOTE: Remember that when you installed DOS, the Installation program created an uninstall disk so that you could return to the previous version of DOS, if desired. If you choose to set up DoubleSpace, you will no longer be able to uninstall DOS, so make sure you are happy with DOS 6 before you set up DoubleSpace.

Setting Up DoubleSpace: Express or Custom Setup?

You can perform either of two setup operations for DoubleSpace: Express Setup or Custom Setup. The following list will help you make the right decision:

Do you want a no-brainer installation? If you have only one hard disk drive (C), and you want the program to do everything for you, perform the Express Setup. The Setup program will automatically compress drive C and create another, uncompressed drive for any files that will not function correctly if compressed.

Does your disk have very little free disk space? If the disk you want to compress has little free disk space, avoid the Custom Setup, because you will have little room for a separate compressed drive.

Do you want more control over the setup operation? The Custom Setup allows you to compress data on a disk other than drive C, specify the compression ratio (to provide a more accurate estimate of the amount of disk space you'll save), and specify how big you want the compressed drive to be. In addition, you can create a compressed drive that does not contain data; later, you can copy only those files you want compressed to the compressed drive.

NOTE: Once you have compressed a drive, you cannot uncompress it. Because of this, I chose to use the Custom Setup to create a separate, empty compressed drive. This way, I have the option of changing my mind later. I can shrink the new compressed drive down in size, essentially destroying it, and use my old, uncompressed drive as usual.

Setting Up DoubleSpace the Easy Way

The Express Setup is the easy way to go. To perform the Express Setup, take the following Quick Steps.

Performing the DoubleSpace Express Setup

1. Exit all programs, including DOS Shell and Windows.

Other programs can interfere with the operation of DoubleSpace.

2. Type `dblspace`, and press `⏎Enter`.

The Microsoft DoubleSpace Setup screen appears.

3. Read the screen, and press `⏎Enter` to continue.

A dialog box appears, as shown in Figure 12.4, asking if you want to perform an Express Setup or Custom Setup.

4. Press `⏎Enter` to accept the Express Setup option.

A screen appears, telling you that drive C will be compressed, and telling how long the compression will take (about one minute per megabyte of data on a 386 25 MHz computer).

5. To start compressing the drive, press `C` for Continue. To quit the DoubleSpace setup, press `F3`. To go back to the previous screen, press `Esc`.

If you press C, the compression starts. When the compression is complete, you'll see a screen that shows how long the setup process took and how much free space is now on the disk.

6. Press `⏎Enter` exit.

DoubleSpace restarts your computer and activates the newly compressed drive.

Figure 12.4

You are prompted to select Express or Custom Setup.

Select Custom or Express Setup.

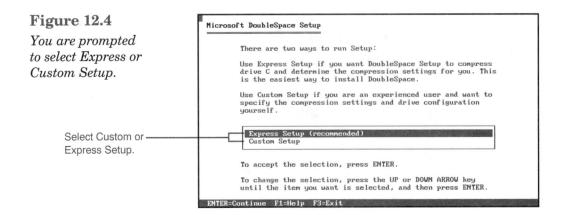

```
Microsoft DoubleSpace Setup

    There are two ways to run Setup:

    Use Express Setup if you want DoubleSpace Setup to compress
    drive C and determine the compression settings for you. This
    is the easiest way to install DoubleSpace.

    Use Custom Setup if you are an experienced user and want to
    specify the compression settings and drive configuration
    yourself.

      Express Setup (recommended)
      Custom Setup

    To accept the selection, press ENTER.

    To change the selection, press the UP or DOWN ARROW key
    until the item you want is selected, and then press ENTER.
 ENTER=Continue  F1=Help  F3=Exit
```

You now have two disk drives: the compressed drive (C) and an uncompressed drive (usually H). The compressed drive contains a file the size of Moby Dick called DBLSPACE.000. This file has swallowed and compressed most of your program and data files. Don't worry, you won't have to work with the file directly; DOS manages the file for you, so drive C will look and act like normal. Don't mess with this file or delete it, because you might end up destroying all your data and program files.

The second disk drive is a small, uncompressed drive that contains any files that would not work properly if compressed. For example, the drive may contain your computer's system files and the Windows swap file.

CAUTION
The files on the uncompressed drive are critical to the operation of your computer. Do not attempt to delete or move these files. I moved a couple of these files once and lost everything on my hard disk. Although I got everything back, it took me two days to do so.

Taking More Control over the DoubleSpace Setup

Although the Custom Setup requires you to make a few more decisions than you would have to make with the Express Setup, Custom Setup is still fairly easy. The following Quick Steps assume you want to create a new compressed drive rather than compressing existing data; however, the Custom Setup does allow you to compress existing drives.

Performing the DoubleSpace Custom Setup

1. Exit all programs, including DOS Shell and Windows.

   Other programs can interfere with the operation of DoubleSpace.

2. Type `dblspace`, and press ↵Enter.

   The Microsoft DoubleSpace Setup screen appears.

3. Read the screen, and press ↵Enter to continue.

   A dialog box appears, asking if you want to perform an Express Setup or Custom Setup.

4. Press the down arrow key to highlight Custom Setup, and press ↵Enter.

   A screen appears, asking if you want to compress an existing drive or create a new compressed drive.

5. Press the down arrow key to highlight Create a new empty compressed drive, and press ↵Enter.

   A screen appears showing the available drives, the amount of free space on each drive, and the actual space you'll have once the drive is compressed.

   continues

continued

6. Use the arrow keys to select the drive whose free space you want to use for the new compressed drive. Press ⏎Enter.

A screen appears, showing the space that will be left on the selected drive for the uncompressed drive, the compression ratio, and the drive letter for the new drive.

7. To change any of the options, use the up arrow key to highlight the option, press ⏎Enter, enter your change, and press ⏎Enter.

When you enter your selection, you are returned to the previous screen, where you can change another setting.

You can press F1 at any time to view a help screen for a selected option.

8. When you are done entering your settings, use the down arrow key to highlight Continue, and press ⏎Enter.

A screen appears, telling you that the drive will be created and indicating how many minutes it will take.

9. Press C to Continue.

DoubleSpace restarts your computer, tests your system, and creates the drive. A screen appears, showing the amount of space on the drive, the compression ratio, and other details.

10. Press ⏎Enter to exit.

DoubleSpace restarts your computer and activates the newly compressed drive.

Once you have created a compressed disk, the disk works just like any other disk. You can create directories on the disk, copy files to the disk, display a directory of files using the DIR command, open compressed files, run programs, and so on. You won't notice much difference between a compressed and an uncompressed disk, except that your compressed disk gives you more room.

> **NOTE:** The compression ratio does not tell DoubleSpace how much to squish the files. How much you can squish a file depends on what kind of file you have. If you have a document, DoubleSpace can compress the file by about 50 percent. With a bit-mapped graphics file, you might get 70 to 90 percent compression. DoubleSpace uses the compression ratio only to give you an estimate of how much space is available on the compressed disk.

Managing a Compressed Disk

Although the compressed disk acts like a normal disk, there are some differences. For example, with a compressed disk, you cannot use the CHKDSK command to find lost file pieces, and you can't use the Defrag program to defragment the disk. In order to perform these tasks, you must use the DoubleSpace versions of Check Disk and Defragment. In addition, you can change the size of the compressed disk, change the compression ratio, and compress the disk even further.

How? By running DoubleSpace again; type `dblspace` at the DOS prompt, and press ⏎Enter. When you run DoubleSpace after you have run DoubleSpace Setup, the screen shown in Figure 12.5 appears. This screen allows you to manage your compressed drive(s), create new compressed drives, and compress floppy disks.

NOTE: You can compress a floppy disk only after you have run the DoubleSpace Setup program to compress one of your hard disks.

Figure 12.5

The DoubleSpace screen allows you to manage your compressed disk(s).

Pull-down menu bar——

Compressed disk——

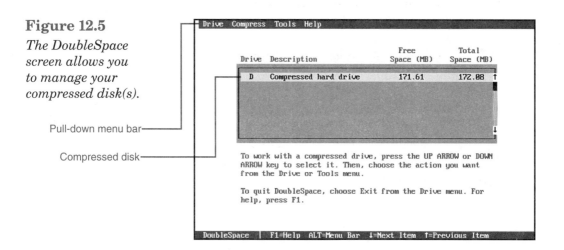

Working with a Compressed Disk

The **Drive** and **Tools** menus allow you to work with an existing compressed disk. To manage a disk, use the up or down arrow key to highlight the letter of the disk you want to manage, and then select the desired option from the Drive or Tools menu. The following commands are available on the **Drive** menu:

Info   Choosing this command displays the Compressed Drive Information dialog box, which shows the drive's free space, used space, and estimated and actual compression ratios.

Change Size   Select this option to change the size of the compressed drive (refer to the Quick Steps later in this section). For example, if you want to store more files on the compressed drive, you may want to make the drive larger. If you want to store more files on the uncompressed drive, use this option to shrink the compressed drive. (If you plan on reducing the size of a compressed drive, run Defragment from the Tools menu first.)

Change **R**atio   Select this option to change the estimated compression ratio. This does not change the actual amount the files are compressed but allows you to get a more accurate estimate of how much space you will save.

Mount   Use this option to tell DoubleSpace that a disk is compressed. Usually, DoubleSpace automatically mounts a compressed hard disk (it "knows" which disk is compressed). However, if you have unmounted a hard disk, or if you need to read a compressed floppy disk, you must use the Mount command first.

Unmount   Use this option to break the link between the compressed disk and DoubleSpace. When you unmount a compressed drive, the drive is no longer accessible.

Format   Allows you to format a compressed drive. This formatting operation is like a normal format; if the compressed disk contains files, formatting will destroy those files.

Delete   Allows you to delete a compressed drive and all the files it contains.

Exit   This quits the DoubleSpace program. However, DoubleSpace remains in memory, allowing you to use your compressed drives.

One of the most common operations you will perform on a compressed disk is to resize it. The following Quick Steps lead you through the process, but you should be aware of one tricky step. You won't change the size of the compressed drive directly; instead, you will increase or decrease the free space on the *uncompressed* drive. Okay, now go to it!

Changing the Size of a Compressed Drive

1. Press Alt + D or click on **D**rive in the menu bar.

The Drive menu appears.

2. Press S or click on **Change S**ize.

The Change Size dialog box appears, as shown in Figure 12.6.

3. Type the number of megabytes of free space you want on the *uncompressed* drive, but make sure the number you type does not exceed the maximum free space for the drive.

As you type, the number you type replaces the existing number in the Free Space box.

4. Select OK.

DoubleSpace changes the size of the compressed drive, remounts the drive, and returns you to the DoubleSpace screen.

5. To exit DoubleSpace, open the **D**rive menu and select **E**xit.

The DoubleSpace screen disappears, but DoubleSpace remains in memory, allowing you to use your compressed drive(s).

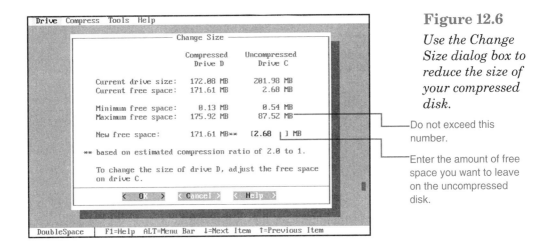

Figure 12.6

Use the Change Size dialog box to reduce the size of your compressed disk.

Do not exceed this number.

Enter the amount of free space you want to leave on the uncompressed disk.

Maintaining a Compressed Disk

Like normal, uncompressed disks, compressed disks need to be maintained. As you copy, delete, and save files to a compressed disk, files get fragmented, and parts of files can get lost. The Tools menu provides the utilities you need to keep your compressed disk in top working order. To open the Tools menu, press Alt+T, or click on Tools in the menu bar. You can then select from the following options:

Defragment   Choose this option to pull all the parts of individual files together on the compressed drive. It is useful to run this option before you reduce the size of a compressed drive.

ChkDsk   This option is similar to the DOS CHKDSK command described earlier. It checks the compressed disk for lost pieces of files and notifies you of any problems. Like CHKDSK, it can also fix any problems it finds.

Options   Allows you to specify the last letter of the drive you want DoubleSpace to use and the number of drives you want to be able to mount after you boot your computer.

Compressing Additional Disks with DoubleSpace

Now that you have one hard disk compressed, you can compress additional disks and floppy diskettes with DoubleSpace. To compress an existing disk, open the Compress menu, and select Existing Drive. Follow the on-screen messages to compress the drive. The process is similar to the procedure you followed for compressing the first drive.

Creating a New Compressed Disk on Your Hard Drive

To create a new compressed drive, first make sure there is enough free space on the uncompressed drive to create a new compressed drive. If there is not enough free space, use the Change Size option on the Drive menu to shrink existing compressed drives, and then choose Create New Drive from the Compress menu. Follow the on-screen messages to create the drive.

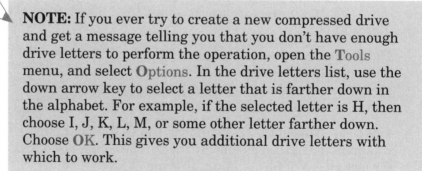

NOTE: If you ever try to create a new compressed drive and get a message telling you that you don't have enough drive letters to perform the operation, open the Tools menu, and select Options. In the drive letters list, use the down arrow key to select a letter that is farther down in the alphabet. For example, if the selected letter is H, then choose I, J, K, L, M, or some other letter farther down. Choose OK. This gives you additional drive letters with which to work.

Compressing a Floppy Disk

What about compressing floppy disks? You can compress a floppy disk by choosing the **E**xisting Drive option from the **C**ompress menu. Before you compress a floppy disk, read the following mild cautions:

- You cannot compress a 360K disk.

- The disk must have at least 650K of free disk space. You cannot compress a full disk.

- You cannot compress an unformatted disk.

- A compressed floppy can be used only on a computer that has DOS 6 and has run DoubleSpace Setup. If you plan on giving the disk to a friend or colleague who does not have DoubleSpace, don't compress the disk.

The following Quick Steps lead you through the process required for compressing a floppy disk.

Compressing a Floppy Disk

1. Insert a formatted floppy disk in one of your floppy disk drives, and close the drive door, if the drive has a door.

2. Press `Alt`+`C`, or click on Compress in the menu bar.

The **C**ompress menu is pulled down.

3. Select **E**xisting Drive.

You will hear your disk drives grind as Double-Space checks your system for compressible disks. DoubleSpace displays a list of compressible drives, as shown in Figure 12.7.

continues

continued

4. Use the up or down arrow key to highlight the drive you want to compress, or click on the drive. Press ⏎Enter, or select OK.

A confirmation screen appears, asking if you are sure you want to compress the drive.

5. Press C to continue.

DoubleSpace defragments the drive, if necessary, mounts the disk, and updates the list of compressed drives.

Figure 12.7

Select the drive that contains the floppy disk you want to compress.

Select the floppy disk drive containing the disk you want to compress.

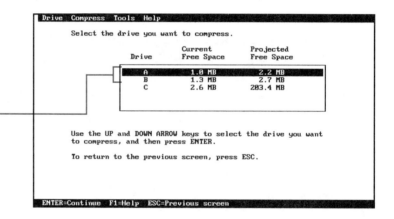

When you first compress a floppy disk, DoubleSpace automatically mounts the disk, so you can use it immediately. However, if you change floppy disks, or restart your computer, the floppy disk is no longer mounted. You can remount the disk by performing the following steps:

1. Insert the compressed floppy disk in the disk drive.

2. Start DoubleSpace by typing `dblspace` at the DOS prompt and pressing ⏎Enter.

3. Press Alt+D or click on **Drive** to open the **Drive** menu.

4. Choose Mount. DoubleSpace searches your system for unmounted disks and displays a list of them.

5. Use the up or down arrow key to select the disk you want to mount, and press ⏎Enter. DoubleSpace mounts the disk and updates the list of compressed drives.

You can now use the compressed floppy disk as you would use any other floppy disk.

> **NOTE:** You cannot run DoubleSpace from Windows, so make sure you mount any floppy disks you want to use before you run Windows.

What's Next?

Your hard disk should now have about 50 percent more space. Good for you. Good for your disk, but what about your computer's memory? Can you wring more space out of it? That's the subject of the next chapter.

In This Chapter

Types of Memory: Conventional, Extended, and Expanded

Using Your Computer's Memory Most Efficiently

Taking Control of SmartDrive, DOS's Memory-Management Program

Using MemMaker to Make More Memory Accessible to Your Programs

Quick Definitions

- *Conventional memory*—Directly usable memory that comes with all computers. Programs use conventional memory to run.
- *Upper memory*—The 384 kilobytes of standard memory that is reserved for system use, such as controlling a disk drive.
- *Expanded memory*—Additional memory that swaps data into and out of conventional memory, making it look as though the computer has more conventional memory than it really has.
- *Extended memory*—Additional memory that some programs can use just like conventional memory.

Determining the Type(s) of Memory Your Computer Has

1. Type mem /p at the DOS prompt.
2. Press ⏎Enter.

Installing MemMaker with Express Setup

1. At the DOS prompt, type memmaker, and press ⏎Enter.
2. Press ⏎Enter to continue.
3. Press ⏎Enter to perform the Express Setup.
4. If you have no programs that use expanded memory, press ⏎Enter to accept No.
5. Remove any floppy disks from the floppy drives, and press ⏎Enter.
6. Wait and watch the screen until MemMaker indicates that it will restart the computer.
7. Press ⏎Enter to continue.
8. Assuming your computer started correctly, press ⏎Enter.

13

Making the Most of Your Computer's Memory

As computer programs get more sophisticated, they require more memory in order to run effectively. But installing a memory board or buying a computer with additional memory isn't enough; you have to manage this memory in order to use it effectively. DOS comes with the following two programs, which are designed to help you get the most out of your computer's memory:

SmartDrive—SmartDrive is a disk-caching program; it stores frequently used data in your computer's memory, where your programs can get to it quickly. Without a disk cache, your computer must read all the data it needs from disk, which is a much slower process.

MemMaker—MemMaker can load some programs into a reserved portion of your computer's memory, so the programs do not consume conventional memory (the memory used by most programs). This gives other programs the memory they need.

NOTE: In DOS 5, several features helped users configure their memory, including EMM386.EXE and HIMEM.SYS. By manually editing your computer's startup files, you could load programs into reserved portions of memory, set up extended and expanded memory for use, and more.

MemMaker is an additional tool that makes this setup procedure easier, by editing your startup files for you. DOS 6 users are still able to set up these features manually, but beginners may prefer to use MemMaker.

Understanding the Different Memory Types

To use SmartDrive or MemMaker you should know at least a little about the four different memory types—conventional, upper memory, extended, and expanded—and how your computer uses these different memory types.

- *Conventional memory* is the memory that comes with all IBM PCs and PC compatibles. Most PCs come with one megabyte (1M) of memory. Of this memory (called upper memory) 384 kilobytes is reserved for system use (see the next item). The other 640 kilobytes of this memory is conventional memory—the memory that DOS uses to run programs, open files, and perform file-management tasks.

- *Upper memory* is the memory reserved for system use, such as controlling a disk drive. Of a computer's first 1 megabyte of memory, upper memory is the 384K left over after conventional memory has been allocated.

- *Expanded memory* is installed in a computer in the form of a board or card. This memory board or card swaps information into and out of conventional memory (640K RAM) at high speeds, giving the user the impression that the computer has more random-access memory (RAM) than the conventional 640K. Some programs are written to use expanded memory, allowing larger programs to run under DOS.

- *Extended memory* is additional memory that can be used in computers with at least an 80286 processor. The additional RAM chips can be installed on the main system board or on a separate card. Although DOS cannot use this additional RAM directly, multitasking programs, such as DESQview and Microsoft Windows, can use the memory indirectly.

TIP: Extended memory can be set up to simulate expanded memory. This is useful if you have a computer with extended memory, but want to run a program that requires expanded memory. For additional details about EMM386.EXE see your DOS manual or type `help emm386.exe` at the DOS prompt, and press `⏎Enter`.

To determine the type and amount of memory in your computer, type `mem /p` at the DOS prompt, and press `⏎Enter`. This displays the Memory Information screen shown in Figure 13.1.

(If all the information does not appear on-screen, press any key to view the next screenful of information.)

FYI
IDEAS

Figure 13.1

The Memory Information screen shows total and available memory.

```
C:\>mem

Memory Type      Total =  Used  +  Free
-----------      -----    ----     ----
Conventional      640K    125K     515K
Upper             187K     91K      96K
Adapter RAM/ROM   384K    384K       0K
Extended (XMS)   2885K   1241K    1644K
                 -----   -----    -----
Total memory     4096K   1841K    2255K

Total under 1 MB  827K    216K     611K

Largest executable program size      515K   (526896 bytes)
Largest free upper memory block       35K   (35904 bytes)
MS-DOS is resident in the high memory area.

C:\>
```

Disk Caching with SmartDrive

Before we get into the nitty gritty of using SmartDrive, you should understand what a disk cache is. A *disk cache* is part of your computer's random-access memory (RAM) that is set aside for storing frequently used data. It basically keeps the information that your computer uses the most at your computer's "fingertips." Instead of having to go to the relatively slow hard disk every time it needs information, your computer can get the information from fast RAM.

Depending on the amount of memory set aside for the cache, entire programs can be stored in the cache. Your work will go faster because your computer won't have to access the disk as much. A disk cache can also prolong the life of your hard disk drive, because the drive doesn't have to work as much.

Using SmartDrive: What Is Involved?

When you installed DOS 6, the installation program set up SmartDrive to run automatically whenever you start your computer. SmartDrive stays in the background and manages your computer's memory, making sure your other programs can make good use of it. So, what do you have to do? Nothing. If you don't want to mess around with SmartDrive, skip the rest of this section and move onto the section about MemMaker. However, if you want more control over SmartDrive, read on.

Taking Control of SmartDrive

Although you don't have to do much with SmartDrive, you can edit the SMARTDRV.EXE command in your AUTOEXEC.BAT file to control the operation of SmartDrive. For example, you can have SmartDrive use more or less of your computer's extended memory for a cache, or you can set aside some extended memory to be used as expanded memory.

> **NOTE:** For more information about editing your AUTOEXEC.BAT file, turn to Chapter 15.

Once you have opened your AUTOEXEC.BAT file to edit it, look for the following command line:

```
C:\DOS\SMARTDRV.EXE
```

This is the command that runs SmartDrive. You can add switches and parameters to this command to control the operation of SmartDrive. For example, you can specify the maximum and minimum amounts of RAM to use for the cache by typing the amounts after the SMARTDRV.EXE command:

```
C:\DOS\SMARTDRV.EXE 2048 1024
```

The number 2048 tells SmartDrive to use a maximum of two megabytes of RAM (1024 plus 1024 kilobytes) for the cache; 1024 tells SmartDrive to reduce the cache size to a minimum of 1 megabyte when running Microsoft Windows.

The following list shows some of the more common parameters and switches you can use:

[drive + or -]   Use this parameter to specify which drives you want to cache. For example, to disable disk caching for your floppy disk drives, you would use the following command:

```
C:\DOS\SMARTDRV.EXE A- B-
```

InitCacheSize   Specifies the cache size that SmartDrive uses when it first starts. In general, the larger the cache size, the greater the increase in performance. Look at Table 13.1 for a list of initial settings. You may want to increase the cache size to improve the performance of your system or decrease the cache size if other programs need more extended memory.

WinCacheSize   Windows is a memory hog, so SmartDrive automatically reduces the amount of memory used for the cache whenever you run Windows. The default settings are shown in Table 13.1. If you want to use more or less memory for the cache when you run Windows, enter your change in the command line. The following command line sets the initial cache size to 2 megabytes and the Windows Cache size to one megabyte:

```
C:\DOS\SMARTDRV.EXE 2048 1024
```

/B:BufferSize   This switch allows you to set the size of the *read-ahead buffer*. This buffer stores data that SmartDrive "thinks" you are about to request. For example, if you display a page of a document on-screen, SmartDrive may read the next page into the buffer so that information will be ready when you need it. The default size of this buffer is 16 kilobytes. You can increase the size, but then SmartDrive will use more conventional memory. For example, the following command line would set the buffer size to 32 kilobytes:

```
C:\DOS\SMARTDRV.EXE /B:32
```

/V   This switch tells SmartDrive to display status messages on startup.

/S   This switch tells SmartDrive to display even more information when it starts.

You can use switches and parameters together as long as you follow the correct syntax for entering the command; that is, the switches and parameters must be typed in the correct order. Here's the correct order:

```
[drive:][path]SMARTDRV [[drive[+|-]]...]
[InitCacheSize] [WinCacheSize]] [/B:BufferSize] [/V]
[/S]
```

[drive:][path] stands for the disk and directory where SMARTDRV.EXE is stored. This is usually C:\DOS. The following example shows a valid SmartDrive command line:

```
C:\DOS\SMARTDRV A- B- D+ /E:4096 2048 1024 /V /S
```

Extended Memory	Initial Cache Size	Windows Cache Size
0 to 1M	All extended memory	No cache
1 to 2M	1M	256K
2 to 4M	1M	512K
4 to 6M	2M	1M
6M or more	2M	2M

Table 13.1
*SmartDrive
Default Cache
Sizes*

Freeing up Conventional Memory with MemMaker

Early in this chapter, you learned that most computers come equipped with at least 1 megabyte of memory. You also learned that 384 kilobytes of this chunk is reserved for system use. If you want to use a mouse or a monitor, you must load the driver into conventional memory—the 640 kilobytes of memory that's left over. This leaves less memory for other programs you want to run.

On some computers, MemMaker can free up part of the 384 kilobytes of memory that's reserved for system use. It does this by moving "background" programs, such as mouse drivers and pop-up programs, out of conventional memory and into some of the unused space in the other 384K. This gives your other programs more conventional memory to work with, allowing you to run larger programs and allowing programs to run faster.

NOTE: DOS 5 allowed you to load programs into upper memory by using the LOADHIGH and DEVICEHIGH commands in your AUTOEXEC.BAT and CONFIG.SYS files. However, you had to do all this manually. MemMaker goes in and does this for you, determining what can and cannot be effectively loaded into upper memory.

What You Need to Use MemMaker

MemMaker will not work on all computers. To use MemMaker, your computer must meet the following minimum requirements:

- An IBM or compatible computer with an 80386 or 386SX processor.

- At least 1 megabyte of RAM.

Setting Up MemMaker: Express or Custom Setup?

Like DoubleSpace, you can set up MemMaker by using either of two setup options: *Express Setup* or *Custom Setup*. The Express Setup can be performed by any advanced primate. The Custom

Setup requires a bit more thought and gives you more control over what MemMaker does. Answer the following questions to decide whether you should use the Express or Custom Setup:

Do you know what you're doing? If not, run Express Setup. When you know more later, you can run the Custom Setup and take more control of the operation.

Does your computer have an EGA or VGA (but not Super VGA) monitor? If you have an EGA or VGA monitor, the Custom Setup will help you free up more upper memory space.

Do you run DOS programs from Windows? If you do not run DOS applications from Windows, you can use the Custom setup to free additional conventional memory for DOS programs when Windows is not running.

TIP: MemMaker is safe to run. Before it starts editing your AUTOEXEC.BAT and CONFIG.SYS files, it makes copies of the files and saves the originals as AUTOEXEC.UMB and CONFIG.UMB in the DOS directory. However, to be on the safe side, copy the files to a floppy disk formatted with the /S switch. (To format a floppy drive with the /S switch, refer to "Using the DOS Format Program" in Chapter 6. This makes the disk bootable.) Insert the floppy disk in drive A. Change to the root directory of drive C (type c:, and press ⏎Enter). Then type cd\, and press ⏎Enter). Type copy autoexec.bat a:, and press ⏎Enter. Type copy config.sys a:, and press ⏎Enter. Store the disk in a safe place.

Setting Up MemMaker the Easy Way

Because MemMaker does everything for you, you don't have to know a lot to use it. Simply perform the Express Setup, by taking the following Quick Steps.

Installing MemMaker
with the Express Setup

1. Type `memmaker`, and press `⏎Enter`.

The Microsoft MemMaker Welcome screen appears, as shown in Figure 13.2.

2. Read the screen, and press `⏎Enter` to continue.

A screen appears asking you to choose the Express or Custom Setup.

3. Press `⏎Enter` to perform the Express Setup.

The next screen asks if you have any programs that use expanded memory.

4. If you have no programs that use expanded memory, or if you are unsure, press the `Spacebar`, and press `⏎Enter` to answer No. Otherwise, press `⏎Enter` to answer Yes.

A screen appears, indicating that MemMaker will now restart your computer.

5. Remove any floppy disks from the floppy drives, and press `⏎Enter`.

MemMaker restarts your computer and watches how your programs are loaded into memory.

6. Wait and watch the screen as MemMaker analyzes your present configuration.

MemMaker edits your CONFIG.SYS and AUTOEXEC.BAT files.

7. Press `⏎Enter` to continue.

MemMaker restarts your computer with its changes now in effect. It then displays a screen asking if your system started correctly.

8. Assuming your computer started correctly, press ⏎Enter to answer Yes. Otherwise, press Spacebar and ⏎Enter to answer No.

If you answer Yes, a screen appears, showing how much conventional memory you just saved. If you answer No, you are given the choice to undo the changes or exit and go on.

9. If your system started correctly, press ⏎Enter. If your system did not start correctly, choose the desired course of action.

Assuming the MemMaker installation proceeded smoothly, your system now has more conventional memory available than before.

```
Microsoft MemMaker

Welcome to MemMaker.

MemMaker optimizes your system's memory by moving memory-resident
programs and device drivers into the upper memory area. This
frees conventional memory for use by applications.

After you run MemMaker, your computer's memory will remain
optimized until you add or remove memory-resident programs or
device drivers  For an optimum memory configuration, run MemMaker
again after making any such changes.

MemMaker displays options as highlighted text. (For example, you
can change the "Continue" option below.) To cycle through the
available options, press SPACEBAR. When MemMaker displays the
option you want, press ENTER.

For help while you are running MemMaker, press F1.

            Continue or Exit? Continue

 ENTER=Accept Selection  SPACEBAR=Change Selection  F1=Help  F3=Exit
```

Press Spacebar to change the selection.

The status line lets you know what actions you can take.

Figure 13.2

The Microsoft MemMaker Welcome screen.

TIP: In step 5, if you answer No, and then find out that one of your programs does not have enough memory, run MemMaker again and answer Yes.

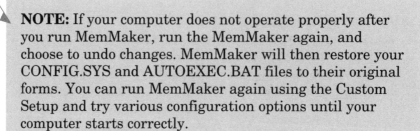

NOTE: If your computer does not operate properly after you run MemMaker, run the MemMaker again, and choose to undo changes. MemMaker will then restore your CONFIG.SYS and AUTOEXEC.BAT files to their original forms. You can run MemMaker again using the Custom Setup and try various configuration options until your computer starts correctly.

Taking More Control Over the MemMaker Setup

To take more control over the MemMaker Setup, run the Custom rather than the Express Setup. When you run the Custom Setup, you will encounter the Advanced Options screen, shown in Figure 13.3. This screen presents the following Yes/No questions. To change an answer, highlight it, and press the (Spacebar).

Specify which drivers and TSRs to include in optimization? Answer Yes if you want to control which programs are loaded into upper memory. For example, if you ran the Express Setup and then had problems with your mouse or monitor, you might want to prevent the driver from being loaded into upper memory.

Scan the upper memory area aggressively? Normally, MemMaker takes an aggressive approach in optimizing your computer's memory. If you run into problems, try running MemMaker so that it takes a more conservative approach.

Optimize upper memory for use with Windows? Answer No to this option unless you run DOS programs from Windows. By answering No, more conventional memory will be available for DOS programs when you are not running Windows. If you run DOS programs from Windows, answering Yes to this question will make more conventional memory available for DOS programs when you run them from Windows, but less memory will be available when you run those programs outside Windows.

Use monochrome region (B000-B7FF) for running programs? If you have an EGA or VGA (but not Super VGA) monitor, answer Yes to this question. This frees up additional upper memory that was reserved for the mono-chrome display driver.

Keep current EMM386 memory exclusions and inclusions? The EMM386 memory manager that comes with DOS controls which parts of upper memory can and cannot be used by certain programs. By answering Yes to this question, you allow EMM386 to retain control. An-swer No, and you give control to MemMaker, which can free up more of this memory.

Move Extended BIOS Data Area from conventional to upper memory? By default, BIOS data is stored in conventional memory. You can choose to move it to upper memory to free up additional conventional memory.

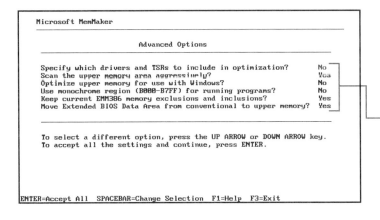

Figure 13.3

The Advanced Options screen lets you customize MemMaker.

Highlight an option, and press the Spacebar to change it.

NOTE: You can always go back. If you choose a more aggressive approach to optimizing your computer's memory and then find that your computer does not start properly, undo MemMaker's changes, as explained in the next section. Then, run MemMaker again, and take a more conservative approach.

To run the Custom Setup, perform the following Quick Steps.

Installing MemMaker with the Custom Setup

1. Type memmaker, and press ⏎Enter.

   The Microsoft MemMaker Welcome screen appears, as shown in Figure 13.2.

2. Read the screen, and press ⏎Enter to continue.

   A screen appears asking you to choose the Express or Custom Setup.

3. Press the Spacebar and then ⏎Enter to perform the Custom Setup.

   The next screen asks if you have any programs that use expanded memory.

4. If you have no programs that use expanded memory, or if you are unsure, press ⏎Enter to answer No. Otherwise, press the Spacebar and then ⏎Enter to answer Yes.

   If you answer No, and then find out that one of your programs does not have enough memory, run the setup again and answer Yes. The Advanced Options screen appears, as shown in Figure 13.3.

5. Select your preferences, as explained earlier, and then press ⏎Enter to continue.

   MemMaker checks to see if Windows is installed. If MemMaker finds Windows, it displays the drive and directory where it thinks Windows is stored.

6. If the Windows drive and directory is correct, press ⏎Enter. Otherwise, type the correct drive and directory, and press ⏎Enter.

   A message appears, telling you that MemMaker is about to restart your computer.

7. Remove any floppy disks from the floppy drives, and press ⏎Enter.

MemMaker restarts your computer and watches how your programs are loaded into memory.

8. Wait and watch the screen until MemMaker indicates that it will restart the computer.

MemMaker edits your CONFIG.SYS and AUTOEXEC.BAT files and displays a message indicating that MemMaker will restart your computer.

9. Press ⏎Enter to continue.

MemMaker restarts your computer with its changes now in effect. It then displays a screen asking if your system started correctly.

10. Assuming your computer started correctly, press ⏎Enter to answer Yes. Otherwise, press Spacebar and ⏎Enter to answer No.

If you answer Yes, a screen appears, showing how much conventional memory you just saved. If you answer No, you are given the choice to undo the changes or exit and go on.

11. If your system started correctly, press ⏎Enter. If your system did not start correctly, choose the desired course of action.

Assuming the MemMaker installation proceeded smoothly, your system now has more conventional memory available than before.

Undoing MemMaker's Changes

When you run the MemMaker setup, MemMaker makes copies of three files: AUTOEXEC.BAT, CONFIG.SYS, and SYSTEM.INI (the Windows startup file). It changes the extensions of the original files to UMB and stores the files in the DOS directory. If you run MemMaker and then later encounter problems when you run one of your programs, you can have MemMaker restore your original AUTOEXEC.BAT, CONFIG.SYS, and SYSTEM.INI files. The following steps lead you through the process:

1. Quit any programs that are currently running, and return to the DOS prompt.

2. Type memmaker /undo, and press ↵Enter. The undo screen appears, as shown in Figure 13.4, asking if you want to restore your original files.

3. Press ↵Enter. A confirmation screen appears. If you edited your AUTOEXEC.BAT, CONFIG.SYS, or SYSTEM.INI files, the confirmation screen warns you that any changes you made to these files since you ran MemMaker will be lost.

4. Press ↵Enter to restore your system to its original condition or F3 to exit.

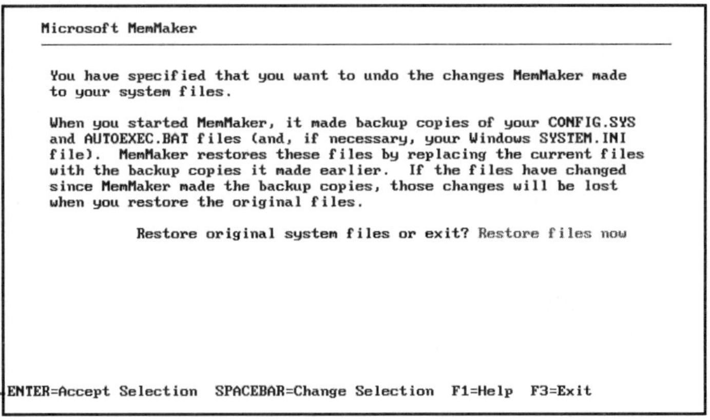

Figure 13.4

You can have MemMaker undo its changes.

You can restore your system to its original condition by pressing Enter.

```
Microsoft MemMaker
───────────────────────────────────────────────────────────────────

You have specified that you want to undo the changes MemMaker made
to your system files.

When you started MemMaker, it made backup copies of your CONFIG.SYS
and AUTOEXEC.BAT files (and, if necessary, your Windows SYSTEM.INI
file). MemMaker restores these files by replacing the current files
with the backup copies it made earlier.  If the files have changed
since MemMaker made the backup copies, those changes will be lost
when you restore the original files.

           Restore original system files or exit? Restore files now




ENTER=Accept Selection   SPACEBAR=Change Selection   F1=Help   F3=Exit
```

Summing It Up

In this chapter, you learned how to change the SmartDrive options to control the way SmartDrive manages your computer's memory. You also learned how to install MemMaker in order to free up conventional memory for use by other programs. In the next chapter, you will learn how to protect your computer against viruses by using Microsoft's new Anti-Virus program.

In This Chapter

Is Your Computer at Risk for Catching a Computer Virus?

Preventing Viruses from Infecting Your Computer

Scanning for Existing Viruses

Scanning for Viruses Each Time You Start Your Computer

Enabling Ongoing Virus Protection with VSafe

Scanning a Drive for Viruses

1. Type msav at the DOS prompt, and press ⏎Enter.

   OR

   In the DOS Shell, select Disk Utilities from the Main Program List, and then select MS Anti-Virus.

2. Press Alt+S, or click on the Select new drive button.

3. Use the arrow keys or mouse to select the drive you want to scan.

4. Select Detect (to find viruses) or Detect & Clean (to find a virus and correct any problem).

5. Read and respond to any dialog boxes that appear.

6. When Anti-Virus is done scanning the files on the current drive, select OK to continue.

Running VSafe to Provide Ongoing Virus Protection

1. At the DOS prompt, type vsafe and press ⏎Enter.

2. Press Alt+V to change the VSafe warning options.

3. Type the number of any option you want to turn on or off.

4. Press Esc to exit and save your changes.

Unloading VSafe from Memory

1. Press Alt+V to display the VSafe Warning Options screen.

2. Press Alt+U.

14

Protecting Your System Against Viruses

A virus is a program specially designed to destroy files and lock up computer systems. A virus can enter your system through its modem, through network lines, or from an infected floppy disk. The virus then spreads to infect your hard disk and any floppy disks you happen to use after contracting the virus. The virus infects files and then works in the background to destroy files on disk, sometimes wiping out an entire disk.

Fortunately, DOS includes Microsoft Anti-Virus to help defend against viruses. Anti-Virus can scan your computer's memory and files for existing viruses and virus activity. You can also run a memory-resident program called VSafe to provide ongoing virus protection as you use your computer. VSafe works in the background, keeping watch for incoming viruses. If your computer gets infected, Anti-Virus provides the tools you need to remove the virus.

How Susceptible Is Your System?

Computer viruses are not airborne diseases that your computer can mysteriously contract. To contract a virus, your computer must be on, and the virus must be introduced to your system through one of its ports or drives. Your computer may be at risk if

- You are connected to other computers via modem, and you obtain (download) and run programs from BBS (Bulletin Board System) services.

- You are connected to other computers on a network. You can't do much to protect your individual computer in this case. Protection is up to the Network Manager.

- Somebody else uses your computer.

- You obtain program or data disks from outside sources.

Almost everyone falls into one of these categories, and almost everyone needs virus protection!

Preventions and Cures

To prevent viruses from damaging your computer or data, you must perform three basic activities: prevention, detection, and removal. The following list provides several steps you can take to prevent your system from getting infected, to detect viruses early (before they can do any damage), to remove viruses, and to recover any lost or damaged information:

- *Check new files for viruses.* Before you use a disk or program obtained from a friend or colleague, scan the files for viruses using Anti-Virus.

- *Write-protect program disks.* Before you install a commercial program, write-protect the disks you purchased. This prevents any existing viruses from writing anything to your original program disks.

- *Back up your data files separately.* Although viruses can wipe out data files, viruses rarely infect data files.

- *Keep track of who is using your computer.* Don't let anyone else use your computer without permission. If your system does contract a virus, then you can track down the source.

- *Keep a bootable disk that contains the Microsoft Anti-Virus programs.* You will learn how to create such a disk later in this chapter.

- *Install Anti-Virus and VSafe to run at startup.* (You'll learn how later in this chapter.) VSafe is a memory-resident program that checks any programs you run for viruses.

Microsoft Anti-Virus and Anti-Virus for Windows

When you installed DOS 6, you were given the option of installing the DOS version of Anti-Virus, the Windows version, or both versions. The procedure for running Anti-Virus depends on the version you plan on using:

- To start the DOS version, type `msav`, and press `↵Enter`. The Microsoft Anti-Virus screen appears, as shown in Figure 14.1.

- To start the Windows version, double-click on the Anti-Virus icon in the Microsoft Tools program group window. You'll see the Microsoft Anti-Virus window, as shown in Figure 14.2.

Both Anti-Virus programs work in a similar fashion. You select the drive you want to check, and then enter a command telling the program to detect any viruses or to detect and clean any discovered viruses from your computer.

Figure 14.1

Microsoft Anti-Virus provides an easy-to-use interface.

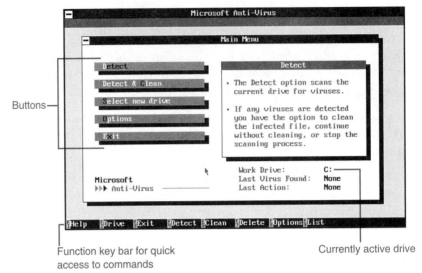

Buttons

Function key bar for quick access to commands

Currently active drive

Figure 14.2

Anti-Virus for Windows.

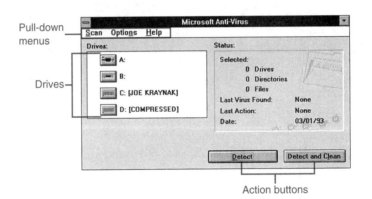

Pull-down menus

Drives

Action buttons

What Does Anti-Virus Do?

Anti-Virus is completely automated; you tell it which drives to scan for viruses, and it does the rest. Anti-Virus scans for the following two indications of virus activity:

- *Signatures of known viruses.* Most virus programs contain data that is unique to that virus. Anti-Virus checks for this unique data and identifies the virus.

• *Changes in executable program files.* When a virus program infects a program file, the virus usually changes the file in some way. Anti-Virus keeps track of file sizes and other information, and lets you know if any program file, such as CONFIG.SYS, has been changed recently. You are then given the option of updating Anti-Virus' records, skipping over the file, or removing the virus.

Scanning the Files on a Disk for Viruses

To use the DOS version of Anti-Virus to scan for viruses, perform the following Quick Steps. The Windows version works much the same way.

Scanning a Disk for Viruses

1. Type msav, and press ↵Enter.

The Microsoft Anti-Virus screen appears, as you saw in Figure 14.1.

2. Press Alt+S, or click on the Select new drive button.

A list of available drives appears at the top of the screen.

3. Use the left or right arrow key to highlight the drive you want to scan, and press ↵Enter, or click on the disk drive with your mouse.

The selected drive appears at the top of the screen.

continues

continued

4. Choose **Detect** (to scan for viruses without getting rid of them) or **Detect & Clean** (to scan for and remove any viruses).

The Scanning Memory for Viruses dialog box appears as Anti-Virus scans your computer's memory for viruses. Anti-Virus then scans all the files on the selected drive. If Anti-Virus detects a known virus, the Virus Found dialog box appears, identifying the virus.

5. If Anti-Virus finds a virus, choose one of the following options: **Clean** (to remove the virus from the infected file), **Continue** (to continue scanning without removing the virus), **Stop** (to stop scanning), or **Delete** (to delete the infected file).

If Anti-Virus detects a suspicious change in a program file, it displays the Verify Error dialog box, shown in Figure 14.3.

6. Choose one of the following options: **Update** (to update the Anti-Virus records, so it won't notify you of this same problem next time), **Delete** (to delete the infected file), **Continue** (to skip this file and continue scanning for viruses), or **Stop** (to stop scanning for viruses).

Choose Update only if you know that you have done something to change a file. For example, if you edited your CONFIG.SYS file, the reason it has changed is because you changed it. Likewise, if you installed a new version of a program, all the program files have changed because they are new.

7. When Anti-Virus is done scanning the files on the current drive, it displays the Viruses Detected and Cleaned dialog box, showing the number of files checked, infected, and cleaned. Select OK to continue.

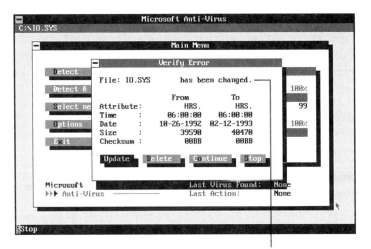

Figure 14.3
Anti-Virus lets you know of any changes in a file that look suspicious.

Anti-Virus has found a file that's been changed.

Setting Anti-Virus Scanning Options

When Anti-Virus scans files for viruses, it performs the scan according to the default option settings. You can change these settings by selecting the Options button on the Microsoft Anti-Virus screen. This displays the Options Setting dialog box, shown in Figure 14.4, which contains the following options:

Verify Integrity works with the Create Ne**w** Checksums option to verify that an executable program file has not changed since the last scan.

Create Ne**w** Checksums pulls together the information that Anti-Virus needs to verify the integrity of a file, such as the file's size, attributes, date, and time. It stores this information in a file called CHKLST.MS on each directory it scans.

Create **C**hecksums on Floppy creates new checksums for the directories on a floppy disk. Use this option the first time you check a floppy, and then write-protect the disk and turn this option off for subsequent checks.

Disable Alarm Sound disables the alarm that sounds when Anti-Virus displays an on-screen message warning you of possible virus activity. You will still see the warning; you just won't hear the beep.

Create **B**ackup tells Anti-Virus to create a copy of an infected file before cleaning it. This option is dangerous, because it leaves the infected file on disk.

Create **R**eport keeps track of any files that were cleaned during a virus scan.

Prompt While Detect tells Anti-Virus to display a message whenever it finds a virus. If you turn this option off, Anti-Virus proceeds without asking for your final okay.

Anti-**S**tealth provides increased protection against viruses that are specifically designed to hide from integrity checks.

Check **A**ll Files tells Anti-Virus to check all files on-disk, including data files. If you turn this option off, Anti-Virus checks only executable program files.

When you are done selecting your preferences, click on the OK button, or press Alt + O .

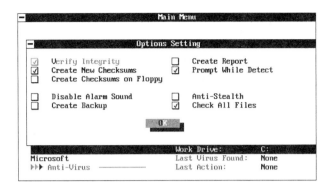

Figure 14.4

*The Options
Setting dialog box
lets you set the
scanning options
for Anti-Virus.*

Creating an Emergency Virus Disk

Once you have checked your system for viruses, and ensured that
no virus is active on your computer, you should make an emergency virus disk. This disk will help you remove any viruses from
your system in the event that a virus infects your computer's hard
disk and makes it inoperable. The following steps lead you
through the process:

1. Get a blank, high-density floppy disk for drive A, or a disk
   that does not contain any useful data.

2. Insert the disk into drive A, and close the drive door, if
   necessary.

3. Type `format a: /s`, and press ↵Enter. DOS displays a
   message telling you to insert a disk in drive A.

4. Press ↵Enter to continue, and then wait until DOS is done
   formatting the disk.

5. When asked to type a volume label, type a label and press
   ↵Enter, or just press ↵Enter to skip this step.

6. Change to the drive and directory that contains the DOS
   files. This is usually C:\DOS.

7. Type `copy msav*.* a:` and press `⏎Enter`. DOS copies all the Microsoft Anti-Virus programs to the disk in drive A.

8. Remove the disk from drive A, and write protect the disk. If your computer ever gets infected by a virus, you can now boot your computer using this disk and run Microsoft Anti-Virus from drive A.

Running Anti-Virus at Startup

Although scanning for viruses ensures that your system is not currently infected, scanning does not prevent viruses from attacking your system in the future. To keep a lookout for viruses, consider setting up Anti-Virus to run whenever you start your computer.

To have Anti-Virus run each time you start your computer, add the following command line to your AUTOEXEC.BAT file:

```
c:\dos\msav /p
```

For information about editing your AUTOEXEC.BAT file, read Chapter 15.

Running VSafe for Continuous Anti-Virus Protection

In addition to running Anti-Virus at startup, you can run a special memory-resident program called VSafe that acts as a virus watchdog. Once you have run VSafe, it stays in your computer's memory and keeps an eye out for any suspicious activity. If VSafe notices anything funny going on (such as unauthorized file activity), VSafe displays a warning, indicating that a virus may be at work.

To run VSafe, type `vsafe` at the DOS prompt, and press `⏎Enter`. To have VSafe loaded automatically whenever you boot your computer, add the following command to your AUTOEXEC.BAT file:

```
c:\dos\vsafe
```

Changing the VSafe Settings

When you load VSafe into memory, the program has several default settings in place. You can change these settings by using VSafe's pop-up options menu. To change an option's setting, perform the following steps:

1. Press `Alt`+`V`. The VSafe Warning Options screen appears.

2. To turn an option on or off, type the number of the option.

3. When you are done entering your preferences, press `Esc`.

   You can change the settings for any of the following options:

   HD low-level format   Warns of any attempt to format your hard disk. Some viruses do their damage by formatting your disk. By default, this option is on.

   Resident   Prevents any program from staying resident in your computer's memory. By default, this option is off. If you turn it on and then get error messages when you try to run a memory-resident program, try turning this option off.

   General write protect   Prevents any program from writing to a disk. By default, this option is off, because you usually want to be able to write to your disks. However, if you know that your system has been infected by a virus, turn this option on to prevent the virus from causing additional damage.

Check executable files   This option tells VSafe to check any programs you run for viruses. By default, this option is on.

Boot sector viruses   Tells VSafe to check the boot sector for viruses. Viruses commonly infect the boot sector of a disk. By default, this option is on.

Protect HD boot sector   Prevents any program from writing to the boot sector of the hard disk. By default, this option is on.

Protect FD boot sector   Prevents any program from writing to the boot sector of a floppy disk. By default, this option is off. If you turn it on and then have trouble formatting a floppy disk, turn this option off.

Protect executable files   Warns you if any program attempts to change an executable program file. By default, this option is off.

Unloading VSafe from Memory

If you need to free up the 46 kilobytes of memory that VSafe occupies, you can unload the program from memory. Just keep in mind that you must unload memory-resident programs from memory in the reverse order in which you loaded them. For example, if you loaded another memory-resident program after loading VSafe, you must unload the other memory-resident program first. Then, perform the following steps to unload VSafe:

1. Press Alt + V to display the VSafe Warning Options screen.

2. Press Alt + U.

Summing It Up

In this chapter, you learned how to run Microsoft Anti-Virus to scan memory and files for viruses. You also learned how to run VSafe for ongoing virus protection. By regularly checking for viruses, you can detect them early and eliminate them before they can do much damage.

In the next chapter, you will learn how to edit your CONFIG.SYS and AUTOEXEC.BAT files to configure your system.

In This Chapter

Configuring Your Computer with CONFIG.SYS and AUTOEXEC.BAT

Viewing the Contents of CONFIG.SYS and AUTOEXEC.BAT

Simple Commands You Can Add to AUTOEXEC.BAT

Setting Up Programs to Run Automatically at Startup

Executing One Startup Command at a Time

Viewing the Contents of a File in the DOS Shell

1. Change to the drive and directory that contains the file whose contents you want to view.
2. Highlight the file in the File List.
3. Press Alt+F, or click on File in the menu bar.
4. Select View File Contents.

Viewing the Contents of a File at the DOS Prompt

1. Change to the drive and directory that contains the file whose contents you want to view.
2. Type type *filename.ext* ¦more, and press Enter. In place of *filename.ext*, type the name of the file you want to view.
3. Press any key to see the next screenful of information contained in the file.

Editing a File with the DOS Edit Program

1. Change to the drive and directory that contains the DOS files.
2. Type edit, and press Enter.
3. Press Esc to skip the survival guide.
4. Open the File menu, and select Open.
5. Use the dialog box that appears to select the file you want to edit, and then select OK.

Executing One Startup Command at a Time

1. Reboot your computer. (Press Ctrl+Alt+Del.)
2. Watch the screen until you see the message Starting MS-DOS...
3. Hold down F8 until DOS displays the message MS-DOS will prompt you to confirm each CONFIG.SYS command.
4. Answer Y or N to each command.

Configuring Your System with AUTOEXEC.BAT and CONFIG.SYS

When you start your computer, it automatically reads two files that contain a series of startup commands: CONFIG.SYS and AUTOEXEC.BAT. CONFIG.SYS contains commands that load device drivers and specify how some of your computer's components operate. For example, your CONFIG.SYS file probably loads the device driver for your monitor and the DOS programs for managing your computer's memory. (A device driver is a set of instructions that tell DOS how to use a part of your computer, such as the monitor or the mouse.)

The AUTOEXEC.BAT file contains additional startup commands. For example, AUTOEXEC.BAT probably contains commands for helping your computer find files, for controlling the appearance of the DOS prompt, and for automatically running other programs at startup.

In this chapter, you will learn how to take more control over your computer by editing these files.

Making a Copy of AUTOEXEC.BAT and CONFIG.SYS

Before you start messing around with your AUTOEXEC.BAT and CONFIG.SYS files, copy the files to a bootable floppy disk so you can return your system to normal if you make any mistakes. Here's how:

1. Get a blank floppy disk for drive A, or a disk that does not contain any useful data. Insert the disk into drive A, and close the drive door, if necessary.

2. Type `format a: /s`, and press `Enter`. DOS displays a message telling you to insert a disk in drive A.

3. Press `Enter` to continue, and then wait until DOS is done formatting the disk.

4. When asked to type a volume label, type a label, and press `Enter`, or just press `Enter` to skip this step.

5. Change to the drive and directory that contains the DOS files. This is usually C:\DOS.

6. Type `copy config.sys a:`, and press `Enter`. Then, type `copy autoexec.bat a:`, and press `Enter`.

7. Remove the disk from drive A and write protect the disk.

If your system does not operate correctly after you've been editing your CONFIG.SYS and AUTOEXEC.BAT files, reboot your computer from the floppy disk, and then copy CONFIG.SYS and AUTOEXEC.BAT from the floppy disk to the root directory of drive C to return your system to its original condition.

Viewing the Contents of AUTOEXEC.BAT or CONFIG.SYS

Before you begin editing AUTOEXEC.BAT and CONFIG.SYS, you might want to take a look at the contents of each file. This look-but-don't-touch approach allows you to see what's in a file without changing it.

The easiest way to view a file is to use the file viewer in the DOS Shell. The following steps lead you through the process:

1. Start the DOS Shell.

2. Change to the root directory of drive C.

3. Highlight the file whose contents you want to view.

4. Open the File menu, and select View File Contents. The contents of the file appear, as shown in Figure 15.1.

NOTE: If the commands you see appear to be in a foreign language, don't worry; you will learn what most of the commands do later in this chapter.

Figure 15.1

The contents of my CONFIG.SYS file displayed in the File Viewer.

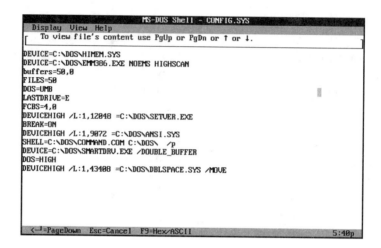

```
                         MS-DOS Shell - CONFIG.SYS
 Display  View  Help
[   To view file's content use PgUp or PgDn or ↑ or ↓.
 DEVICE=C:\DOS\HIMEM.SYS
 DEVICE=C:\DOS\EMM386.EXE NOEMS HIGHSCAN
 buffers=50,0
 FILES=50
 DOS=UMB
 LASTDRIVE=E
 FCBS=4,0
 DEVICEHIGH /L:1,12040 =C:\DOS\SETVER.EXE
 BREAK=ON
 DEVICEHIGH /L:1,9072 =C:\DOS\ANSI.SYS
 SHELL=C:\DOS\COMMAND.COM C:\DOS\ /p
 DEVICE=C:\DOS\SMARTDRV.EXE /DOUBLE_BUFFER
 DOS=HIGH
 DEVICEHIGH /L:1,43408 =C:\DOS\DBLSPACE.SYS /MOVE




 <─┘=PageDown  Esc=Cancel  F9=Hex/ASCII                             5:40p
```

If you want to view the contents of a file at the DOS prompt, use the TYPE command. The following steps explain how to view the contents of the AUTOEXEC.BAT file:

1. At the DOS prompt, change to the root directory of drive C. (Type `c:` and press ⏎Enter. Then type `cd\`, and press ⏎Enter.)

2. Type `type autoexec.bat ¦more`, and press ⏎Enter. DOS displays as much of the file as will fit on one screen, as shown in Figure 15.2.

3. To see more of the file, press any key.

Figure 15.2

The contents of my AUTOEXEC.BAT file displayed with the TYPE command.

```
C:\>type autoexec.bat ¦more

LH /L:0;1,42384 /S C:\DOS\SMARTDRV.EXE
ECHO OFF
VERIFY OFF
PROMPT $P$G
PATH C:\DOS;C:\;C:\WINDOWS;C:\EXECUTE;C:\ZIP;C:\WORD5;C:\NC;C:\WP51;c:\pctools
set temp=C:\WINDOWS\TEMP
SET PCTOOLS=C:\PCTOOLS\DATA
REM SET COMSPEC=C:\DOS\COMMAND.COM
C:\DOS\DOSKEY
numlock -
MIRROR C:
LH /L:1,56928 mouse
commute /r1

C:\>
```

Using the DOS Editor

To edit CONFIG.SYS or AUTOEXEC.BAT, you should open the file in a *text editor*. What's a text editor? It is a program that allows you to edit and save files without saving the file in a special format. In general, you should avoid editing CONFIG.SYS and AUTOEXEC.BAT in a word-processing program, because these programs add formatting codes that can prevent the commands from running correctly. Fortunately, DOS 6 comes with its own text editor.

You can run the editor from the DOS prompt by typing `edit`, and pressing ⏎Enter. Or to run the editor from the DOS Shell, perform the following Quick Steps.

Opening a File in the Text Editor

1. In the Main Program List, double-click on `Editor`, or highlight it and press ⏎Enter.

The File to Edit dialog box appears, asking which file you want to edit.

2. Type `c:\autoexec.bat`, and press ⏎Enter to open the AUTOEXEC.BAT file, or type `c:\config.sys`, and press ⏎Enter to open CONFIG.SYS.

The contents of the file appear in the text editor, as shown in Figure 15.3.

3. Use the edit keys as shown in Table 15.1 to edit the file.

More information about commands you can add to AUTOEXEC.BAT and CONFIG.SYS is provided later in the chapter.

continues

continued

4. To save your changes, open the File menu, and select Save.

The file is saved to disk under its original name.

5. Open the File menu and select Exit.

This closes the text editor and returns you to the DOS prompt.

NOTE: Changes you make to AUTOEXEC.BAT and CONFIG.SYS are not immediately activated. You must reboot your computer to put the new commands into effect.

Figure 15.3

The contents of my AUTOEXEC.BAT file displayed in the text editor.

```
 File  Edit  Search  Options                                    Help
                        AUTOEXEC.BAT
C:\DOS\SMARTDRV.EXE
ECHO OFF
VERIFY OFF
PROMPT $P$G
PATH C:\DOS;C:\;C:\WINDOWS;C:\EXECUTE;C:\ZIP;C:\WORD5;C:\WP51
set temp=C:\WINDOWS\TEMP
SET PCTOOLS=C:\PCTOOLS\DATA
REM SET COMSPEC=C:\DOS\COMMAND.COM
C:\DOS\DOSKEY
MIRROR C:
C:\DOS\MOUSE.EXE
win




MS-DOS Editor  <F1=Help> Press ALT to activate menus            00012:004
```

Table 15.1

Use These Keys to Edit Your File

Press	To
↑	Move up one line.
↓	Move down one line.
←	Move left one character.
→	Move right one character.
Home	Move to the beginning of a line.
End	Move to the end of a line.

Press	To
Del	Delete the character that the cursor is under.
◆Backspace	Delete the character to the left of the cursor.
⏎Enter	Start a new line above the cursor.

Editing Your AUTOEXEC.BAT File

Because the AUTOEXEC.BAT file contains the more simple commands, let's edit it first. The following sections start with some simple commands and then move on to more complex commands. As you edit your file, keep in mind that you have the original files stored safely on a floppy disk; so don't be afraid to make mistakes.

Changing the Look of the DOS Prompt

The DOS prompt normally shows only the letter of the active disk drive (for example, A>, B>, or C>). You can change the look of the DOS prompt by using the PROMPT command. Try adding one of the following PROMPT commands to the end of your AUTOEXEC.BAT file.

- Type `prompt $n$q`, and press ⏎Enter. $n displays the current drive, and $q displays the equal sign (=). The prompt should now look like C=.

- Type prompt `$v $n$b`, and press ⏎Enter. $v displays the DOS version number, and $b displays a vertical line (¦). The prompt should now look something like

```
MS-DOS Version 6.00 C¦
```

- Type `prompt $p$g`, and press `⏎Enter`. $p displays the current drive letter and directory name, and $g displays a right angle bracket (>). The prompt should now look something like `C:\>`. (This is one of the most commonly used prompts.)

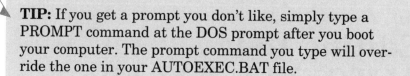

TIP: If you get a prompt you don't like, simply type a PROMPT command at the DOS prompt after you boot your computer. The prompt command you type will override the one in your AUTOEXEC.BAT file.

Helping Your Computer Locate Files with a Path Statement

Chances are your AUTOEXEC.BAT file already contains a path statement that looks something like this:

```
PATH=C:\;C:\DOS
```

This statement tells DOS where to look for program files when you enter a command to start a program. For example, if you are in the root directory, and you enter `dblspace` to run the DoubleSpace program, the path command will look in the root directory first and then in C:\DOS to find the file that initiates DoubleSpace. Without the path command, DOS would not know where to look; whenever you wanted to run DoubleSpace, you would have to use the CD command to change to the DOS directory.

If your AUTOEXEC.BAT file does not contain a path statement, add a statement to the beginning of the file. Start with the path statement shown above. You can add drives and directories to the path statement by typing a semicolon (;) to separate the entries. For example, to add the D:\WORD5 directory to your path statement, you would move the cursor to the end of the statement and type `;d:\word5`. Your path statement would then look like this:

```
PATH=C:\;C:\DOS;d:\word5
```

> **TIP:** As you edit your files, consider entering your changes in lowercase characters. That way, you can quickly see the changes you entered.

Preventing Commands from Appearing On-Screen

Whenever you start your computer, you will notice that DOS displays the commands in AUTOEXEC.BAT as it carries out those commands. If you want to prevent the commands from appearing on-screen, add the following command:

```
echo off
```

Add the command before the commands that you want to prevent from appearing on-screen. You can add an `echo on` command later in the file if you want to resume displaying commands on-screen.

Setting Up Programs to Run Automatically

Have you ever used a computer that starts Windows or some other program automatically when you turn the computer on? Whoever set up the computer added a command line to the end of the AUTOEXEC.BAT file to run the program. In the case of Windows, the program line probably looks like this:

```
c:\windows\win
```

> **TIP:** If you added the Windows directory to your path statement, you can omit the directory from the command line. For example, you could add the command line `win` to run Windows. The path statement tells DOS to look to the Windows directory to find WIN.EXE, the file that starts Windows. (Of course, this only works if the path line comes before the line that starts Windows.)

If you don't have Microsoft Windows, you might consider entering a command line to run DOS Shell at startup. It would look like this:

```
c:\dos\dosshell
```

CAUTION   When setting up programs to run automatically, make sure you type the command line at the *end* of the file. Otherwise, AUTOEXEC.BAT might start the program before it finishes entering its other commands.

Running DOSKey

In Chapter 5, you learned how to use DOSKey to help you edit command lines at the DOS prompt. You can add the DOSKey command to your AUTOEXEC.BAT file to have DOSKey run each time you start your computer. To run DOSKey, add the following command line:

```
c:\dos\doskey
```

Again, if the DOS directory is in your path statement, you can omit the directory from the command line. Simply type `doskey`.

Running VSafe

In Chapter 14, you learned how to run VSafe from the DOS prompt to load it in your computer's memory. Recall that VSafe stays in memory and keeps a lookout for any suspicious activity that may indicate the presence of a virus. To have VSafe run each time you start your computer, add the following command line to AUTOEXEC.BAT:

```
c:\dos\vsafe
```

Add the command near the end of the file (but before any programs you're starting, like Windows).

In addition, you can have Anti-Virus scan your computer's memory and drive C for computer viruses each time you start your computer, by adding the following line:

```
c:\dos\msav /p
```

Using the REM Command to Temporarily Disable a Command Line

So far, I have talked about adding command lines to AUTOEXEC.BAT, but what about deleting command lines? In general, you should avoid deleting command lines until you are absolutely sure you will never want the command line in your file. Instead, type the REM command and a space before any command line that you want to prevent from running. For example,

```
rem c:\dos\doskey
```

prevents DOSKey from running. If you ever want to enable the command line again, simply open the file in the text editor and delete the REM command and the space.

NOTE: When you are done entering changes to your
AUTOEXEC.BAT file, remember to save the file. Open the
File menu, and select Save.

Editing Your CONFIG.SYS File

Your CONFIG.SYS file contains slightly more advanced commands than the ones you find in AUTOEXEC.BAT. The CONFIG.SYS commands load programs that control your computer's memory, its monitor, the number of files that can be open at one time, and other programs that control your system. To be safe, if you don't know what a command is for, don't change it.

To edit your CONFIG.SYS file, first display its contents in the text editor as explained earlier in this chapter. Figure 15.4 shows what my CONFIG.SYS file looks like. The following sections explain some of the commands you are likely to encounter in CONFIG.SYS.

Figure 15.4

The contents of a sample CONFIG.SYS file displayed in the text editor.

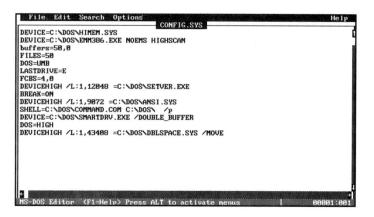

Device Commands and What They Do

Device commands are the meat and potatoes of any CONFIG.SYS file. These commands load programs (device drivers) that control the various pieces of hardware that make up your computer, including the mouse driver, memory board drivers, and video drivers. If you ran MemMaker, you may notice some commands that start with DEVICEHIGH. These device commands load the device drivers into upper memory in order to free up space in conventional memory. The following list explains some of the more common device commands you will encounter:

DEVICE=C:\DOS\HIMEM.SYS   On a 286 or better computer with extended memory, HIMEM.SYS manages the use of extended memory. This command *must* be the first command in your CONFIG.SYS file.

DEVICE=C:\DOS\EMM386.EXE NOEMS   On a 386 or better computer, EMM386.EXE allows the computer to use extended memory as expanded memory and to access upper memory. If you ran MemMaker, MemMaker automatically added this command line for you, directly after the HIMEM.SYS command line.

DEVICE=C:\DOS\SETVER.EXE   This command line loads the DOS version table into memory. This is useful if you have a program that is conflicting with DOS 6. The version table helps the program find a DOS version that is more compatible with the program.

DEVICE=C:\DOS\ANSI.SYS   ANSI stands for American National Standards Institute. This driver tells your keyboard and monitor to follow ANSI standards when typing and displaying characters.

DEVICE=C:\MOUSE\MOUSE.SYS   When you buy and install a mouse, the setup program that came with the mouse will add a command such as this to your CONFIG.SYS file or a command such as C:\MOUSE\MOUSE.COM to your AUTOEXEC.BAT file. Either command line loads the program that tells your computer how to use your mouse.

**DEVICE=C:\DOS\SMARTDRV.EXE /
DOUBLE_BUFFER**   When you installed DOS 6, the
setup program added this command line to your
CONFIG.SYS file to help SmartDrive (the disk cache
program) run more efficiently on your computer. For more
information about SmartDrive, see Chapter 13.

DEVICE=C:\DOS\DBLSPACE.SYS   If you installed
DoubleSpace on your computer, the installation added
this command line to load the memory-resident part of
DoubleSpace into memory. This program controls the
operation of any drives you compressed with DoubleSpace.

Setting the Number of Buffers and Files

Buffers are used by application programs to temporarily store
data that is being used. Most programs recommend a minimum
number of buffers. If that number is greater than the number in
your BUFFERS= command line, you should edit the line to
increase the number of buffers. For example, the following command line creates 50 buffers:

```
buffers=50
```

The FILES= command sets the number of files that DOS can
manage at one time. Most programs recommend a minimum
number for the FILES setting. If you are working in a program
and you get a message such as Too many files are open, you should
edit the FILES= line to increase the number of files. For example,
type files=50 to allow 50 files to be open at once.

CAUTION   Increasing the number of buffers and files
            consumes more memory, so try to keep each
number at or below 50.

Allowing DOS to Use Upper Memory

If you ran MemMaker in Chapter 13, the MemMaker setup program added two DOS commands to your CONFIG.SYS file:

```
DOS=UMB

DOS=HIGH
```

The first command allows DOS to use upper memory (UMB stands for Upper Memory Blocks). The second command loads DOS into high memory in order to free up additional conventional memory for your other programs. Note that both of these commands must come after HIMEM.SYS and EMM386.EXE are loaded.

If you want, you can combine these two lines into one, and they will still work the same. It would look like this:

```
DOS=HIGH,UMB
```

Turning Your NumLock Key Off at Startup

If you're like me, you use the cursor keys on the numeric keypad to move around on-screen. (That way, you can use the edge of the keyboard to help position your fingers.) The only problem with this is that most keyboards start with NumLock on, so you have to press the NumLock key whenever you start your computer. DOS 6 comes with a nifty program that automatically does this for you. Type the following command in your CONFIG.SYS file:

```
numlock=off
```

Other CONFIG.SYS Commands

It would be nearly impossible to cover all the CONFIG.SYS commands in this book. However, I can tell you a quick way to learn more about these commands using the DOS Help system. At the DOS prompt, type `help` followed by the name of the command in the list and press `⏎Enter`. For example, for information about the LASTDRIVE command, type `help lastdrive`, and press `⏎Enter`.

Try typing `help` and some of the following commands:

BREAK	COUNTRY	DRIVPARM
INSTALL	LASTDRIVE	SET
SHELL	STACKS	FCBS

NOTE: You can use several commands in both the AUTOEXEC.BAT and CONFIG.SYS files. For example, you can use the REM command in both files to disable individual command lines. In addition, you can use the BREAK and SET commands in both files.

Rebooting Your Computer to Put Your Changes into Effect

When you are done entering your changes to CONFIG.SYS and AUTOEXEC.BAT, save the file you are currently editing, exit the text editor (choose Exit from the File menu), and then press `Ctrl`+`Alt`+`Del` to reboot your computer.

As your computer reboots, it reads and carries out the commands in CONFIG.SYS and AUTOEXEC.BAT. Watch the screen, and look for any messages that might indicate a problem in one of these files. For example, if DOS does not recognize a command in CONFIG.SYS, it displays a messages such as

```
Unrecognized command in CONFIG.SYS

Error in CONFIG.SYS Line 8
```

If you see such an error message, reopen the file that contains the bad command line, and then edit the line to fix it. Remember to save the file.

> **TIP:** After you're done adding lines to your CONFIG.SYS and AUTOEXEC.BAT, run MemMaker again to load as many of the new commands as possible into upper memory. This prevents your newly added commands from taking up valuable conventional memory. See Chapter 13 for details.

Troubleshooting Startup Problems

When you start your computer (assuming you did not add an echo off command to your CONFIG.SYS or AUTOEXEC.BAT file), DOS displays each command it carries out. However, these commands can scroll by too quickly for you to read them. To slow down the display, reboot your computer like this:

1. Press Ctrl+Alt+Del to reboot your computer.

2. Watch the screen until you see the message
   `Starting MS-DOS...`

3. Press F8. DOS carries out the CONFIG.SYS commands one at a time, asking you to confirm the command by pressing Y or skip it by pressing N.

4. Answer Ⓨ or Ⓝ to each command. (You can press Ⓔsc to have DOS carry out each command without asking for your okay, or you can press Ⓕ5 to skip all commands.)

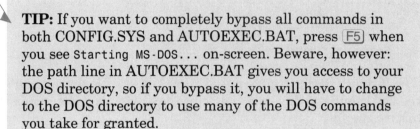

TIP: If you want to completely bypass all commands in both CONFIG.SYS and AUTOEXEC.BAT, press Ⓕ5 when you see `Starting MS-DOS...` on-screen. Beware, however: the path line in AUTOEXEC.BAT gives you access to your DOS directory, so if you bypass it, you will have to change to the DOS directory to use many of the DOS commands you take for granted.

Summing It Up

In this chapter, you learned how to take control of your computer's startup by editing the AUTOEXEC.BAT and CONFIG.SYS files. If this is your first try at editing these files, go back and practice on the AUTOEXEC.BAT file. Try entering various PROMPT commands, or add directories to your path statement. Once you get comfortable with editing these files, you will begin to realize how much time you can save by having your system customized for the way you work.

In This Chapter

Using InterInk to Transfer Files Between Computers

How to Connect Two Computers with a Null-Modem Cable

Conserving Power on Your Laptop Computer

Connecting Two Computers with a Null-Modem Cable

1. Obtain a null-modem serial cable from a computer or electronics store.
2. Turn both computers off.
3. Plug one end of the cable into an open COM port on one of the computers.
4. Plug the other end of the cable into an open COM port on the other computer.

Establishing a Connection Between Two Computers

1. Make sure both computers have DOS 6 installed or at least have the following two InterInk files: INTERLNK.EXE and INTERSVR.EXE.
2. On the laptop computer, type `edit c:\config.sys`, and press `Enter`.
3. Type the following command at the end of the CONFIG.SYS file: `device=c:\dos\interlnk.exe`.
4. Save your changes (File Save), and exit the editor (File Exit).
5. Press `Ctrl`+`Alt`+`Del` to reboot your computer.
6. On the desktop computer, type `intersvr`, and press `Enter`.

Conserving Battery Power on Your Laptop Computer

1. At the DOS prompt, type `edit c:\config.sys`, and press `Enter`.
2. Move to the end of the CONFIG.SYS file, and press `Enter` to start a new line.
3. Type the following command line: `device=c:\dos\power.exe`.
4. Save your changes (File Save), and exit the editor (File Exit).
5. Press `Ctrl`+`Alt`+`Del` to reboot your computer.

16

Special Programs for Laptop Computers

DOS 6 comes with two programs specially designed for laptop computers: Interlnk and Power. Interlnk allows you to connect two computers with a special cable and transfer files from one computer to another. This provides you with an easier and faster way to transfer files from one computer to another without using floppy disks.

The Power program is designed to conserve battery power on a laptop computer. When applications and hardware devices are idle, the Power program reduces the power needed to keep the system running, conserving energy consumption 5 to 25 percent.

Using Interlnk to Transfer Files between Two Computers

If you have two computers—a laptop to take home and a desktop at work, for instance—and you transfer files between the two, you can save time by using Interlnk. Once the two computers are connected and running Interlnk, you simply copy files from one to the other, just as you would copy files from one disk or directory to another.

What You Need to Use Interlnk

To use Interlnk, your system must meet the following hardware and software requirements:

- Both computers must have a free serial port. (Serial ports are commonly used for modems and mice.)

- You must have a null-modem serial cable or a bidirectional parallel cable. Throughout this chapter, I assume you will be using a null-modem serial cable. (The next section explains what you need in greater detail.)

- You must have MS-DOS 6 on one computer and MS-DOS 3 or later on the other. (You can have MS-DOS 6 on both computers.)

- The laptop computer (or the computer you will use to control the file transfer) must have 16 kilobytes free memory. The desktop computer must have 130 kilobytes free memory. (That's no big deal; computers normally have between 400 and 600K free.)

Connecting the Two Computers

The first step in establishing a connection is to purchase the proper serial null-modem cable. You need a cable to connect a COM port on one computer to a COM port on the other computer.

To figure out what kind of connectors the cable should have, check the ports on the back of the computer. If they're marked, you're in luck; if not, refer to the documentation that came with your computer, or call your dealer to figure out which is the serial (COM) port.

Write down how many pins each COM port has (9 or 25) and whether the port is male (has pins) or female (has receptacles for pins). The serial ports are usually male, but don't bet on it. When you've figured out what you need, obtain the required cable and any necessary adapters from your local computer store.

> CAUTION
>
> Make sure the cable is a null-modem cable—not just a standard serial cable (it should be marked). You can convert a serial cable to a null-modem cable by connecting a *null-modem adapter* to the cable.

> **NOTE:** Your printer is probably connected to the parallel port at the back of your computer. If you have a mouse or modem, it's probably connected to your serial port. If you have only one COM port on your computer, you'll have to disconnect any device that's connected to it before you can proceed.

With both computers turned off (to protect them), connect the COM ports on the two computers using the cable. Then, boot (turn on) each computer.

Setting Up the Client and Server

Before you perform the next step, decide which computer will control the transfer of data (usually the laptop computer). This computer will be the *client*. The other computer (usually the desktop) will be the *server*; it will do only what the client computer tells it to do. (See Figure 16.1.)

Figure 16.1

Connection of a laptop (client) and desktop (server) computer using a null-modem cable.

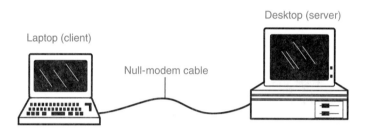

Desktop (server)

Laptop (client)

Null-modem cable

Interlnk requires you to run a different program on each computer; you'll run INTERLNK.EXE on the client (laptop) and INTERSVR.EXE on the server (desktop). To run INTERLNK.EXE on the client, perform the following steps:

1. Make sure INTERLNK.EXE is in the DOS directory of the client's hard disk. (If you installed DOS 6 on the client, INTERLNK.EXE is on its hard disk. If not, transfer the file by using a floppy disk or by using the remote copy procedure, as explained later.)

2. Open the client's CONFIG.SYS file in the MS-DOS text editor, as explained in Chapter 15.

3. Type the following command at the end of the CONFIG.SYS file:

   ```
   device=c:\dos\interlnk.exe
   ```

   (You can add switches to control the operation of Interlnk. Refer to the examples following these steps.)

4. Save your changes (File Save), and exit the editor (File Exit).

5. Press `Ctrl`+`Alt`+`Del` to reboot your computer.

Here are those examples that I promised in step 3. You can use them, instead of the command line given in step 3, to control Interlnk's operation more precisely.

`c:\dos\interlnk /drives:6` Tells Interlnk to redirect 6 drives on the server rather than the default number (3). If you have problems with redirecting too many drives, check your CONFIG.SYS file for a command that starts `LASTDRIVE=`. Change the last drive letter to a letter that comes later in the alphabet.

`c:\dos\interlnk /noprinter` Tells Interlnk not to redirect the printer ports. Normally, Interlnk redirects all available printer ports.

`c:\dos\interlnk /com:3F8` Normally, Interlnk scans all serial and parallel ports to redirect any available ports. The /COM switch specifies the serial port number and address to use for the connection. If you use the /COM switch without a serial port number or address, Interlnk scans all of the COM ports, and only the COM ports, to find the one that's connected to the server.

`c:\dos\interlnk /auto` By default, Interlnk loads into memory whether or not it can connect to the server. The /AUTO switch tells Interlnk to load into memory only if a connection can be established.

`c:\dos\interlnk /noscan` The /NOSCAN switch loads Interlnk into memory but does not allow it to automatically scan ports. Interlnk will not scan for or redirect ports until you enter the INTERLNK command at the DOS prompt.

`c:\dos\interlnk /baud:57600` By default, Interlnk transfers files at a maximum baud rate of 115200. If you are getting communications error messages at this rate, use the /BAUD switch to try a slower setting.

NOTE: You can combine switches in the INTERLNK command line. For example, the following command line is valid:

C:\DOS\INTERLNK.EXE /DRIVES:5 /AUTO/BAUD:5700

Setting up the server (desktop) computer is easy, because you don't have to edit its CONFIG.SYS file. Just make sure you have the two Interlnk files in your DOS directory: INTERLNK.EXE and INTERSVR.EXE. (If you installed DOS 6 on the server, these files are in the DOS directory. If not, use the Remote Copy procedure explained in the next section to copy the files.) Then simply type the following command at the DOS prompt of the server:

```
intersvr
```

and press ⏎Enter. You'll see the screen shown in Figure 16.2, indicating the redirected drives.

Figure 16.2

When you run INTERSVR on the server, a screen appears showing you the letters of the redirected drives.

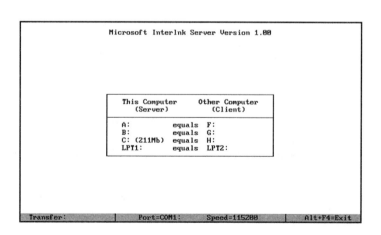

Using the Remote Copy Procedure

Even before you use Interlnk to connect two computers, you can use the program to copy files from one computer to the other. This allows you to transfer the Interlnk files from the computer that has DOS 6 installed to the computer that does not have DOS 6. Here's how to do it:

1. Connect the two computers with a 7-pin, null-modem, serial cable. (If you have a bidirectional parallel cable or a 3-pin null-modem cable, you cannot perform remote copy. Instead, you will have to use a floppy disk to transfer the files.)

2. If you are using a COM port other than COM1 on the computer to which you are copying the files, make sure the SHARE program is not loaded on that computer.

> **TIP:** How do you find out if SHARE is loaded? Check the AUTOEXEC.BAT or CONFIG.SYS file as explained in Chapter 15. If SHARE is there, add the REM command at the beginning of the command line to disable it. Then save the file, exit, and reboot the computer.

3. On the computer to which you want to copy the Interlnk files, change to the DOS directory.

4. Move over to the computer from which you will copy the files. Type `intersvr /rcopy`, and press ⏎Enter. A dialog box appears, asking you to select a COM port.

5. Use the up arrow and down arrow keys to select a COM port, and then press ⏎Enter. The Interlnk Remote Installation screen appears, as shown in Figure 16.3, providing additional instructions.

6. Follow the instructions on-screen. When you are done, Interlnk copies the two Interlnk files (INTERLNK.EXE and INTERSVR.EXE) to the DOS directory on the computer that needs the files.

Figure 16.3

The Interlnk Remote Installation program tells you what to do depending on which COM port you are using.

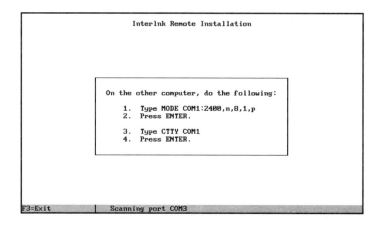

Establishing the Connection Between Computers

Okay, you have INTERLNK.EXE running on the client computer and INTERSVR.EXE running on the server. You can now establish a connection between the two computers by performing any of the following steps:

- Reboot the client computer while the server is on, by pressing Ctrl+Alt+Del on the client computer's keyboard.

- On the client computer, type `interlnk`, and press ⏎Enter.

- On the client computer, change to one of the drives that corresponds to the drive on the server.

What happens when a connection is established? The drives on the server are *appended* to the drives on the client. For example, if the client computer has drives A, B, and C and the server has drives A, B, C, and D, the client's drives retain their letter assignments, and the server's drives are added as D, E, F, and G. This gives the client computer seven drives: its original drives (A, B, and C) and four additional drives (D, E, F, and G).

> **TIP:** To view the redirected drives on the client, type `interlnk` at the DOS prompt, and press ⏎Enter.

Using the Redirected Drives

Now that the drives are redirected, you can change to any of the drives using the client computer. The drives act as normal disk drives, allowing you to run programs, copy and delete files, and even edit files on the server. For example, if you run DOS Shell on the client computer, icons for the redirected drives appear at the top of the shell, as shown in Figure 16.4. You can then work with the files as you normally would.

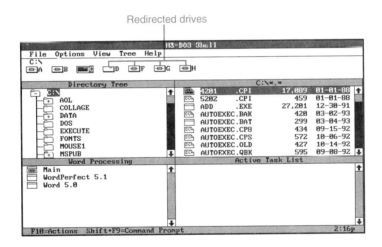

Redirected drives

Figure 16.4
When you run DOS Shell, you will see icons for the redirected drives.

Breaking the Connection Between Computers

When you are done transferring files between the two computers, you can break the connection between the computers. To break the connection, press ⌊Alt⌋+⌊F4⌋ on the server's keyboard. To reestablish the connection, type intersvr on the server, and press ⌊↵Enter⌋.

After breaking the connection, you can turn off both computers and disconnect the null-modem cable.

CAUTION   Before connecting or disconnecting any cable to a computer, make sure the power to the computer is off. Otherwise, you might damage one of the computers.

Conserving Power on Your Laptop Computer

DOS 6 comes with a program called Power that can conserve battery power on your laptop computer. If your laptop conforms to the APM (Advanced Power Management) specifications, your computer will experience a savings of up to 25 percent. If your laptop does not conform to these specifications, it will experience a savings of about 5 percent. To use the Power program, perform the following steps:

1. Open your CONFIG.SYS file in the DOS text editor. (At the DOS prompt, type edit c:\config.sys, and press ⌊↵Enter⌋.)

2. Move to the end of the CONFIG.SYS file, and press ⌊↵Enter⌋ to start a new line.

3. Type the following command line:

   device=c:\dos\power.exe

4. Save your changes (File Save), and exit the editor (File Exit).

5. Press Ctrl + Alt + Del to reboot your computer.

To view your power savings, type **power** at the DOS prompt, and press ↵Enter. You'll see a screen like the one in Figure 16.5 showing the power setting and the percent of time that your computer's CPU (central processing unit) is idle.

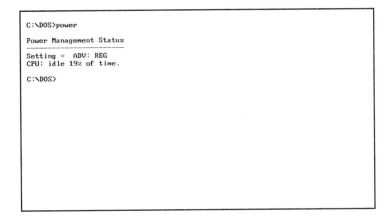

```
C:\DOS>power

Power Management Status
-----------------------
Setting =  ADV: REG
CPU: idle 19% of time.

C:\DOS>
```

Figure 16.5
Power shows you the amount of time your CPU is idle.

Summing It Up

At first glance, the procedures in this chapter may seem a little complicated. However, once you establish a connection between two computers for the first time, future connections go smoothly. You simply connect the cable, establish the connection, and transfer your files.

DOS
Command
Reference

Throughout this book, you learned a few of the more important and more commonly used DOS commands. You learned how to make a directory with MD, copy files with COPY, and run DoubleSpace with DBLSPACE. This reference provides a more extensive list of DOS commands, complete with an explanation of what each command does, when you are most likely to use it, and examples. This list even covers commands that were not covered anywhere else in the book.

TIP: To get more information about any of the commands listed here, use the DOS Help system. Type `help` followed by the name of the command and press ⏎Enter. For example, to view a help screen for the APPEND command, type `help append` and press ⏎Enter. The first screen displays general information about the command and how to enter it. Press Alt+N to see the next screen, which displays notes about the command, such as when not to run it. Press Alt+N again to see sample command entries. You can back through the help screens by pressing Alt+B. For more information about entering commands, look back to Chapter 5 of this book.

APPEND

APPEND is like the PATH command, which tells DOS where to look for program files. Unlike PATH, APPEND tells DOS where to look for data files, such as overlay files (files that contain information that tells the program how to create a display). When you install a program, the installation process may add an APPEND command to your AUTOEXEC.BAT file. The command might look something like this:

```
APPEND C:\PROGRAM;C:\PROGRAM\DATA
```

ATTRIB

ATTRIB allows you to set the file attributes for a file, or group of files, to control the way DOS treats the file. For example, you can turn on a file's Hidden attribute to prevent the file from being displayed in a directory listing. To change a file's attributes in the DOS Shell, select the file, and then choose Change Attributes from the File menu. To change attributes from the DOS prompt, type a command such as this:

```
ATTRIB +R +S +H C:\DIRECTORY\FILENAME.EXT
```

The plus sign (+) tells DOS to turn the attribute on. R stands for Read Only; S stands for System; and H stands for Hidden. (For more information about changing attributes, refer to "Changing File Attributes" in Chapter 8.)

BREAK

The BREAK command tells DOS how often to check to see if the Break key or Ctrl + Break is pressed. For example,

```
BREAK OFF
```

tells DOS to check for the Break key only when an operation uses the keyboard, mouse, communications port, or screen.

```
BREAK ON
```

tells DOS to check the Break key whenever the system is called on to perform an operation, including reading or writing from disk.

Normally, you put the BREAK command in your AUTOEXEC.BAT or CONFIG.SYS file. In the AUTOEXEC.BAT file, leave a space between BREAK and ON or OFF. In the CONFIG.SYS file, insert an equal sign; for example, type `BREAK=ON`. By default, BREAK is off.

BUFFERS

Buffers are used by application programs to temporarily store data that is being used. Most programs recommend a minimum number of buffers. If that number is greater than the number in your BUFFERS= command line, you should edit the line to increase the number of buffers. For example, the following com mand line creates 50 buffers:

```
buffers=50
```

Although you can have up to 255 buffers, each buffer takes a little extra memory, so try to keep the number at or below 50. For more information about adding the BUFFERS command to your CONFIG.SYS file, see Chapter 15.

CD (CHDIR)

CD stands for Change Directory. Use the CD command to activate a directory on the current hard disk. For example, to change to the TEMP\DATA directory, type

```
CD \TEMP\DATA
```

and press ⏎Enter. (Refer to Chapter 5 for more information about changing directories at the DOS prompt.) If you are using the DOS Shell, you can activate a directory simply by selecting it from the Directory Tree (see Chapter 4).

CHKDSK

CHKDSK tells DOS to check your computer's hard disk for lost pieces of files. You usually use the CHKDSK command at the DOS prompt with the /F (fix) switch to tell DOS to fix any problems it finds. For example, type

```
CHKDSK /F
```

at the DOS prompt, and press ⏎Enter. For more information on using CHKDSK, refer to Chapter 12.

CLS

CLS stands for Clear Screen. You enter this command at the DOS prompt to clear any text that is displayed on-screen.

COPY

The COPY command lets you copy one or more files from one drive and directory to another. The easiest way to copy files is to use the DOS Shell, as explained in Chapter 8. You can also copy files by entering the COPY command at the DOS prompt:

```
COPY D1:\DIR1\FILE1.EXT D2:\DIR2\FILE2.EXT
```

where *D1:\DIR1\FILE1.EXT* is the path and file name of one of the files you want to copy, and *D2:\DIR2\FILE2.EXT* is the path and file name of the new copy. You can copy a file using the same file name to a different drive or directory, or you can copy the file to the same drive and directory by using a different file name.

DATE

The DATE command displays the current date according to the clock inside your computer. It also allows you to type a new date, if the displayed date is incorrect. To enter the DATE command, simply type

```
DATE
```

at the DOS prompt, and press ↵Enter). If the date is correct, press ↵Enter) to accept it. If the date is incorrect, type the new date in the requested format, and press ↵Enter).

DEFRAG

DEFRAG runs a program that defragments the files on your hard disk. This pulls all the pieces of each individual file together and places the pieces on neighboring areas of the disk. By storing the parts of each file next to one another, the program makes it easier for your hard disk drive to read the file. To run DEFRAG, make sure no other memory-resident programs are running (such as DOS Shell or Windows); then type

```
DEFRAG
```

and press ↵Enter). For more information about Defrag, refer to Chapter 12.

DEL (ERASE)

The DEL or ERASE command allows you to delete or erase one or more files from a disk. The easiest way to delete files is to use the DOS Shell. Select the files you want to delete, and then select Delete from the File menu. To delete files from the DOS prompt, change to the drive and directory that contains the files you want to delete, and then enter the following command:

```
DEL FILENAME.EXT
```

You can use wild-card characters to delete groups of files. (For more information about deleting files, refer to Chapter 8.)

DELOLDDOS

When you installed DOS 6, the installation program stored the files of the previous DOS version in a directory called OLD_DOS.1, so you could uninstall DOS 6 if you didn't like it. If you are satisfied with DOS 6, type

```
DELOLDDOS
```

at the DOS prompt and press ↵Enter) to get rid of the old DOS files.

DELTREE

In previous versions of DOS, you could delete only empty directories at the DOS prompt. If you wanted to remove an entire directory, its subdirectories, and its files, you first had to delete all the files in each directory. With DELTREE, you can delete a directory, its subdirectories, and all its files. For example, to delete a directory called TEMP on drive C, you would type

```
DELTREE C:\TEMP
```

DOS displays a message asking you to confirm the deletion. Press Y) to confirm or N) to cancel the operation, and then press ↵Enter).

DEVICE and DEVICEHIGH

The DEVICE and DEVICEHIGH commands are used in the CONFIG.SYS file to load programs (device drivers) that control various hardware devices, such as your mouse and your computer's memory. The DEVICE command loads the device driver into conventional memory (the memory that most programs use). DEVICEHIGH loads the device into upper memory (a reserved portion of memory); this frees space in conventional memory for other programs. Here's a sample DEVICE command for loading a mouse driver:

```
DEVICE=C:\MOUSE\MOUSE.SYS
```

For more information, refer to "Device Commands and What They Do" in Chapter 15.

DIR

The DIR command displays a list of files and subdirectories in the current drive and directory. The easiest way to view a directory and its contents is to use the DOS Shell. However, you can enter the DIR command at the DOS prompt to see a list of directories and files. You can add switches to the DIR command to control the display. For example,

```
DIR /P
```

pauses the list after each screenful, to prevent long lists from scrolling off the screen before you can read them. For more information, refer to "Viewing a List of Files" in Chapter 5.

DISKCOMP

The DISKCOMP command allows you to compare two disks to make sure the disks are identical. This command is useful if you use the DISKCOPY command (explained next) to create a duplicate disk for a friend or colleague. To use the DISKCOMP command, type the following at the DOS prompt:

```
DISKCOMP D1: D2:
```

where *D1* is the letter of the drive that contains one of the disks, and *D2* is the letter of the drive that contains the same disk. (You can use the same disk drive for both disks.)

DISKCOPY

The DISKCOPY command lets you create exact duplicates of floppy disks. This is useful for creating a backup set of program disks. (It's smart to make a backup set of program disks for any program you purchase, so you can use the backups to install and run the program without risking damage to your original disks.) To use the DISKCOPY command, type the following at the DOS prompt:

```
DISKCOPY D1: D2:
```

where *D1* is the letter of the drive that contains one of the disks, and *D2* is the letter of the drive that contains the same disk. (You can use the same disk drive for both disks.)

DOSHELP

Used alone, DOSHELP displays a complete list of DOS commands with a brief description of each command. If you type DOSHELP followed by a command name, DOSHELP displays specific information about the command. For example,

```
DOSHELP DISKCOPY
```

displays specific information about the DISKCOPY command. Although this information may be just what you need, you can get more information by using the HELP command explained later.

DOSKEY

DOSKey is a handy program if you commonly enter commands at the DOS prompt. DOSKey stores previously entered commands in a special buffer and allows you to recall the commands by pressing F3. DOSKey also lets you edit commands without having to delete the entire command. To run DOSKey, type

```
DOSKEY
```

at the DOS prompt, and press ⏎Enter. You can add the DOSKEY command to your AUTOEXEC.BAT file, as explained in Chapter 15, to have DOSKey run whenever you start your computer. (For more information about using DOSKey, refer to "Saving Time with DOSKey" in Chapter 5.)

DOSSHELL

DOSSHELL runs the DOS Shell, the program that allows you to manage disks, directories, and files more easily than you can from the DOS prompt. To start the Shell, type

```
DOSSHELL
```

at the DOS prompt, and press ⏎Enter. You can add the DOSSHELL command to your AUTOEXEC.BAT file, as explained in Chapter 15, to have the DOS Shell run whenever you start your computer. Chapter 4 provides in-depth details on running and using the DOS Shell.

DBLSPACE

DBLSPACE runs DOS's new DoubleSpace program. This program compresses the files on your hard disk to provide more free disk space. To install DoubleSpace, type the following command at the DOS prompt:

```
DBLSPACE
```

and press ⏎Enter. For more information about DoubleSpace, refer to "Getting More Disk Space with DoubleSpace" in Chapter 12.

ECHO

The ECHO ON or ECHO OFF command is commonly added to the CONFIG.SYS or AUTOEXEC.BAT file to prevent commands from appearing on-screen as DOS carries them out. You can also use the ECHO command to display a string of text on-screen. For example, add the following ECHO command to your AUTOEXEC.BAT file to display "Good Morning Neighbor!" when you start your computer:

```
ECHO Good Morning Neighbor!
```

EDIT

Starts the MS-DOS text editor. This editor is useful for editing plain text files, such as AUTOEXEC.BAT and CONFIG.SYS. To start the editor, type `edit` at the DOS prompt, and press ⏎Enter. The following command starts the editor and opens the AUTOEXEC.BAT file that's in the root directory of drive C:

```
EDIT C:\AUTOEXEC.BAT
```

To open the CONFIG.SYS file in the editor, enter the following command:

```
EDIT C:\CONFIG.SYS
```

EXIT

EXIT returns you to the DOS Shell or Windows or any other program that you may have suspended to go temporarily to the DOS prompt. For example, if you select Command Prompt from the Main Program list in Shell, the Shell displays the DOS prompt. You can run programs and perform other tasks from this prompt. When you want to return to the Shell, type

```
EXIT
```

and press ⏎Enter.

FORMAT

Format prepares a disk to store information. The easiest way to format a disk is to run the Format program from the Shell. Select Disk Utilities from the Main Program list, and then choose Format. You can also format disks by typing a command at the DOS prompt. For example, the following command formats the disk in drive A:

```
FORMAT A:
```

For more information about formatting disks, refer to "Preparing a Disk for Storing Data" in Chapter 6.

HELP

Entered alone, the HELP command displays the DOS 6 Help system. This system allows you to get information about any of the DOS 6 commands. To get help about a specific command, type help followed by the name of the command. For example, to get help for the FORMAT command, type

```
HELP FORMAT
```

and press ⏎Enter. For more information about using the DOS Help system, refer to "Getting Help at the DOS Prompt" in Chapter 5. (You can get help for DOS Shell commands by using the Help menu inside the Shell. For more information, refer to "Getting Help in the DOS Shell" in Chapter 4.)

INTERLNK and INTERSVR

New to DOS, the Interlnk program allows you to connect two computers (usually a laptop and a desktop computer) and transfer files between them. To use Interlnk, the two computers must be connected with a null-modem cable. The following command must be in the CONFIG.SYS file of one of the computers:

```
DEVICE=C:\DOS\INTERLNK
```

On the other computer, you must run INTERSVR.EXE by entering INTERSVR at the DOS prompt. Interlnk adds drive letters to one of the computers; these drive letters correspond to the other computer's disk drives. Copying files between computers is then as easy as copying a file from one disk to another, although it takes more time. For more information, see Chapter 16.

LABEL

LABEL allows you to add a volume label to a disk. Labeling a disk is useful for helping you determine the contents of a disk. The label appears in a directory listing. To label a disk, type the LABEL command followed by the letter of the disk drive that contains the disk you want to label; for example

```
LABEL A:
```

LH (LOADHIGH)

The LH (LOADHIGH) command allows you to load certain memory-resident programs into the upper memory area that is normally reserved for specific device drivers. This command is usually used in the AUTOEXEC.BAT file. For example, if you ran MemMaker in Chapter 13, MemMaker probably added LH before the command to load the mouse driver:

```
LH C:\DOS\MOUSE.COM
```

MEM

MEM displays the types of memory installed on your system and the amounts of each type in use and free to be used. To view information about the memory in your system, enter the following command at the DOS prompt:

```
MEM /P
```

The /P switch tells the display to pause if there is more than one screenful of information.

MEMMAKER

A new program in DOS 6, MemMaker optimizes your computer's memory by freeing and making use of upper memory (memory previously reserved for specific device drivers). MemMaker includes an Express Setup that does everything for you. To start MemMaker, enter the following command at the DOS prompt:

```
MEMMAKER
```

MD (MKDIR)

MD stands for Make Directory. Use this command to make a directory under the current directory. To make a directory, change to the drive and directory under which you want the new directory created. Type

```
MD DIRNAME
```

where *dirname* is the name of the new directory. Press ⏎Enter.

PATH

The PATH command tells DOS where to look for executable program files. Normally, if you enter a command to run a program, DOS looks only in the current drive and directory to find the file that initiates the program. The PATH command provides DOS with additional places to look. For example, the following command

```
PATH=C:\;C:\DOS;C:\WORD5
```

tells DOS to look in the root directory of drive C, in the DOS directory, and in the WORD5 directory. Usually, you add a PATH command to your AUTOEXEC.BAT file. (For more information about adding a PATH statement to AUTOEXEC.BAT, see Chapter 15.)

PROMPT

The PROMPT command allows you to control the appearance of the DOS prompt. For example, you can enter the following command to have the DOS prompt display the letter of the current drive and the name of the current directory:

```
PROMPT $P$G
```

$P tells DOS to display the current drive and directory. $G displays the right angle bracket (>). For more information about using the PROMPT command, refer to Chapter 15.

REM

The REM command disables any command in your CONFIG.SYS or AUTOEXEC.BAT files. For more information about using the REM command, refer to "Using the REM Command to Temporarily Disable a Command Line" in Chapter 15.

REN (RENAME)

The RENAME command lets you change the name of a file or group of files (but not the name of a directory). The easiest way to rename files is to use the DOS Shell. Select the file(s) you want to rename, and then select Rename from the File menu. To rename a file at the DOS prompt, change to the drive and directory that contains the file you want to rename, and then type this command:

```
REN FILE1.EXT FILE2.EXT
```

where *FILE1.EXT* is the current name of the file and *FILE2.EXT* is the new name. Press ⏎Enter. You can also use wild-card characters to rename groups of files. For example, to change the extension of all files that have the .BAK extension to .OLD, type `ren *.bak *.old` and press ⏎Enter.

RD (RMDIR)

RD stands for Remove Directory. It allows you to remove an empty directory from your hard disk. The easiest way to remove a directory is to use the DOS Shell. Highlight the directory you want to delete, open the File menu, and select Delete. To remove a directory at the DOS prompt, change to the directory above the directory you want to delete, and enter the following command:

```
RD DIRNAME
```

where *DIRNAME* is the name of the directory you want to delete. If the directory is empty, DOS will delete it.

SETVER

The SETVER command tricks a program into thinking that it is running under a previous version of DOS. This is useful if you have problems running a program under DOS 6. Add the following command to your CONFIG.SYS file:

```
DEVICE=C:\DOS\SETVER
```

For more information about this command, see "Device Commands and What They Do" in Chapter 15.

SMARTDRV

SMARTDRV loads DOS's disk-caching program, SmartDrive. This program stores often-used data in a special buffer in memory. When your computer needs more information in order to perform a task, the computer can get the information from memory rather than having to read it off a disk. To run SmartDrive, type the following command at the DOS prompt:

    SMARTDRV

and press ⏎Enter. If SmartDrive is already running, you'll see a screen showing you the types of memory installed on your computer. When you installed DOS 6, the installation program automatically added the SMARTDRV command to your AUTOEXEC.BAT file. For more details, refer to "Disk Caching with SmartDrive" in Chapter 13.

TIME

The TIME command displays the current time according to the clock inside your computer. It also allows you to type a new time, if the displayed time is incorrect. To enter the TIME command, simply type

    TIME

at the DOS prompt, and press ⏎Enter. If the time is correct, press ⏎Enter to accept it. If the time is incorrect, type the new time in the requested format, and press ⏎Enter.

TREE

The TREE command displays a directory tree for the current disk. You can add the ¦more switch as follows to prevent the tree from scrolling off your screen:

    TREE ¦MORE

A more efficient way to display a directory tree is to use the DOS Shell. In Shell, you can move around in the tree while you are viewing it.

TYPE

The TYPE command displays the contents of the file you specify on-screen. To display the contents of the file, change to the drive and directory that contains the file. Then use the TYPE command. You can add the |more switch as follows to prevent the contents from scrolling off the screen before you can read it:

```
TYPE FILENAME.EXT |MORE
```

where *FILENAME.EXT* is the name of the file you want to view. This command is especially useful for viewing README.TXT files that commonly come with programs. (An easier way to view the contents of such files is to use the DOS Shell. Highlight the file, and select View File Contents from the File menu.)

UNDELETE

Undelete allows you to recover accidentally deleted files. To undelete files, change to the drive and directory that contains the files you want to undelete. Then, enter the following command:

```
UNDELETE
```

If you installed Undelete for Windows, you can run the Windows Undelete program by double-clicking on the Undelete icon in the Microsoft Tools program group window. (For more information about Undelete and Undelete for Windows, see "Undeleting Files" in Chapter 8.)

UNFORMAT

The Unformat program allows you to recover accidentally formatted disks. If you accidentally formatted a disk that contains data, you will have a better chance of recovering the disk if you use Unformat immediately after you discover the accident.

For example, to unformat the disk in drive A, enter the following command:

```
UNFORMAT A:
```

For more information about unformatting disks, refer to "Unformatting a Disk" in Chapter 6.

VER

The VER command displays the number of the DOS version you have. Type the following command at the DOS prompt, and press ⏎Enter:

```
VER
```

DOS should display the version number MS-DOS 6.0.

VERIFY

The VERIFY command tells DOS to turn file-writing verification on or off. By default, VERIFY is off. If you want DOS to verify that every single character of a file is saved correctly on disk, enter the

```
VERIFY ON
```

command. Usually this is unnecessary, but if you are working with highly critical data, and you don't mind the drag on your system, try running VERIFY.

VOL

The VOL command displays the label of the specified disk drive. This is similar to the LABEL command but does not allow you to change the label of the disk. The following command would display the volume label of the disk in drive A:

```
VOL A:
```

Index

Symbols

— (minus sign) by directory
  names, 52
$B switch, PROMPT command, 283
$G switch, PROMPT command, 71,
  284, 322
$N switch, PROMPT command, 283
$P switch, PROMPT command, 71,
  284, 322
$Q switch, PROMPT command, 283
$V switch, PROMPT command, 283
* (asterisk) wild-card character
  copying groups of files, 123, 125
  deleting groups of files, 133
  listing files, 75
  renaming groups of files, 131
  searching for files, 145
+ (plus sign) by directory names, 51
/? switch, 67
/1 switch, Disk Copy program, 93
/4 switch, FORMAT command, 86
? (question mark) wild-card
  character
  copying groups of files, 123, 125
  deleting groups of files, 133
  listing files, 75
  renaming groups of files, 131
  searching for files, 145

3 1/2-inch floppy disks, write-
  protecting, 30
5 1/4-inch floppy disks, write-
  protecting, 31

A

+/-A switch, ATTRIB command, 144
/A switch, TREE command, 72
active disk letter, 42, 45
Active Task List, 168-170
  deleting programs from, 170
Add Group dialog box, 156-157
Add mode, 120
Add Program dialog box, 158-159
Advanced dialog box, 160-161
Advanced Options screen, 256-259
Advanced Power Management
  (APM) specifications, 306
/ALL switch, UNDELETE
  command, 137-138
alphanumeric keys, 5
Alt key, 6
Anti-Virus (Microsoft)
  emergency virus disk, 271-272
  running at startup, 272
  scanning for viruses, 265-270
APM (Advanced Power
  Management) specifications, 306

APPEND command, 310
applications, *see* programs
Archive attribute, 143, 174-175
arrow keys, 6
ASCII display, changing to
hexadecimal code, 140
Associate File dialog box, 166-167
associating data files with
programs, 165-167
asterisk (*) wild-card character
copying groups of files, 123, 125
deleting groups of files, 133
listing files, 75
renaming groups of files, 131
searching for files, 145
ATTRIB command, 144, 310
attributes, files, 142-144
archive, 174-175
/AUTO switch, INTERLNK
command, 301
AUTOEXEC.BAT file
adding path statements, 284-285
backing up, 278-279
bypassing all commands at
startup, 294
customizing DOS prompt,
283-284
disabling command lines,
287-288
preventing on-screen command
display, 285
rebooting computers after
changing, 292-293
running automatically at startup
DOS Shell, 286
DOSKey, 286
programs, 285-286
VSafe, 287
viewing contents, 279-280
automatically
running at startup
DOS Shell, 149, 286
DOSKey, 286
programs, 285-286
VSafe, 287
turning off NumLock key at
startup, 291

B

/B:BufferSize switch, SMARTDRV
command, 250
Backup (Microsoft)
backups
full, 186-189
incremental, 189-191
preparing for, 183-186
selected directories and files,
191-198
comparing backup files to
originals
choosing backup catalogs,
204-206
choosing sources and
destinations, 206-207
comparing, 209-210
selecting files, 207-208
starting, 203-204
configuring, 177-182
restoring files to hard disks
full restorations, 202, 212-215
partial restorations, 215-218
preparing for, 202, 211-212
running, 182
starting, 172
Backup Complete dialog box, 180
Backup Devices dialog box, 178-179
Backup for Windows (Microsoft),
running, 172, 199-200
Backup Set Catalog dialog box,
205-206, 209, 215-216
Backup To dialog box, 179
backups
archive attributes for, 174-175
AUTOEXEC.BAT and
CONFIG.SYS files, 278-279
catalogs, 186, 204-206
lost or damaged, 219
names, 186
differential, 176
files
comparing to originals,
203-210
reasons for, 174

restoring to hard disks, 202, 210-218
full (hard disks), 172, 175, 186-189
    before installing DOS 6, 32
incremental, 175-176, 189-191
options for, 184-186
selected directories and files, 191-192
    including/excluding groups of files, 192-194, 196
    selecting directories, 194-195
    selecting files, 195-196
selecting
    disk drives for, 183
    types, 184
storing
    floppy disks of, 188-189
    selecting disk drives for, 183-184
strategies for, 174, 176-177
bad sectors, 89
.BAK file extension, 123
base names, files, 23
.BAT file extension, 152
batteries of laptop computers, conserving power, 296, 306-307
/BAUD switch, INTERLNK command, 301
BIOS (basic input-output system), 11
bits, 19
booting computers, 12, 39
    clean, 225
    from floppy disks, 28, 40-41
    from hard disks, 28, 40
    warm versus cold boots, 41
BREAK command, 310-311
buffers
    read-ahead, setting size, 250
    setting number of, CONFIG.SYS file, 290
BUFFERS command, 290, 311
bytes, 19

C

cable, null-modem serial, connecting computers with, 296, 299
caching memory, 248-251
cancelling commands, 69
capacity, floppy disks, 19-20
capitalization of commands, 67
care and handling of floppy disks, 20-21
.CAT file extension, 205
catalogs, backup, 186, 204-206
    lost or damaged, 219
    names, 186
CD (CHDIR) command, 70-71, 311-312
central processing units (CPUs), 4
Change Attributes dialog box, 143-144
Change Size dialog box, 238
check boxes, 54
chips, memory, 4
.CHK file extension, 222
CHKDSK command, 222, 312
CHKDSK program, 220, 222-223
clean boots, 225
clicking, 7, 46
client computers
    breaking connections with server computers, 305-306
    drives redirected to, 305
    setting up, 300-302
CLS command, 312
cold boots, 41
collapsing directory trees, 52
Color Scheme dialog box, 58-59
.COM file extension, 152
COM ports, 299
/COM switch, INTERLNK command, 301
command bar, 42, 45
command buttons, 55
commands
    APPEND, 310
    ATTRIB, 144, 310

in AUTOEXEC.BAT file
bypassing all at startup, 294
disabling, 287-288
preventing on-screen
display, 285
BREAK, 310-311
BUFFERS, 290, 311
cancelling, 69
capitalization, 67
CD (CHDIR), 70-71, 311-312
CHKDSK, 222, 312
CLS, 312
in CONFIG.SYS file
bypassing all at startup, 294
device commands, 289-290
executing one at a time at
startup, 276, 293
using Help system to learn
about, 292
COPY, 123-125, 312
DATE, 313
DBLSPACE, 231, 233-234, 317
DEFRAG, 226, 313
DEL (ERASE), 313-314
DELOLDDOS, 314
DELTREE, 108-109, 314
DEVICE, 289-290, 314-315
DEVICEHIGH, 289, 314-315
DIR, 73-75, 114-115, 315
DISKCOMP, 96-97, 315
DISKCOPY, 95, 316
DOS=HIGH, 291
DOS=UMB, 291
DOSHELP, 316
DOSKEY, 80-81, 316-317
DOSSHELL, 44, 317
ECHO, 285, 317-318
EDIT, 281, 318
editing, 69
only errors, 79-80
elements, 66-67
entering at DOS prompt, 66
ERASE, 313-314
EXIT, 56, 318
external, 70
File Associate, 166-167

File Change Attributes, 143-144
File Copy, 122-124
File Create Directory, 102-103
File Delete, 106, 132, 164
File Deselect All, 118
File Exit, 63, 79
File Move, 128
File New, 156-159
File Open, 150, 152-153
File Print, 142
File Properties, 160, 162-163
File Rename, 104-105, 130-131
File Reorder, 165
File Run, 90-92, 96-97, 150-151
File Save Setup As, 197
File Search, 145
File Select All, 118
File View File Contents,
140, 279
FILES, 290
FORMAT, 85-87, 319
HELP, 76, 79, 319
Help information about specific,
79, 309
Help menu, 61
INTERLNK, 301-302, 304,
319-320
internal, 70
INTERSVR, 302-303, 306,
319-320
LABEL, 91-92, 320
LH (LOADHIGH), 320
MD (MKDIR), 104, 321
MEM, 320-321
MEMMAKER, 254-256,
258-259, 321
MSAV, 265, 267-269
MSBACKUP, 177, 182
NUMLOCK=OFF, 291
Options Colors, 58-59
Options Confirmation, 127
Options Display, 59-60
Options Display Options,
113-114
Options Enable Task Swapper,
168-169

Options Select Across
  Directories, 121
PATH, 284-285, 321-322
POWER, 307
PRINT, 142
PROMPT, 71, 283-284, 322
RD (RMDIR), 107, 323
recalling, 80-81
REM, 287-288, 322
REN (RENAME), 322-323
Search Find, 78
selecting, 47-49
SETUP, 33-34, 38
SETVER, 323
SMARTDRV, 249-252, 323-324
syntax, 67-69
TIME, 324
TREE, 71-72, 324
TYPE, 141, 280, 325
UNDELETE, 137-140, 325
UNFORMAT, 90-91, 325-326
VER, 326
VERIFY, 326
View All Files, 116
View Dual File Lists, 115
View Program List, 58, 87,
  93, 154
View Program/File Lists, 57, 154
View Single File List, 58, 115
VOL, 91, 326
VSAFE, 273
Compare Complete dialog box,
  180-181
Compare Files screen, 209
Compare screen, 204-210
comparing
  backup files to originals
    choosing backup catalogs,
      204-206
    choosing sources and
      destinations, 206-207
    comparing, 209-210
    selecting files, 207-208
    starting, 203-204
  floppy disks, 95-97
Compatibility Test dialog box, 181

compressed disks
  creating, 233-235
  floppy, 241-243
  maintaining, 239
  managing, 235-237
  resizing, 237-238
compressing
  drives, 240
  files, 220, 228-235
  floppy disks, 241-243
computers
  booting, 12
    actions during, 2, 10-11
    bypassing all commands in
      CONFIG.SYS and
      AUTOEXEC., 294
    from floppy disks, 28, 40-41
    from hard disks, 28, 40
    troubleshooting, 293-294
    warm versus cold boots, 41
  components, 2
    keyboards, 5-6
    monitors, 8
    mouse, 6-7
    printers, 8
    system units, 4-5
  rebooting after changing
    AUTOEXEC.BAT or
    CONFIG.SYS files, 292-293
  remote connections
    breaking connections, 305-306
    connecting, 296, 304-305
    redirected drives, 305
    remote copy between, 303-304
    setting up servers and clients,
      300-302
    with null-modem serial cable,
      296, 299
  running application
    programs, 12
  viruses, risk susceptibility, 264
CONFIG.SYS file
  allowing DOS into upper and
    high memory, 291
  backing up, 278-279

bypassing all commands at
startup, 294
device commands, 289-290
rebooting computers after
changing, 292-293
running commands one at a time
at startup, 293
setting number of buffers and
files, 290
turning off NumLock Key at
startup, 291
using Help system to learn about
commands, 292
viewing contents, 279-280
Configure dialog box, 181
configuring
Defrag program, 227-228
Microsoft Backup, 177-182
Confirm Mouse Operation dialog
box, 126
confirmation warnings, turning
off, 127
conserving laptop battery power,
296, 306-307
context-sensitive help, 42, 62-63
conventional memory, 244, 246
freeing, 251-260
COPY command, 123-125, 312
copying
files, 110, 122
AUTOEXEC.BAT and
CONFIG.SYS, to bootable
disks, 278-279
dragging with mouse, 125-126
name conflicts, 127
to different directories/disks,
124-125
to same directories/disks,
122-123
floppy disks, 82, 92-95
remote, between computers,
303-304
CPUs (central processing units), 4
Create Directory dialog box,
102-103
Ctrl key, 6

D

data files, 23
associating with programs,
165-167
DATE command, 313
DBLSPACE command, 231,
233-234, 317
DEFRAG command, 226, 313
Defrag program, 220, 223-228
Defrag screen, 226
defragmenting hard disks, 220,
223-228
DEL (ERASE) command, 313-314
Delete Directory Confirmation
dialog box, 106
Delete File Confirmation dialog
box, 132
Delete File dialog box, 132
Delete Item dialog box, 164
Delete Sentry program, 138-140
Delete Tracker program, 138-140
deleting
command lines from
AUTOEXEC.BAT file, 287
directories, 106-109
files, 110, 132-133
programs from Active Task
List, 170
delimiters, 66
DELOLDDOS command, 314
DELTREE command, 108-109, 314
density, floppy disks, 20
DEVICE command, 289-290,
314-315
device drivers, device commands for
loading, 289-290
DEVICEHIGH command, 289,
314-315
dialog boxes
Add Group, 156-157
Add Program, 158-159
Advanced, 160-161
Associate File, 166-167
Backup Complete, 180
Backup Devices, 178-179

Backup Set Catalog, 205-206, 209, 215-216
Backup To, 179
Change Attributes, 143-144
Change Size, 238
Color Scheme, 58-59
Compare, 204-210
Compare Complete, 180-181
Compatibility Test, 181
Configure, 181
Confirm Mouse Operation, 126
Create Directory, 102-103
custom, creating for programs, 162-163
Delete Directory Confirmation, 106
Delete File, 132
Delete File Confirmation, 132
Delete Item, 164
Disk Backup Options, 185-186
Disk Copy, 93-94
Disk Restore Options, 211-212
elements, 54-55
Exclude Files, 193
File Display Options, 113-114
File to Edit, 281
Find, 78
Finished Condensing, 226
Floppy Disk Compatibility Test, 179
Floppy Drive Change Line Test, 178
Format, 87-88
Include Files, 192-193
Microsoft Backup, 182-191
Move File, 128
New Program Object, 156-159
Options Setting, 269-270
Program Group Properties, 160
Program Item Properties, 160, 162-163
Recommendation, 226
Rename Directory, 105
Rename File, 130-131
Replace File Confirmation, 127
Restore, 211-218

Run, 90, 96-97, 151
Scanning Memory for Viruses, 268
Screen Display Mode, 60
Search File, 145
Select Backup Files, 191-198
selecting items in, 55
Setup Files, 198
Special Selections, 196
Undelete, 135, 136
Verify Error, 268
Video and Mouse Configuration, 178
Viruses Detected and Cleaned, 269
.DIF file extension, 186
differential backups, 176
DIR command, 73-75, 114-115, 315
directories, 16, 24-26
    backing up selected, 191-198
    changing, 50-51
        at DOS prompt, 64, 70-71, 100
        in DOS Shell, 100
    creating, 98, 102-104
    deleting, 106-109
    guidelines, 98, 101-102
    naming, 102
    renaming, 98, 104-105
Directory Tree window, 42, 45, 50-52
directory trees, 16
    collapsing, 52
    expanding, 52
    viewing at DOS prompt, 71-72
Disk Backup Options dialog box, 185-186
disk caching, 248-251
Disk Compare program, 95-97
Disk Copy dialog box, 93-94
Disk Copy program, 92-95
disk drives, 5, 18-19
    changing, 42, 49-50
        at DOS prompt, 64, 70, 82-83
        in DOS Shell, 82-83
    compressed, creating, 240

floppy, 18
   types, 84-85
hard, 18-19
letters, 16
   active, 42, 45
logical, 19
physical, 19
redirected, client/server remote
   connections, 304-305
scanning for viruses, 265-270
selecting
   for backing up, 183
   for storing backups, 183-184
disk icons, 42, 45
Disk Restore Options dialog box,
  211-212
Disk Utilities program group
  Disk Copy, 93-95
  displaying, 82
  Format, 87-89
  MS Backup, *see* Backup
  Undelete, 134-138
DISKCOMP command, 96-97, 315
DISKCOPY command, 95, 316
disks
  saving to, 14
  versus memory, 18
  see also floppy disks; hard disks
DOS, 2, 9-10
  disk-drive letters, 16
  loading into high memory, 291
  using upper memory, 291
  version numbers, 10
DOS 6
  DELTREE command, 108-109
  installing
    on floppy disks, 38-39
    on new computers, 28, 32-33
    over earlier versions, 28, 32-37
    preparing for, 28
  uninstalling, 37
DOS prompt, 11, 65
  customizing, 283-284
  displaying current directory
    name, 71
  entering commands at, 66-69

help, 64, 75-79
  temporary, 55-56
DOS Shell
  changing drives, 49-50
  dialog boxes, 54-55
  Directory Tree window, 50-52
  exiting, 63
  File List window, 53
    displaying, 56-58
  listing files, 112-116
  navigating, 46-47
  Program List
    adding program groups,
      156-157
    assigning keyboard shortcuts
      to programs in, 170
    deleting programs from, 164
    displaying, 56-58
    reordering programs, 164-165
    running programs from, 148,
      150, 154-155
  running automatically at
    startup, 149, 286
  screen
    changing colors, 58-59
    elements, 42, 44-46
  selecting commands, 47-49
  starting, 42, 44
  temporary DOS prompt, 55-56
  toggling graphics/text modes,
    59-60
DOS=HIGH command, 291
DOS=UMB command, 291
DOSHELP command, 316
DOSKEY command, 80-81, 316-317
DOSKey program, 79-81
  running automatically at
    startup, 286
DOSSHELL command, 44, 317
double-clicking, 7, 46
double-sided floppy disks, 20
  double-density (DSDD), 85
  high-density (DSHD), 85
DoubleSpace program, 220
  advantages and disadvantages,
    228-229

compressed disks
 floppy, 241-243
 maintaining, 239
 managing, 235-237
 resizing, 237-238
Custom Setup, 233-235
Express Setup, 230-232
guidelines for determining setup
 methods, 229-230
DoubleSpace screen, 235-238
dragging, 7, 46
drives
 disk, *see* disk drives
 MS-DOS, 184
/DRIVES switch, INTERLNK
 command, 301
DSDD (double-sided, double-
 density) floppy disks, 85
DSHD (double-sided, high-density)
 floppy disks, 85
Dual File Lists display, 115-116

E

ECHO command, 285, 317-318
EDIT command, 281, 318
editing
 AUTOEXEC.BAT file, 283-288
 commands, 69
 only errors, 79-80
 CONFIG.SYS file, 288-292
 Include/Exclude List, 193-194
 program groups or items, 160
 with text editors, 281-283
ejecting floppy disks, 21-22
emergency virus disks
 creating, 271-272
ERASE (DEL) command, 313-314
Error in CONFIG.SYS Line *x*
 message, 293
error messages, *see* messages
Esc key, 6
Exclude Files dialog box, 193
.EXE file extension, 152

executable files
 running programs from, 148,
 150, 152-153
 scanning for changes caused by
 viruses, 267
EXIT command, 56, 318
exiting
 DOS Shell, 63
 help, 79
 programs, 169-170
expanded memory, 244, 247
expanding directory trees, 52
extended memory, 244, 247
extensions, *see* files, extensions
external
 commands, 70
 hard drives, 18

F

/F switch, CHKDSK command, 312
/F:size switch, FORMAT
 command, 86
FAT (file allocation table), 84
File Associate command, 166-167
File Change Attributes command,
 143-144
File Copy command, 122-124
File Create Directory command,
 102-103
File Delete command, 106, 132, 164
File Deselect All command, 118
File Display Options dialog box,
 113-114
File Exit command, 63, 79
File List window, 42, 45, 53
 displaying, 56-58
File Move command, 128
File New command, 156-159
File Open command, 150, 152-153
File Print command, 142
File Properties command, 160,
 162-163
File Rename command, 104-105,
 130-131
File Reorder command, 165

File Run command, 90-91, 96-97,
    150-151
File Save Setup As command, 197
File Search command, 145
File Select All command, 118
File to Edit dialog box, 281
File View File Contents command,
    140, 279
files, 16, 22
    attributes, 142-144
    AUTOEXEC.BAT
        backing up, 278-279
        bypassing all commands at
            startup, 294
        editing, 283-288
        rebooting computers after
            changing, 292-293
        viewing contents, 279-280
    backing up, 172, 175, 186-189
        reasons for, 174
        selected, 191-198
    backups
        comparing to originals,
            203-210
        restoring to hard disks, 202,
            210-218
    compressing, 220, 228-235
    CONFIG.SYS
        backing up, 278-279
        bypassing all commands at
            startup, 294
        editing, 288-292
        rebooting computers after
            changing, 292-293
        running commands one at a
            time at startup, 293
        viewing contents, 279-280
    copying, 110, 122
        dragging with mouse, 125-126
        name conflicts, 127
        remote, between computers,
            303-304
        to different directories/disks,
            124-125
        to same directories/disks,
            122-123

data, 23
    associating with programs,
        165-167
defragmenting, 220, 223-228
deleting, 110, 132-133
executable, running programs
    from, 148, 150, 152-153
extensions, 23
    .BAK, 123
    .BAT, 152
    .CAT, 205
    .CHK, 222
    .COM, 152
    .DIF, 186
    .EXE, 152
    .FUL, 186
    .INC, 186
    .SET, 197
listing
    at DOS prompt, 64, 73-75
    filtering or sorting, 112-115
    in two windows, 115-116
moving, 127-130
naming, 16, 23
opening, 14-15
organizing
    on floppy disks, 24
    on hard disks, 24-26
printing, 141-142
program, 23
renaming, 130-131
saving to disks, 23
scanning for viruses, 265-270
searching for, 144-145
    lost allocation units, 220,
        222-223
selecting, 53, 117
    all in current directory,
        117-118
    in different directories, 121
    individually, 110, 117
    neighboring, 110, 118-119
    non-neighboring, 119-120
setting number of, CONFIG.SYS
    file, 290

setup, for backup selections,
197-198
undeleting, 133-140
uninstall, 32
viewing contents, 140-141, 276
FILES command, 290
filtering file lists, 112-115
Find dialog box, 78
finding, *see* searching
Finished Condensing dialog
box, 226
Floppy Disk Compatibility Test
dialog box, 179
floppy disk drives, 18
floppy disks
backups, storing, 188-189
booting computers from, 28,
40-41
care and handling, 20-21
characteristics, 19-20
comparing, 95-97
compressing, 241-243
copying, 82, 92-95
emergency virus, creating,
271-272
formatting, 22, 82, 84-89
inserting and removing, 21-22
installing DOS 6 on, 38-39
organizing files, 24
renaming, 91-92
swapping, 22
types, 84-85
unformatting, 89-91
volume labels, viewing, 91
write-protecting, 30-31
Floppy Drive Change Line Test
dialog box, 178
FORMAT command, 85-87, 319
Format dialog box, 87-88
Format program, 85-89
formatting floppy disks, 22, 82,
84-89
freeing conventional memory,
251-260
.FUL file extension, 186

full
backups, 172, 175, 186-189
restorations, 202, 212-215
function keys, 6

G-H

graphics mode, toggling with text
mode, 59-60

+/-H switch
ATTRIB command, 144
hard disks, 18-19, 22
backing up, 172, 175, 186-189
before installing DOS 6, 32
booting computers from, 28, 40
compressed
creating new drives, 240
maintaining, 239
managing, 235-237
resizing, 237-238
compressing, 220, 228-235
defragmenting, 220, 223-228
organizing files, 24-26
restoring backup files, 202,
210-218
hardware requirements, Interlnk
program, 298
help, 42
about specific commands, 79
at DOS prompt, 64, 75-79
command information, 309
about CONFIG.SYS
commands, 292
Command Reference, 76-77
context-sensitive, 42, 62-63
exiting, 79
searching for topics, 77-78
screens, 76-79
window elements, 62
HELP command, 76, 79, 319
Help menu, 61
hexadecimal display, changing to
ASCII, 140
Hidden attribute, 143
high memory, loading DOS
into, 291

I

icons, 42, 45
.INC file extension, 186
Include Files dialog box, 192-193
incremental backups, 175-176,
    189-191
individual catalogs, 205
input
    devices, 7-8
        keyboards, 5-6
        mouse, 6-7
    ports, 4
Insert system disk in drive A
    message, 33
installing
    DOS 6
        on floppy disks, 38-39
        on new computers, 28, 32-33
        over earlier versions, 28, 32-37
        preparing for, 28
    DoubleSpace program
        with Custom Setup, 233-235
        with Express Setup, 230-232
    MemMaker program
        with Custom Setup, 256-259
        with Express Setup, 244,
            253-256
    Interlnk program
        breaking connections between
            computers, 305-306
        connecting computers, 304-305
            with null-modem serial
                cable, 299
        hardware and software require-
            ments, 298
        redirected drives, 305
        remote copy between computers,
            303-304
        setting up client and server
            computers, 300-302
    INTERLNK command, 301-302,
        304, 319-320
    Interlnk Remote Installation
        screen, 303-304
    INTERLNK.EXE program, 300-302

internal commands, 70
INTERSVR command, 302-303,
    306, 319-320
INTERSVR.EXE program, 302

J-K

jumps, 76

keyboard ports, 5
keyboard shortcuts
    active-program switching, 169
    Add mode toggle (Shift+F8), 120
    assigning to programs in
        Program List, 170
    break remote connection
        (Alt+F4), 306
    bypassing all commands in
        CONFIG.SYS and
        AUTOEXEC.BAT files at
        startup (F5), 294
    cancel
        Ctrl+Break, 69
        Ctrl+C, 69
    Copy (F8), 122
    Deselect All Files (Ctrl+\), 118
    DOS Shell navigation, 47
    DOSKey editing, 80
    Exit DOS Shell (Alt+F4), 63
    Help (F1), 61
    Move (F7), 128
    reboot (warm) (Ctrl+Alt+Del),
        41, 292
    recalling commands, 80-81
    return to DOS Shell (Ctrl+Esc),
        168
    running CONFIG.SYS com-
        mands one at a time at startup
        (F8), 293
    Select All Files (Ctrl+/), 118
    View File Contents (F9), 140
keyboards, 2, 5-6
keypads, numeric, 6
keys
    alphanumeric, 5
    Alt, 6

arrow, 6
Ctrl, 6
Delete, 132
Esc, 6
function, 6
NumLock, turning off at
    startup, 291
text editor, 282-283
kilobytes (K), 19

L

LABEL command, 91-92, 320
laptop computers
    breaking connections, 305-306
    connecting, 296, 304-305
        with null-modem serial cable,
            296, 299
    conserving battery power, 296,
        306-307
    drives redirected to, 305
    remote copy between, 303-304
    setting up client and server
        computers, 300-302
LD (low-density) floppy disks, 85
LH (LOADHIGH) command, 320
list boxes, 54
/LIST switch, UNDELETE
    command, 135, 137-138
logical drives, 19
low-density (LD) floppy disks, 85

M

master catalogs, 204-205
MD (MKDIR) command, 104, 321
megabytes (M), 19
MEM command, 320-321
MEMMAKER command, 254-256,
    258-259, 321
MemMaker program, 245
    freeing comventional memory,
        251-252
    guidelines for determining setup
        methods, 252-253

installing
    with Custom Setup, 256-259
    with Express Setup, 244,
        253-256
    requirements, 252
    undoing changes, 259-260
memory
    conventional, 244, 246
        freeing, 251-260
    determining types, 244, 247
    disk caching, 248-251
    expanded, 244, 247
    extended, 244, 247
    high, loading DOS into, 291
    RAM (random-access
        memory), 12
    ROM (read-only memory), 11
    unloading VSafe program, 274
    upper, 244, 246
        allowing DOS to use, 291
    versus disks, 18
memory chips, 4
Memory Information screen, 247
menu bar, 42, 45
menus
    Help, 61
    selecting commands, 47-49
messages
    Error in CONFIG.SYS Line x,
        293
    Insert system disk in drive A, 33
    Too many files are open, 290
    Unrecognized command in
        CONFIG.SYS message, 293
Microsoft Anti-Virus (DOS and
    Windows)
    emergency virus disk, 271-272
    running at startup, 272
    scanning for viruses, 265-270
Microsoft Anti-Virus screen, 265,
    267-269
Microsoft Backup
    backups, 183-198
    comparing backup files to
        originals, 203-210
    configuring, 177-182

restoring backup files to hard
disks, 210-218
running, 182
starting, 172
Microsoft Backup screen, 182-191
Microsoft Backup for Windows,
running, 172, 199-200
Microsoft DoubleSpace Setup
screen, 231, 233-234
Microsoft Welcome screen, 254, 258
minus sign (–) by directory
names, 52
modes
Add, 120
graphics, toggling with text
mode, 59-60
monitors, 2, 8
¦MORE switch
DIR command, 74
TREE command, 72, 324
TYPE command, 141, 325
mouse, 2, 6-7, 46
mouse pointer, 45
Move File dialog box, 128
moving
files, 127-130
program groups/items within
Program List, 164-165
MS-DOS (Microsoft disk operating
system), *see* DOS
MS-DOS drives, 184
MS-DOS Help: Command
Reference window, 76-77
MS-DOS 6 Setup screen, 34-37
MSAV command, 265, 267-269
MSBACKUP command, 177, 182

N

naming
backup catalogs, 186, 205
directories, 102
files, 16, 23
see also renaming
New Program Object dialog box,
156-159

/NOPRINTER switch, INTERLNK
command, 301
/NOSCAN switch, INTERLNK
command, 301
null-modem
adapters, 299
serial cable, connecting
computers with, 296, 299
numeric keypads, 6
NumLock key, turning off at
startup, 291
NUMLOCK=OFF command, 291

O

/O:attributes switch, DIR
command, 114-115
opening files, 14-15
option buttons, 55
Options Colors command, 58-59
Options Confirmation
command, 127
Options Display command, 59-60
Options Display Options command,
113-114
Options Enable Task Swapper
command, 168-169
Options Select Across Directories
command, 121
Options Setting dialog box, 269-270
output
devices, 9
monitors, 8
printers, 8
ports, 4

P

/P switch
DIR command, 74, 315
MEM command, 321
parameters, 66
partial restorations, 215-218
partitioning hard drives, 19
passwords for program groups,
forgetting, 157

PATH command, 284-285, 321-322
paths, 16, 25-26
    statements, adding to
        AUTOEXEC.BAT file, 284-285
physical drives, 19
plus sign (+) by directory names, 51
pointing, 7
ports
    COM, 299
    input and output, 4
    keyboard, 5
    printer, 142
power, conserving in laptop
    batteries, 296, 306-307
POWER command, 307
Power program, 306-307
PRINT command, 142
PRINT.COM program, 142
printer ports, 142
printers, 2, 8
printing files, 141-142
program files, 23
Program Group Properties dialog
    box, 160
program groups, 154
    adding
        items, 157-159
        to Program List, 156-157
    deleting from Program List, 164
    Disk Utilities, *see* Disk Utilities
        program group
    editing, 160
    forgetting passwords for, 157
    moving within Program List,
        164-165
Program Item Properties dialog
    box, 160, 162-163
program items, 154
    adding to groups, 157-159
    deleting from Program List, 164
    editing, 160
    moving within Program List,
        164-165
Program List, 42, 45
    adding program groups, 156-157
    assigning keyboard shortcuts to
        programs in, 170

deleting programs from, 164
displaying, 56-58
reordering programs, 164-165
running programs from, 148,
    150, 154-155
programs
    active, switching between, 169
    assigning keyboard shortcuts to,
        in Program List, 170
    associating data files with,
        165-167
    CHKDSK, 220, 222-223
    creating custom dialog boxes for,
        162-163
    Defrag, 220, 223-228
    Delete Sentry, 138-140
    Delete Tracker, 138-140
    deleting from Program List, 164
    Disk Compare, 95-97
    Disk Copy, 92-95
    DOSKey, 79-81, 286
    DoubleSpace, 220, 228-243
    exiting, 169-170
    Format, 85-89
    Interlnk, 298-306
    INTERLNK.EXE, 300-302
    INTERSVR.EXE, 302
    MemMaker, 244-245, 251-260
    Microsoft
        Anti-Virus (DOS/Windows),
            265-272
        Backup for Windows, 199-200
        Backup, *see* Backup
    moving within Program List,
        164-165
    Power, 306-307
    PRINT.COM, 142
    running, 12
        advanced options for, 160-161
        automatically at startup,
            285-286
        from executable files, 148,
            150, 152-153
        from Program List, 148, 150,
            154-155
        multiple, 168-169
        with Run command, 148,
            150-151

Setup, 33-39
SmartDrive, 245, 248-251
Undelete, 134-138
VSafe, 272-274, 287
PROMPT command, 71,
283-284, 322
protecting against viruses
emergency virus disks, 271-272
guidelines for preventions and
cures, 264-265

Q

/Q switch, FORMAT command, 86
question mark (?) wild-card
character
copying groups of files, 123, 125
deleting groups of files, 133
listing files, 75
renaming groups of files, 131
searching for files, 145

R

+/-R switch, ATTRIB command, 144
RAM (random-access memory), 12
/RCOPY switch, INTERSVR
command, 303
RD (RMDIR) command, 107, 323
Read only attribute, 142
read-ahead buffer, setting size, 250
rebooting computers after changing
AUTOEXEC.BAT or
CONFIG.SYS files, 292-293
recalling commands, 80-81
Recommendation dialog box, 226
redirected drives, client/server
remote connections, 304-305
REM command, 287-288, 322
remote computer connections
breaking connections, 305-306
connecting, 304-305
redirected drives, 304-305
remote copy between, 303-304
setting up servers and clients,
300-302

with null-modem serial
cable, 299
remote copy between computers,
303-304
REN (RENAME) command,
322-323
Rename Directory dialog box, 105
Rename File dialog box, 130-131
renaming
directories, 98, 104-105
files, 130-131
floppy disks, 91-92
see also naming
Replace File Confirmation dialog
box, 127
resizing compressed disks, 237-238
Restore screen, 211-218
restoring files to hard disks
full restorations, 202, 212-215
partial restorations, 215-218
preparing for, 202, 211-212
ROM (read-only memory), 11
Run dialog box, 90, 96-97, 151

S

+/-S switch, ATTRIB command, 144
/S switch
FORMAT command, 86
SMARTDRV command, 251
UNDELETE command, 139
saving
backup selections in setup files,
197-198
files to disks, 14, 23
scanning for viruses, 265-270
Scanning Memory for Viruses
dialog box, 268
Screen Display Mode dialog box, 60
screens
Advanced Options, 256-259
Compare, 204-210
Compare Files, 209
Defrag, 226
displaying one at a time, 72, 74,
141, 324-325

DOS Shell
  changing colors, 58-59
  elements, 42, 44-46
DoubleSpace, 235-238
help, 76-79
Interlnk Remote Installation, 303-304
Memory Information, 247
Microsoft Anti-Virus, 265, 267-269
Microsoft Backup, 182-191
Microsoft DoubleSpace Setup, 231, 233-234
Microsoft Welcome, 254, 258
MS-DOS 6 Setup, 34-37
Restore, 211-218
Select Compare Files, 207-208
undo, 260
VSafe Warning Options, 273-274
Search File dialog box, 145
Search Find command, 78
searching
  files for lost allocation units, 220, 222-223
  for files, 144-145
  for help topics, 77-78
sectors, bad, 89
Select Backup Files dialog box, 191-198
Select Compare Files screen, 207-208
server computers
  breaking connections with client computers, 305-306
  redirected drives, 305
  setting up, 300-302
.SET file extension, 197
SETUP command, 33-34, 38
setup files, for backup selections, 197-198
Setup Files dialog box, 198
Setup program, 33-39
SETVER command, 323
signatures of known viruses, 266
single-sided floppy disks, 20
size, floppy disks, 19

SmartDrive program, 245, 248-251
SMARTDRV command, 249-252, 323-324
software
  Interlnk program requirements, 298
  see also programs
sorting file lists, 112-115
Special Selections dialog box, 196
starting
  computers
    actions during, 2, 10-11
    bypassing all commands in CONFIG.SYS and AUTOEXEC., 294
    executing commands one at a time, 276
    running Delete Sentry or Delete Tracker, 139-140
    running DOS Shell automatically, 149, 286
    running DOSKey automatically, 286
    running Microsoft Anti-Virus (DOS/Windows), 272
    running programs automatically, 285-286
    running VSafe automatically, 287
    troubleshooting, 293-294
    turning off NumLock key, 291
  DOS Shell, 42, 44
  Microsoft Backup, 172
storing backup floppy disks, 188-189
subdirectories, 24
swapping floppy disks, 22
switches, 66-67
  $B, PROMPT command, 283
  $G, PROMPT command, 71, 284, 322
  $N, PROMPT command, 283
  $P, PROMPT command, 71, 284, 322
  $Q, PROMPT command, 283
  $V, PROMPT command, 283

/?, 67
/1, Disk Copy program, 93
/4, FORMAT command, 86
+/-A, ATTRIB command, 144
/A, TREE command, 72
/ALL, UNDELETE command, 137-138
/AUTO, INTERLNK command, 301
/B:BufferSize, SMARTDRV command, 250
/BAUD, INTERLNK command, 301
/COM, INTERLNK command, 301
/DRIVES, INTERLNK command, 301
/F, CHKDSK command, 312
/F:size, FORMAT command, 86
+/-H, ATTRIB command, 144
/LIST, UNDELETE command, 135, 137-138
¦MORE
    DIR command, 74
    TREE command, 72, 324
    TYPE command, 141, 325
/NOPRINTER, INTERLNK command, 301
/NOSCAN, INTERLNK command, 301
/O:attributes, DIR command, 114-115
/P
    DIR command, 74, 315
    MEM command, 321
/Q, FORMAT command, 86
+/-R, ATTRIB command, 144
/RCOPY, INTERSVR command, 303
+/-S, ATTRIB command, 144
/S
    FORMAT command, 86
    SMARTDRV command, 251
    UNDELETE command, 139
/T, UNDELETE command, 139

/UNDO, MEMMAKER command, 260
/V
    Disk Copy program, 93
    SMARTDRV command, 251
/V:label, FORMAT command, 86
/W, DIR command, 74
switching between active programs, 169
syntax, commands, 67-69
System attribute, 143
system units, 2, 4-5

T

/T switch, UNDELETE command, 139
tables, file allocation (FAT), 84
Task Swapper, 168-169
temporary DOS prompt, 55-56
text boxes, 54
text editors, 281
    editing AUTOEXEC.BAT file, 283-288
    editing CONFIG.SYS file, 288-291
text mode, toggling with graphics mode, 59-60
TIME command, 324
title bar, 42, 45
Too many files are open message, 290
TREE command, 71-72, 324
troubleshooting startup, 293-294
TYPE command, 141, 280, 325

U

UNDELETE command, 137-140, 325
Undelete dialog box, 135, 136
Undelete program, 134-138
undeleting files, 133-138
undo screen, 260
/UNDO switch, MEMMAKER command, 260

undoing MemMaker changes, 259-260
UNFORMAT command, 90-91, 325-326
unformatting floppy disks, 89-91
uninstall files, 32
uninstalling DOS 6, 37
unloading VSafe program from memory, 274
Unrecognized command in CONFIG.SYS message, 293
upper memory, 244, 246
    allowing DOS to use, 291

V

/V switch
    Disk Copy program, 93
    SMARTDRV command, 251
/V:label switch, FORMAT command, 86
VER command, 326
VERIFY command, 326
Verify Error dialog box, 268
version numbers, 10
Video and Mouse Configuration dialog box, 178
View All Files command, 116
View Dual File Lists command, 115
View Program List command, 58, 87, 93, 154
View Program/File Lists command, 57, 154
View Single File List command, 58, 115
viruses, 263
    checking for at startup, 272
    displaying warnings about, 272-274
    emergency virus disks
        creating, 271-272
    guidelines for preventions and cures, 264-265
    risk susceptibility, 264
    scanning for, 265-270

Viruses Detected and Cleaned dialog box, 269
VOL command, 91, 326
volume labels, viewing, 91
VSAFE command, 273
VSafe program, 272-274
    running automatically at startup, 287
VSafe Warning Options screen, 273-274

W-Z

/W switch, DIR command, 74
warm boots, 41
wild-card characters
    copying groups of files, 123, 125
    deleting groups of files, 133
    listing files, 74-75
    renaming groups of files, 131
    searching for files, 145
windows
    Directory Tree, 42, 45, 50-52
    File List, 42, 45, 53
        displaying, 56-58
    help, elements, 62
    see also screens
    MS-DOS Help: Command Reference, 76-77
write-protecting floppy disks, 30, 31